The Theory of Poker

By

David Sklansky

A product of Two Plus Two Publishing

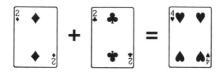

FOURTH EDITION

SIXTH PRINTING
October 2004

Printing and Binding
Creel Printing Co.
Las Vegas, Nevada

Printed in the United States of America

The Theory of Poker

For information contact: **Two Plus Two Publishing**
600 West Sunset; Suite 103
Henderson NV 89015
(702) 896-1326

ISBN #1-880685-00-0

To my Parents, Mae and Irving

Table of Contents

About David Sklansky

David Sklansky is generally considered the number one authority on gambling in the world today. Besides his nine books on the subject, David also has produced two videos and numerous writings for various gaming publications. His occasional poker seminars always receive an enthusiastic reception including those given at the Taj Mahal in Atlantic City and the World Series of Poker in Las Vegas.

More recently David has been doing consulting work for casinos, Internet gaming sites, and gaming device companies. He has recently invented a new game called *Poker Challenge,* soon to appear in casinos.

David attributes his standing in the gambling community to three things:

1. The fact that he presents his ideas as simply as possible (sometimes with Mason Malmuth) even though these ideas frequently involve concepts that are deep, subtle, and not to be found elsewhere.
2. The fact that what he says and writes can be counted on to be accurate.
3. The fact that to this day a large portion of his income is still derived from gambling (usually poker but occasionally blackjack, sports betting, horses, video games, casino promotions, or casino tournaments).

Thus, those who depend on David's advice know that he still depends on it himself.

Other Books by David Sklansky

Hold 'em Poker
Getting The Best of It
Sklansky on Poker

Poker, Gaming, and Life
Sklansky Talks Blackjack

Gambling for a Living by David Sklansky and Mason Malmuth
Hold 'em Poker For Advanced Players by David Sklansky and
   Mason Malmuth
Seven-Card Stud for Advanced Players by David Sklansky,
   Mason Malmuth, and Ray Zee

Preface

This book is about the general theories and concepts of poker play, which are operative in nearly every variation of poker from five-card draw to Texas hold 'em. It is not a how-to book in the sense of providing the basic rules and a step-by-step procedure for playing the various games. Beginning poker players sometimes ask, "What do you do in this particular situation?" There is really no correct answer to that question because it's the wrong question. Rules of thumb that say to fold one hand, call with another, and raise with yet another simply won't get a poker player beyond the beginning stages.

The right question is: "What do you *consider* in this particular situation before determining what to do?" *The Theory of Poker* addresses itself to such considerations. It analyzes every aspect of a poker hand from the ante structure to play after the last card has been dealt. By explaining the logic of poker, the book will, I hope, show the reader what kinds of things to think about in order to become a better player.

To illustrate the concepts presented, I use primarily five games — five-card draw, seven-card stud, hold 'em, draw lowball, and razz or seven-card lowball. For readers who may not be familiar with one or another of these games, I give brief summaries of their rules in the Appendix. I also use standard poker terms like *flop, on board, sixth street, back-door flush,* and the like. As much as possible, I explain these terms in the text, but readers can avail themselves of the Glossary of Poker Terms at the back of the book to check the definitions of any terms about which they are uncertain.

The Theory of Poker is an expansion and total revision of the book *Sklansky on Poker Theory,* written by David Sklansky and originally published by Gambler's Book Club of Las Vegas in 1978. That book was directed primarily to professional poker players. This book is directed to poker players in general, who know the basics, who may even be good players, but who want to delve deeper into the inner workings of the game. It is not an easy book, but a careful reading of it should reap rich rewards.

Note: This book was formerly titled *Winning Poker.*

Chapter One

Beyond Beginning Poker

The beauty of poker is that on the surface it is a game of utter simplicity, yet beneath the surface it is profound, rich, and full of subtlety. Because its basic rules are so simple, anyone can learn poker in a few minutes, and novice players may even think they're pretty good after a few hours. From the expert's point of view, the veneer of simplicity that deludes so many players into thinking they're good is the profitable side of the game's beauty. It doesn't take long for pool players or golfers to realize they're outclassed and to demand that a match be handicapped, but losers in poker return to the table over and over again, donating their money and blaming their losses on bad luck, not bad play.

It's true that in any given session the best of players can get unlucky. Going into the final day of the 1981 world championship of poker, Bobby Baldwin of Tulsa, Oklahoma, had a substantial lead over the eight other surviving players. Within a couple of hours he had two hands beat when his opponents outdrew him on the final card on 21-to-1 shots. Suddenly he was out of the tournament. Coincidentally, in both hands Baldwin's opponent needed one of the two remaining queens among the 44 unseen cards, and he got it.

However, it is more likely for a good player like Baldwin to suffer these *bad beats,* as they are called, than for an average player or a weak player to suffer them. "I've heard good players complain to me about how they get drawn out on all the time," Baldwin said after the 1981 tournament. "But if they want to better their game and better their emotional state while playing, they should realize it's a mirage. If you are an excellent player, people are going to draw out on you a lot more than you're going to draw out on them because they're simply going to have the worst hand against you a lot more times than you have the worst hand against them. There's no way you're going to draw out on anybody if you don't get all your money in there on the worst hand."

As Baldwin implies, expert players do not rely on luck. They are at war with luck. They use their skills to minimize luck as much as possible. They figure they're getting the best of it, and they leave lucky draws to their weaker opponents. To the extent that they are getting the best of it, they will win more often than they lose. Over the long run everybody gets the same proportion of good and bad cards, of winning and losing hands. Beginning poker players rely on big hands and lucky draws. Expert poker players use their skills to minimize their losses on their bad hands and maximize their profits on their big hands. They also are able to judge better than others when a big hand is not the best hand and when a small hand is the best hand.

Whatever your level of play, the succeeding chapters will introduce you to theories and concepts of poker that will eliminate your reliance on luck and lead you to become an expert who relies on his skills. For above all, you must remember that poker is not primarily a game of luck. It is a game of skill.

The Forms of Poker

Poker is a generic name for literally hundreds of games, but they all fall within a few interrelated types. There are high games like seven-card stud and Texas hold 'em, in which the highest hand in the showdown wins, and low games like draw lowball and razz, in which the lowest hand wins. There are also high-low split games, in which the best high hand and the best low hand split the pot. Among high, low, and high-low split games there are those like five-card draw, in which the hands are closed, and those like seven-card stud, in which some of the players' cards are exposed for all to see.

Jokers, wild cards, and special rules may be introduced into any of these games to create such aberrations as Baseball, Follow the Queen, Anaconda, and scores of other variations that have spiced up home poker for decades. Paradoxically, the two types of players who favor these exotic poker variations are generally amateurs who want a lot of action and hustlers who prey on these amateurs because their long experience allows them to adjust more easily to unusual games than their amateur opponents can. However, before a player can become an expert at exotic games, he must understand the basic concepts of standard games.

Another significant distinction among poker games is their betting structure. Most home games and most games in Las Vegas, Gardena, California, and elsewhere are limit games — that is, games in which limits are set on the minimum and maximum bets. Normally, in the smaller-limit games of Las Vegas, such as $1-$3 seven-card stud, there is no ante, and the low card starts the action for 50 cents. In subsequent rounds, the high hand on board may check or bet $1, $2, or $3. In the higher-limit Las Vegas games and in the limit draw games of the card rooms of Gardena, the betting is rigidly structured. In Gardena the bets double after the draw. In Las Vegas they double in the later rounds of betting. In $5-$10 seven-card stud, for example, there is a 50-cent ante, low card starts the action, or *brings it in,* for $1, and on the next round the bets and raises must be $5, no more and no less. With an open pair after four cards, a player generally has the option of betting $5 or $10, but anyone who raises must raise $10. After the fifth, sixth, and seventh cards, the bets and raises must be $10 whether or not anyone has a pair showing.

In other poker games the betting structure might be pot-limit or no-limit. In a pot-limit game, bets and raises may be for any amount up to the size of the pot. Thus, with a $10 pot, someone might bet $10 and be called by three players. The last player to call can raise $50, the current size of the pot. If one player calls the raise, the size of the pot would then be $150 so that in the next round the first bet could be anything up to that amount.

In no-limit poker, a player may bet or raise any amount up to what he has in front of him/her at any time. If he has $500 in front of him, he can bet that. If he has $50,000 in front of him, he can bet that. He cannot, however, raise a player with less money out of a pot. That player may simply call with the money in front of him and a side pot is created for any remaining players. If his hand prevails, the player who is "all-in" can win only the money he called in the main pot, and the best hand among those remaining wins the side pot. (The same mechanics apply to limit games when a player is all-in.)

Notwithstanding the great variety of poker games — high games and low games, stud games and draw games, limit games and no-limit games — there is an inner logic that runs through all of them, and there are general precepts, concepts, and theories that apply to all of them. However experienced a player may be with the rules and methods of a specific game, like, say, five-card draw, only by understanding and applying the underlying concepts of poker can he move confidently to the expert level. The principles of such stratagems as the semi-bluff (Chapter Eleven) and slowplaying (Chapter Fifteen) are essentially the same in limit five-card draw poker as in no-limit hold 'em poker, and they are equally important.

Poker Logic

Poker logic is not tricks and ploys. In weaker games tricks and ploys may sometimes work — for example, gesturing as though to fold your hand and then raising after the third man in the pot has called. However, a super hustler with an arsenal of tricks and ploys who is not also a good player will not get the money against tough competition. Some poker writers make tricks and ploys the essence of poker; the best that can be said of them is they are misguided. Some players substitute tricks and ploys for sound precepts and sound play. They act surly, try to anger other players in the game — in a word, use almost any gimmick other than good play to win the money on the table. In the world of professional Las Vegas poker, such players never rise to the bigger games, and eventually, their tricks and ploys played out, they fade into the Las Vegas night like so many failed gamblers, earning a living driving a cab.

Nor is poker logic purely mathematical. Knowing the mathematics of poker can certainly help you play a better game. However, mathematics is only a small part of poker logic, and while it is important, it is far less important than understanding and using the underlying concepts of poker.

It is important to understand that poker is a much more difficult game than most people realize, that it can be more complex than bridge or backgammon. The concepts in this book are intended to make you understand the depth of the game and to make you a good player against tough competition. (Obviously if you can beat tough games, you will have little trouble destroying easier games.) While the concepts discussed often apply to all poker games, they relate particularly to limit games. Properly adjusted, they also relate to pot-limit and no-limit games. However, they do not always relate to games like high-low split, in which there are two winners in a pot.

The Object of Poker

Whether you are playing $1-limit poker at the kitchen table or pot-limit poker at the Stardust in Las Vegas, whether you are playing poker for fun or for a living, once a week or every day, you have to understand that the object of the game is to make money. That's where the profits are. That's where the fun is. That's the way the game is scored. Jack Straus, 1982 poker champion, has said he'd bust his own grandmother if she was in a pot with him, which is pretty much the only attitude a serious poker player can have when he or she sits down behind a stack of chips. Whatever the environment and whoever your opponents happen to be, you must play the game tough; you must play the game to win money. That does not mean you cannot joke or socialize, whether at the kitchen table or in a Las Vegas card room. Quite to the contrary. In a public card room people seem to mind losing their money to a sociable person less than losing it to a mole. However, when the cards are dealt, you are no longer a grandson, a friend, or a nice guy; you are a player.

To say a poker player is out to make money does not necessarily mean he is out to win pots. Of course, you can't win money without winning pots, but attempting to win every pot or too many pots is a losing proposition. If you win $100 in one pot but lose $120 trying to win four others, you have a net loss of $20. You may occasionally be in a game where the best strategy is to win as many pots as possible, but such games are exceptions. In most games the bets you save are as important as the bets you win, because your real goal is to maximize your wins and minimize your losses. Ideally you want the pots you win to be as big as possible and the pots you lose to contain nothing more than your ante. You must remember that reducing losses — by not making the calls, for example, that a weaker player would make — adds that much more to your win when the game is over.

Many players don't follow this precept, however obvious it may seem. They play as though they want to win the pot, an individual pot, at all costs. The worst of them, to put it bluntly, are the suckers in the game. On the other hand, a good player develops the patience to wait for the right situations to play a pot and develops the discipline to release a hand he judges to be second-best.

Just as it is important not to think in terms of individual pots — not to chase money you have contributed to an individual pot — so it is important to realize you are not playing in individual games. Each individual game is part of one big poker game. You cannot win every game or session you play, anymore than a golfer or bowler can win every match he or she plays. If you are a serious poker player, you must think in terms of your win at the end of the year or the end of the month — or, as sometimes happens, of your loss at the end of the year or the end of the month, which, of course, you want to keep as small as possible.

Thus, whether you are winning or losing on a given night is not in itself important, and above all it must not affect your play. It's easy to get *steamed,* or disgruntled or discouraged, when you're losing. However, you must be disciplined enough to play every hand correctly, regardless of how you are doing.

Similarly, you should not allow the fact that you are winning or losing to affect your decision to stay in or quit a game. From a money making point of view the only criterion for playing is whether you're a favorite in the game or an underdog. If you're a significant favorite, then it's a good game, and you should stay in it; if you're an underdog, then it's a bad game which you should quit. Never quit a good game as a small winner just to ensure a winning session. By the same token, don't continue playing in a bad game just to get even.

Even for tough professionals, quitting a game, particularly when they're *stuck* — that is, when they've lost money — is sometimes a hard thing to do. So long as you remain a big favorite, you should stay, even if it means using toothpicks to prop up your eyelids. But if the game has changed so that you're an underdog, you should quit whether you're a winner or loser. When you're stuck, you should examine the reasons why you're stuck. It may be just bad luck, but it may not. Are there too many players better than you? Is there cheating going on? Perhaps you yourself are playing worse than you normally do. Are you tired or distracted? Are you thinking about the football game you bet or the woman who's been "busy" the last four times you asked her out? Are you shaken up over a bad beat earlier in the session when someone drew a fourth deuce to beat your aces full? Making money is the object of poker, and making money involves saving it on bad nights as well as winning it on good nights. So don't worry about quitting a loser. If you have the best of it, you will win in the long run just as surely as a roulette wheel will win for the casino in the long run.

Chapter Two

Expectation and Hourly Rate

Mathematical Expectation

Mathematical expectation is the amount a bet will average winning or losing. It is an extremely important concept for the gambler because it shows him how to evaluate most gambling problems. Using mathematical expectation is also the best way to analyze most poker plays.

Let's say you are betting a friend $1, even money, on the flip of a coin. Each time it comes up heads, you win; each time it comes up tails, you lose. The odds of its coming up heads are 1-to-1, and you're betting $1-to-$1. Therefore, your mathematical expectation is precisely zero since you cannot expect, mathematically, to be either ahead or behind after two flips or after 200 flips.

Your hourly rate is also zero. Hourly rate is the amount of money you expect to win per hour. You might be able to flip a coin 500 times an hour, but since you are getting neither good nor bad odds, you will neither earn nor lose money. From a serious gambler's point of view, this betting proposition is not a bad one. It's just a waste of time.

But let's say some imbecile is willing to bet $2 to your $1 on the flip of the coin. Suddenly you have a positive expectation of 50 cents per bet. Why 50 cents? On the average you will win one bet for every bet you lose. You wager your first dollar and lose $1; you wager your second and win $2. You have wagered $1 twice, and you are $1 ahead. Each of these $1 bets has earned 50 cents.

If you can manage 500 flips of the coin per hour, your hourly rate is now $250, because on average you will lose one dollar 250

9

times and win two dollars 250 times. $500 minus $250 equals a $250 net win. Notice again that your mathematical expectation, which is the amount you will average winning per bet, is 50 cents. You have won $250 after betting a dollar 500 times: That works out to be 50 cents per bet.

Mathematical expectation has nothing to do with results. The imbecile might win the first ten coin flips in a row, but getting 2-to-1 odds on an even-money proposition, you still earn 50 cents per $1 bet. It makes no difference whether you win or lose a specific bet or series of bets as long as you have a bankroll to cover your losses easily. If you continue to make these bets, you will win, and in the long run your win will approach specifically the sum of your expectations.

Anytime you make a bet with the *best of it,* where the odds are in your favor, you have earned something on that bet, whether you actually win or lose the bet. By the same token, when you make a bet with the *worst of it,* where the odds are not in your favor, you have lost something, whether you actually win or lose the bet.

You have the best of it when you have a positive expectation, and you have a positive expectation when the odds are in your favor. You have the worst of it when you have a negative expectation, and you have a negative expectation when the odds are against you. Serious gamblers bet only when they have the best of it; when they have the worst of it, they pass.

What does it mean to have the odds in your favor? It means winning more on a result than the true odds warrant. The true odds of a coin's coming up heads are 1-to-1, but you're getting 2-to-1 for your money. The odds in this instance are in your favor. You have the best of it with a positive expectation of 50 cents per bet.

Here is a slightly more complicated example of mathematical expectation. A person writes down a number from one to five and bets $5 against your $1 that you cannot guess the number. Should you take the bet? What is your mathematical expectation?

Four guesses will be wrong, and one will be right, on average. Therefore, the odds against your guessing correctly are

4-to-1. Chances are that in a single try you will lose the dollar. However, you are getting $5-to-$1 on a 4-to-1 proposition. So the odds are in your favor, you have the best of it, and you should take the bet. If you make that bet five times, on average you will lose $1 four times and win $5 once. You have earned $1 on five bets for a positive expectation of 20 cents per bet.

A bettor is *taking* the odds when he stands to win more than he bets, as in the example above. He is *laying* the odds when he stands to win less than he bets. A bettor may have either a positive or a negative expectation, whether he is taking the odds or laying them. If you lay $50 to win $10 when you are only a 4-to-1 favorite, you have a negative expectation of $2 per bet, since you'll win $10 four times but lose $50 once, on average, for a net loss of $10 after five bets. On the other hand, if you lay $30 to win $10 when you're a 4-to-1 favorite, you have a positive expectation of $2, since you'll win $10 four times again but lose only $30 once, for a net profit of $10. Expectation shows that the first bet is a bad one and the second bet is a good one.

Mathematical expectation is at the heart of every gambling situation. When a bookmaker requires football bettors to lay $11 to win $10, he has a positive expectation of 50 cents per $10 bet. When a casino pays even money on the pass line at the craps table, it has a positive expectation of about $1.40 per $100 bet since the game is structured so that the pass line bettor will lose 50.7 percent of the time and win 49.3 percent of the time, on average. Indeed it is this seemingly minuscule positive expectation that provides casinos around the world with all their enormous profits. As Vegas World casino owner Bob Stupak has said, "Having one-thousandth of one percent the worst of it, if he plays long enough, that one-thousandth of one percent will bust the richest man in the world."

In most gambling situations like casino craps and roulette, the odds on any given bet are constant. In others they change, and mathematical expectation can show you how to evaluate a particular situation. In blackjack, for instance, to determine the right play, mathematicians have calculated your expectation playing a hand one way and your expectation playing it another way. Whichever play gives you a higher positive expectation or a lower negative expectation is the right one. For example, when you have a 16 against the dealer's 10, you're a favorite to lose. However, when that 16 is 8,8, your best play is to split the 8s, doubling your bet. By splitting the 8s against the dealer's 10, you still stand to lose more money than you win, but you have a lower negative expectation than if you simply hit every time you had an 8,8 against a 10.

Mathematical Expectation in Poker

Poker plays can also be analyzed in terms of expectation. You may think that a particular play is profitable, but sometimes it may not be the best play because an alternative play is more profitable. Let's say you have a full house in five-card draw. A player ahead of you bets. You know that if you raise, that player will call. So raising appears to be the best play. However, when you raise, the two players behind you will surely fold. On the other hand, if you call the first bettor, you feel fairly confident that the two players behind you will also call. By raising, you gain one unit, but by only calling you gain two. Therefore, calling has the higher positive expectation and is the better play.

Here is a similar but slightly more complicated situation. On the last card in a seven-card stud hand, you make a flush. The player ahead of you, whom you read to have two pair, bets, and there is a player behind you still in the hand, whom you know you have beat. If you raise, the player behind you will fold. Furthermore, the initial bettor will probably also fold if he in fact does have only two pair; but if he made a full house, he will reraise. In this instance, then, raising not only gives you no positive expectation, but it's actually a play with negative expectation. For if the initial bettor has a full house and reraises, the play costs you two units if you call his reraise and one unit if you fold.

Taking this example a step further: If you do *not* make the flush on the last card and the player ahead of you bets, you might *raise* against certain opponents! Following the logic of the situation when you did make the flush, the player behind you will fold, and if the initial bettor has only two pair, he too may fold. Whether the play has positive expectation (or less negative expectation than folding) depends upon the odds you are getting for your money — that is, the size of the pot — and your estimate of the chances that the initial bettor does not have a full house and will throw away two pair. Making the latter estimate requires, of course, the ability to read hands and to read players, which I discuss in later chapters. At this level, expectation becomes much more complicated than it was when you were just flipping a coin.

Mathematical expectation can also show that one poker play is less unprofitable than another. If, for instance, you think you will average losing 75 cents, including the ante, by playing a hand, you should play on because that is better than folding if the ante is a dollar.

Another important reason to understand expectation is that it gives you a sense of equanimity toward winning or losing a bet: When you make a good bet or a good fold, you will know that you have earned or saved a specific amount which a lesser player would not have earned or saved. It is much harder to make that fold if you are upset because your hand was outdrawn. However, the money you save by folding instead of calling adds to your winnings for the night or for the month. I actually derive pleasure from making a good fold even though I have lost the pot.

Just remember that if the hands were reversed, your opponent would call you, and as we shall see when we discuss the Fundamental Theorem of Poker in the next chapter, this is one of your edges. You should be happy when it occurs. You should even derive satisfaction from a losing session when you know that other players would have lost much more with your cards.

Hourly Rate

As suggested in the coin-flip example at the opening of this chapter, hourly rate is closely related to expectation, and it is a concept especially important to the professional player. When you go into a poker game, you should try to assess what you think you can earn per hour. For the most part you will have to base your assessment on your judgment and experience, but you can use certain mathematical guidelines. For instance, if you are playing draw lowball and you see three players calling $10 and then drawing two cards, which is a very bad play, you can say to yourself that each time they put in $10 they are losing an average of about $2. They are each doing it eight times an hour, which means those three players figure to lose about $48 an hour. You are one of four other players who are approximately equal, and therefore you four players figure to split up that $48 an hour, which gives you $12 an hour apiece. Your hourly rate in this instance is simply your share of the total hourly loss of the three bad players in the game.

Of course, in most games you can't be that precise. Even in the example just given, other variables would affect your hourly rate. Additionally, when you are playing in a public card room or in some private games where the operator *cuts the pot,* you need to deduct either the house *rake* or the hourly *seat charge.* In Las Vegas card rooms the rake is usually 10 percent of each pot up to a maximum of $4 in the smaller seven-card stud games and 5 percent of each pot to a maximum of $3 in the larger seven-card stud games, in the Texas hold 'em games, and in most other games.

In the long run a poker player's overall win is the sum of his mathematical expectations in individual situations. The more plays you make with a positive expectation, the bigger winner you stand to be. The more plays you make with a negative expectation, the bigger loser you stand to be. Therefore, you should almost always try to make the play that will maximize your positive expectation or minimize your negative expectation in order to maximize your hourly rate.

Once you have decided what your hourly rate is, you should realize that what you are doing is earning. You are no longer gambling in the traditional sense. You should no longer be anxious to have a good day or upset when you have a bad day. If you play regularly, you should simply feel that it is better to be playing poker making $20 an hour, able to come and go as you please, than to be working an eight-hour shift making $15 an hour. To think of poker as something glamorous is very bad. You must think that you are just working as a poker player and that you are not particularly anxious about making a big score. If it comes, it comes. Conversely, you won't be so upset if you have a big loss. If one comes, it comes. You are just playing for a certain hourly rate.

If you have estimated your hourly rate correctly, your eventual winnings will approximate your projected hourly rate multiplied by the total hours played. Your edge comes not from holding better cards, but from play in situations where your opponents would play incorrectly if they had your hand and you had theirs. The total amount of money they cost themselves in incorrect play, assuming you play perfectly, minus the rake, is the amount of money you will win. Your opponents' various mistakes per hour will cost them various amounts of money. If the hands were reversed, you wouldn't make these mistakes, and this difference is your hourly rate. That's all there is to it. If they play a hand against you differently from the way you would play it five times an hour, and if it's a $2 mistake on average, that's a $10-an-hour gain for you.

To assume you play perfectly is, of course, a big assumption. Few if any of us play perfectly all of the time, but that is what we strive for. Furthermore, it is important to realize that there is not one particular correct way to play a poker hand as there is in most bridge hands. On the contrary, you must adjust to your opponents and mix up your play, even against the same opponents, as we shall explain in later chapters.

Furthermore, it is sometimes correct to play incorrectly! You may, for example, purposely make an inferior play to gain in a future hand or future round of betting. You also may play less than optimally against weak opponents who have only a limited amount to lose or when you yourself are on a short bankroll. In these cases it is not correct to push small edges. You should not put in the maximum raises as a small favorite. You should fold hands that are marginally worth calling. You have reduced your hourly rate but have ensured yourself a win. Why give weaker players any chance to get lucky and quit big winners or get lucky and bust you if you are on a short bankroll? You'll still get the money playing less than optimally. It will just take a few more hours.

You should try to assess most poker games in terms of your expected hourly rate by noticing what mistakes your opponents are making and how much these mistakes are costing them. Don't sit in a game with an insufficient hourly rate projection unless you think the game will become better — either because you expect some weaker players to arrive soon or because some good players in the game have a tendency to start playing badly when they are losing. If these good players jump off winners, you should quit if you can. However, it is sometimes good to continue in a game with a low hourly rate projection for political reasons — you do not want to get a reputation for gambling only when you have much the best of it. Such a reputation can make enemies, cost you money in the long run, and even get you barred from some games.

Chapter Three

The Fundamental
Theorem of Poker

There is a Fundamental Theorem of Algebra and a Fundamental Theorem of Calculus. So it's about time to introduce the Fundamental Theorem of Poker. Poker, like all card games, is a game of incomplete information, which distinguishes it from board games like chess, backgammon, and checkers, where you can always see what your opponent is doing. If everybody's cards were showing at all times, there would always be a precise, mathematically correct play for each player. Any player who deviated from his correct play would be reducing his mathematical expectation and increasing the expectation of his opponents.

Of course, if all cards were exposed at all times, there wouldn't be a game of poker. The art of poker is filling the gaps in the incomplete information provided by your opponent's betting and the exposed cards in open-handed games, and at the same time preventing your opponents from discovering any more than what you want them to know about your hand.

That leads us to the Fundamental Theorem of Poker:

Every time you play a hand differently from the way you would have played it if you could see all your opponents' cards, they gain; and every time you play your hand the same way you would have played it if you could see all their cards, they lose. Conversely, every time opponents play their hands differently from the way they would have if they could see all your cards, you gain; and every time they play their

hands the same way they would have played if they
could see all your cards, you lose.

The Fundamental Theorem applies universally when a hand
has been reduced to a contest between you and a single opponent.
It nearly always applies to multi-way pots as well, but there are
rare exceptions, which we will discuss at the end of the chapter.

What does the Fundamental Theorem mean? Realize that if
somehow your opponent knew your hand, there would be a
correct play for him to make. If, for instance, in a draw poker
game your opponent saw that you had a pat flush before the draw,
his correct play would be to throw away a pair of aces when you
bet. Calling would be a mistake, but it is a special kind of mistake.
We do not mean your opponent played the hand badly by calling
with a pair of aces; we mean he played it differently from the way
he would play it if he could see your cards.

This flush example is very obvious. In fact, the whole
theorem is obvious, which is its beauty; yet its applications are
often not so obvious. Sometimes the amount of money in the pot
makes it correct to call, even if you could see that your opponent's
hand is better than yours. Let's look at several examples of the
Fundamental Theorem of Poker in action.

Examples of The
Fundamental Theorem of Poker

Example 1

Suppose your hand is not as good as your opponent's when
you bet. Your opponent calls your bet, and you lose. But in fact
you have not lost; you have gained! Why? Because obviously
your opponent's correct play, if he knew what you had, would be
to raise. Therefore, you have gained when he doesn't raise, and if
he folds, you have gained a tremendous amount.

This example may also seem too obvious for serious discussion, but it is a general statement of some fairly sophisticated plays. Let's say in no-limit hold 'em you hold the

and your opponent holds an *offsuit*

The flop comes:

You check, your opponent bets, and you call. Now the ace of diamonds comes on fourth street, and you bet, trying to represent aces. If your opponent knew what you had, his correct play would be to raise you so much it would cost too much to draw to a flush or a straight on the last card, and you would have to fold. Therefore, if your opponent only calls, you have gained. You have gained not just because you are getting a relatively cheap final card but because your opponent did not make the correct play. Obviously if your opponent folds, you have gained tremendously since he has thrown away the best hand.

Example 2

Suppose there is $80 in the pot, and you have two pair. You are playing draw poker, and you bet $10, which we will assume is all you can bet. Your single opponent has a *four-flush* — that is, four cards to a flush. The question is — are you rooting for him to call or fold? Naturally you want him to do what is most profitable for you. The Fundamental Theorem of Poker states that what is most profitable for you is for your opponent to make the incorrect play based on complete information about both hands. Since your opponent is getting 9-to-1 odds (his $10 call might win him $90) and is only about a 5-to-1 underdog to make a flush, it is correct for him to call because a call has positive expectation. Since it is correct for him to call, following the Fundamental Theorem, you are therefore rooting for him to fold.

This sort of situation comes up frequently. You have the best hand, but your opponent is getting odds good enough to make it correct to call if he knew what you had. Therefore, you want your opponent to fold. By the same token, it is correct for you to chase when you are getting sufficient pot odds. If you don't chase, you are costing yourself money and, therefore, making money for your opponent.

Example 3

Since it is correct for your opponent to call when he is getting sufficient pot odds, you can sometimes make an opponent fold incorrectly by showing more strength than you actually have on an early betting round. Suppose in seven-card stud you bet with:

An opponent calls with:

You are fairly sure he has kings. You now proceed to make a pair of 6s on board, and you bet. Your opponent will almost certainly fold a pair of kings since he is afraid you have made aces up.

Some people might say, "Well, wait a second. Why don't I want my opponent to call as long as his pair of kings is worse than my two small pair?" The answer is that if there are cards to come and your opponent is getting proper odds, you do better to win the pot right there. A pair of kings versus two smaller pair needs very short odds to justify a call. Since your opponent would have been correct to call, you gain when you make him fold.

Example 4

In razz, a seven-card stud lowball game in which the lowest hand wins, we can see another example of showing more strength than you have to make an opponent fold incorrectly. Let's say your opponent has

showing, and you have something like

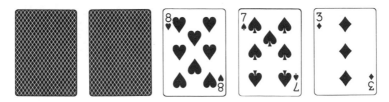

If you think your opponent has a four-card 8 — and you have a pair and only a four-card 8-7 — it is important to bet, even though you know you will be called. The bet gains you some extra equity, should you happen to catch a little card on sixth street, giving you an 8-7 low. If your opponent catches a big card or a pair, still having a draw to a better 8 than yours, he will fold, since your previous bet indicated you had an 8 made already. The little card you've now caught suggests you have made a 7 low, which makes your opponent think he is *drawing dead* — that is, drawing with no chance of winning.

Notice that once again you want your opponent to fold even though you have the best hand. You have an 8,7 low and are drawing to a 7, while all your opponent has is a draw to a better 8. However, you gain by his folding because, had he known you had only an 8,7, he would be getting proper odds to call in the hope of drawing out on you. By not calling he made a mistake, and you have gained. (You gain even more when that sixth street card makes you two pair, and your opponent folds the best hand.)

Example 5

Just as you are rooting for an opponent to fold when he is getting sufficient pot odds, you are rooting for him to call when he is getting insufficient pot odds. Thus, it is frequently correct to play a strong hand weakly on an early round — the converse of your plays in the previous two examples — so that your opponent will make a bad call when you do improve. Look at the following two hands from seven-card razz:

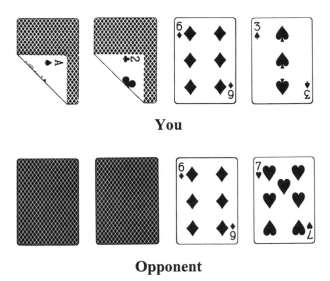

You

Opponent

A good play against some people with this hand would be to check and just call if your opponent bets. Many players would now put you on a pair or a bad card in the hole. If you do catch a 4, 5 or 7 on board, giving you a 6 or 7 low, your opponent will probably still call, even if he is drawing dead, because your earlier play along with his pot odds make him think it's worth a call. This is exactly what you are hoping for. Your deceptive play early has caused your opponent to make an incorrect play on a later round.

Example 6

Any time an opponent is not getting close to proper odds against you, you are rooting for him to call, even if by calling he has a chance of drawing out on you. If in the flush example at the beginning of this chapter, the pot were $20 instead of $80, you would be rooting for your opponent with the four-flush to call your $10 bet because he is a 5-to-1 underdog getting only 3-to-1 for his money. If he calls and makes a flush, those are the breaks. Nevertheless, his play is incorrect because it has negative expectation, and you gain any time he makes it.

When you have a hand that is rooting for a call, you should not try to make your opponent fold by betting an exorbitant amount in a no-limit or pot-limit game. Such a situation came up one day when I was playing no-limit hold 'em. There was one card to come, and I had a straight which, at that point, was the *nuts* — that is, the best possible hand. I bet something like $50, the player to my left called, and the player behind him called the $50 and raised the rest of his money, which was about $200.

Since I had the best possible hand, the question was, should I raise or just call? There was something like $500 in the pot. Because the third man was all-in, I only had to think about the man behind me. I knew if I reraised, say, $400, making it $600 to him, he definitely would fold; in fact, if I raised almost any amount he would fold. But if I just called the $200, he would probably call.

What did I want him to do? I was pretty sure he had two pair. If I called the $200, there would be about $700 in the pot, which would give him 7-to-2 odds to call $200 with his two pair. However, the odds against his making a full house with two pair were 10-to-1 (there were 40 cards in the deck that didn't help him and 4 that did). Therefore, if he knew I had a straight, it would be incorrect for him to take 7-to-2 odds on a 10-to-1 shot. So I just called the $200, and as I expected and wanted, he did too.

The sad conclusion to this story is that he made a full house and bet a very small amount, which I paid off. Many people argued I had been wrong to let him in rather than raise him out, but in fact they are wrong. I had to give him a chance to make a mistake, which he did, because whenever my opponent makes a mistake, I gain in the long run.

"Mistakes" According to The Fundamental Theorem of Poker

It is very important to understand that when we talk about making a mistake according to the Fundamental Theorem of

Poker, we're not necessarily talking about playing badly. We're talking about a very strange kind of mistake — playing differently from the way you would if you could see all your opponents' cards. If I have a royal flush and someone has a king-high straight flush, that player is making a mistake to call me. But a player surely cannot be accused of playing badly by calling or, as is much more likely, raising with a king-high straight flush. Since he doesn't know what I have, he is making a mistake in a different sense of the word.

In advanced poker you are constantly trying to make your opponent or opponents play in a way that would be incorrect if they knew what you had. Anytime they play in the right way on the basis of what you have, you have not gained a thing. According to the Fundamental Theorem of Poker, you play winning poker by playing as closely as possible to the way you would play if you could see all your opponents' cards; and you try to make your opponents play as far away from this Utopian level as possible. The first goal is accomplished mainly by reading hands and players accurately, because the closer you can come to figuring out someone else's hand, the fewer Fundamental Theorem mistakes you will make. The second goal is accomplished by playing deceptively.

Multi-Way Pots

We stated at the start of the chapter that the Fundamental Theorem of Poker applies to all two-way pots and to nearly all multi-way pots. The reason we qualify multi-way pots is that there are certain situations with two or more opponents when you actually want one or more of them to play as they would if they knew what you had. Let's say that with cards still to come, you have a 30 percent chance of winning a pot. Opponent A has a 50 percent chance, and Opponent B has a 20 percent chance. If you bet, you might not mind Opponent A's raising with the best hand to force Opponent B out. A's chances of winning may now increase to 60 percent, but yours increase to 40 percent. You have both profited at the expense of C. You might, for example, bet a pair of aces. Opponent A has two pair, and Opponent B has a straight draw. You'd like Opponent A to know you have only aces, not aces up, so that he will raise and drive the straight draw out. You would be getting good enough odds to call the raise and at the same time wouldn't have to worry about Opponent B's drawing a straight.

Summary

The Fundamental Theorem of Poker states that the best way for players to play is the way they would play if they knew their opponent's cards. Anytime a player sees an opponent's cards when the hand is over and says, "Oh, if I'd known that's what he had, I would have played differently," that player has cost himself money and made (or saved) money for his opponents.

Chapter Four

The Ante Structure

All poker starts as a struggle for the antes. If there were no ante, there would be no reason to play. It's true that some players would play anyway, but a good player in such a game would simply wait for the pure nuts and nearly always win. A good player would have no reason to play anything but big starter hands — three aces, say, in seven-card stud — because with no money yet in the pot, there would be nothing to shoot for. To play with anything less would be to risk getting picked off by someone else who played nothing but the pure nuts. If all players in the game played nothing but the pure nuts, there could be no game. Any time one person bet, everyone else would fold. Obviously, then, there has to be an ante to establish a game.

On the other hand, if the ante were ridiculously large in relation to the betting limits, the game would pretty much deteriorate into a crap shoot. It would be like someone walking by a $5-$10 game and tossing a $100 bill on the table saying, "Play for it, boys." With that big an initial pot, in which you would be getting at least 21-to-1 odds on your first $5 call, it would be worth playing just about any hand right to the end.

These two extremes — no ante and an absurdly high ante — suggest a general principle of play. The lower the ante in comparison to future bets, the fewer hands you should play; the higher the ante, the more hands you should play. A different way of looking at it is: The lower the ante, the higher your starting requirements should be, and the higher the ante, the lower your starting requirements should be. Or in the language of the poker room: The lower the ante, the tighter you should play; the higher the ante, the looser you should play. I consider 5 percent or less of the average future bets a small ante and 15 percent or more of the average future bets a large ante. Anything in between is an

27

average ante. Thus, $100 would be an average ante in a $1,000-$2,000 game, while in a $5-$10 game, 50 cents would be an average ante.

The antes are not always the only things that make up the initial pot. There may be forced bets, or *blinds* — forced bets that rotate around the table from hand to hand. In Las Vegas seven-card stud, for example, the low card on board starts the action with a small bet. In most $1-$2, $1-$3, and $1-$4 stud games the forced bet (50 cents) actually replaces the ante. In razz the high card starts the action with a small bet. And in hold 'em there is almost always at least one and sometimes two or even three blinds. When we talk about antes in this chapter, we are including any forced bets or blinds.

To repeat, all poker starts as a struggle for the ante. This struggle for the antes is what determines all future action. It is a struggle that increases and builds up, but it should never be forgotten that the initial struggle for the antes is what started the war. Players who do forget this, no matter how well they play otherwise, frequently find themselves in trouble. Most often they play too many hands in relation to the size of the ante; sometimes they play too few.

The best way to evaluate the size of the ante is to think about it in terms of pot odds and expectation. Let's say you sit down in an eight-handed $10-$20 game, and everybody antes $1. That creates an $8 pot. Starting with that $8, you should play your hand in terms of the odds you're getting for each bet in relation to your expectation of winning. If you bet $10, you are laying $10 to win $8. If someone calls you, he is getting $18-to-$10.

The fact that $1 or one-eighth of that ante money was originally yours is of no consequence. In truth, it is no longer yours. The moment you place your $1 ante in the pot, it belongs to the pot, not to you, and eventually to the winner of the hand. It is a common fallacy for players to think in terms of the money they have already put in the pot. They make a bad call because they called one or two bets on earlier rounds. However, it is absolutely irrelevant whether you put the money in there or someone else did. It is the total amount, no part of which belongs to you any longer, that should determine how you play your hand. In home games the dealer often antes for everybody. Some players play much more loosely when they are dealing, thinking that the ante is somehow theirs. But to play differently just because you anted, rather than someone else, is absurd. It is the same amount of money out there, no matter from whose stack of chips it came.

On the other hand, when you have the blind in hold 'em, for example, you can and should play a little looser, not because that blind is yours, but because you're getting better pot odds. A single example should make this clear. Let's say you have the $5 blind in hold 'em, and someone behind you raises it to $10. It now costs everyone else $10 to call, but when it comes back around to you, it costs you only $5. If the pot grows to $35, someone calling the $10 would be getting 3½-to-1, but since it's only $5 to you, you're getting 7-to-1 for your money. So you don't need quite so strong a hand to justify a call. You are considering your present pot odds, not the $5 you already have in the pot.

Large Antes

The size of the ante in a particular game determines how you play. The larger the ante in comparison to later bets, the more hands you should play. Since there's more money in the pot, you're obviously getting better odds, but there are other reasons for playing more loosely. Should you wait to get an extremely good hand in a high ante game, you'll have lost more than the size of the pot in antes by the time you win a pot. Furthermore, the pots you do win will be comparatively small because the other players, if they are decent players, will notice you are playing very tight and won't give you much action when you do play a hand. In fact, when you do get action, you're very likely to be beat.

As the antes go up, your opponents reduce their playing requirements, and unless you want to be eaten up by the antes, you too must reduce your playing requirements. These lower requirements continue to the next round of betting and progress right on to the end of the hand. In a large-ante game you might bet for value marginal hands you would throw away in a small-ante game. The principle holds true especially in head-up situations. In a large-ante seven stud game you might see two good players betting and calling right up to the last card, and then at the end one of them bets a pair of 7s for value and gets called by his opponent with a pair of 5s. As it happens, though, larger antes tend to make multi-way pots more numerous since more players are getting good pot odds to draw to a big hand. With many players in the pot, *drawing hands* (like four-flushes and open-end straights) go up in value, while mediocre pairs like those 7s and 5s go down in value.

Another reason for loosening up when the ante is comparatively high is that if you are playing too tight, it becomes correct for other players to try to steal the ante from you without any kind of a hand. I've been in games where some players played too tight for the ante. When they were the only players in the pot, I knew I could try to steal the antes, no matter what I had. Let's say it costs me $7 to raise the pot in order to try to steal $10 in antes. That is, I put in $7, hoping the remaining players will fold. I figure I will get away with the play approximately 60 percent of the time. Since I need to be successful only about 41 percent of the time to show a profit, I can try to steal with anything. The point is you cannot play too tightly for the antes unless you want to give up this edge to your opponents. To the contrary, as the ante increases, you yourself should try to steal more antes, especially if you are up against tight players.

If it makes sense to try to win antes right away when they are large, it makes abundant sense not to slowplay a good hand.[1] The reason is that if you don't raise with a good hand on the first

---

[1] *Slowplaying,* or *sandbagging,* is playing a strong hand weakly in a round of betting to induce a call by a worse hand in the later rounds. (*See also* Chapter Fifteen.)

round, you are giving an opponent with a mediocre hand the chance to come in cheaply and possibly draw out on you. With a large ante, he is not making a mistake on the basis of the Fundamental Theorem of Poker because he is getting good odds. In other words, if a player is getting 8-to-1 odds or 10-to-1 odds on that first round, it is worth it for him to come in and hope to catch a perfect card on the next round — even when he is pretty sure you are slowplaying a big hand. However, when you raise, you wreck the odds he is getting, and he has to throw away his mediocre hand. With almost any good hand, it is not worth letting opponents in cheaply when the ante gets up there. You are satisfied with winning only the antes. On the other hand, when the ante is low, it becomes more reasonable to slowplay big hands in order to suck worse hands in; you want to get more value for your big hands.

Let us summarize this discussion of games with large antes before moving on to small-ante games.

1. As the ante increases, you loosen up your starting-hand requirements. There are four reasons for you to loosen up. First, you are getting better pot odds. Second, it costs too much money in antes to wait for big hands. Third, your opponents are playing weaker hands. And finally, when you play too tight against observant opponents, they will give you no action when you do get a big hand.

2. As the ante increases, you loosen up on later rounds, too, because the initial weaker requirements carry over into later rounds. However, in multi-way pots, hands like mediocre pairs decrease in value while drawing hands increase in value.

3. As the ante increases, you try to steal antes, especially against tight players, because the play has good positive expectation.

4. As the ante increases, you raise with a good hand rather than try to slowplay it because a large ante makes it likely your opponents are getting their proper odds when you do *not* raise and let them in cheaply. Furthermore, when the ante is large, opponents may even call your raise when they are not getting proper odds, which, according to the Fundamental Theorem, is exactly what you want. They are even more likely to call your raise if they suspect you have been stealing antes with your raises on previous hands.

Small Antes

Not playing loose enough in high-ante games is a much less common problem among poker players than playing too loose in low-ante and average-ante games. When players in a game cry out, "Here comes a live one," what they mean is, "Here comes a player who plays too many pots, who always wants to get into the action, who doesn't consider the odds before calling, who calls to the end with next to nothing when two aces are staring him in the face." Put more succinctly, what they mean is, "Here comes a sucker."

What happens when you play too loose for the ante? Well, even if you play very well from then on, you have the problem of playing a worse hand on average than your opponents who are playing correctly according to the ante. Consequently, you figure to lose to them as long as they play as well as you. Even if they don't play quite as well as you, you figure to lose to them because their starting requirements are higher than yours, and so the hands they play against you will, on average, be better than yours.

There used to be a no-limit hold 'em game with a very small ante in Las Vegas, and there were a couple of excellent players in the game. But they insisted on raising almost every pot before the flop, not to steal the small antes, but just to get more money in the pot since they felt they could outplay everybody else from that point on. However, when a mediocre player who simply played tight came into the game, they found they couldn't beat him. What was happening, of course, was that the hands they played were on average much worse than the mediocre player's, and even a world champion with a pair of kings is an underdog against a nobody with a pair of aces. No matter how great a player is, if he plays much too loose for the ante, he is giving away an edge to those players who play correctly for the ante.

With a small ante, you should play just the opposite of the way you would play with a large ante. You play fewer hands, you steal fewer antes, and you slowplay big hands to draw people in. Let the aggressive players control the game if they choose to. Let them steal the antes. Give them a false sense of security. Then, when you are in a pot against them, your hand will be so much stronger than theirs on average that you'll win any antes they might have stolen from you and much more.

As long as you play tight in a small-ante game most of the time, it will be possible for you too to steal antes occasionally. However, when you are called or reraised, especially by players you know to be tight, you must give up on your bluff immediately since you are up against too big a hand.

The general rule is that as the ante decreases, you must tighten up. But when you are at least as good as or better than your opponents in a game with a very low ante, you should not tighten up so much that you never seem to play a hand. As the ante gets to a very low level, there is a limit to how much you should tighten up, because you need to give yourself the chance to outplay weaker opponents in later rounds. As the best player in the game, you want to play as many hands as possible to allow yourself to use your full arsenal of weapons.

Some games have a small ante and also a small initial bet. In such cases you should play loose for the *initial bet only,* calling with a marginal hand but folding on the next round of betting if your hand has not improved. When you do develop a hand, your small investment will pay big dividends. There is a $3-$6 game in Nevada with a tiny dime ante. Tight players think they have a gold mine in this game, but against decent players they don't. The reason is that the first bet is only 50 cents. It's worth playing a marginal hand to see one card for half a dollar in the hope of making a hand that will win a big pot. While the immediate pot odds may not justify the call, the implied odds you're getting, which are explained in detail in Chapter Seven, do justify it. You can call that half-dollar 20 times without improving your hand, but if, when you make a hand, you get just one opponent to call you to the end, you stand to win more than twice what you had to pay for those 20 hands that did not improve. Remember, however, to resist any temptation you may have to continue calling when your hand has not improved on fourth street.

Summary

The concepts discussed in this chapter may be summed up in a few sentences. All poker begins as a struggle for the antes. The size of the ante determines the way you play to a large extent, because if you don't struggle properly for the antes, you cost yourself money one way or the other — either by playing too many hands when there's a small ante or too few when there's a large ante. With a low ante you should play tight (except in the cases noted above), and as the ante increases, you should loosen up.

Chapter Five

Pot Odds

Pot odds are the odds the pot is giving you for calling a bet. If there is $50 in the pot and the final bet was $10, you are getting 5-to-1 odds for your call. It is essential to know pot odds to figure out expectation. In the example just given, if you figure your chances of winning are better than 5-to-1, then it is correct to call. If you think your chances are worse than 5-to-1, you should fold.

Calling on the Basis of Pot Odds When All the Cards are Out

When all the cards are out, you must decide whether your hand is worth a call, and that depends upon the odds you are getting from the pot and what you think of your chances of having the best hand. It is a judgment problem more than a math problem because there is no way to calculate your chances of winning precisely. If you can beat only a bluff, you have to evaluate the chances that your opponent is bluffing. When you have a decent hand, you must evaluate the chances that your opponent is betting a worse hand than yours. Making these evaluations is often not easy, especially when you have a marginal hand like two pair in seven-card stud. Your ability to do so depends upon your experience, especially your ability to read hands and players. Some things can be learned only through trials by fire at the poker table.

Calling on the Basis of Pot Odds With More Cards to Come

What about deciding whether to call before the draw in draw poker and in stud games when there is one card to come? Now the math becomes important. If you know you have to improve your hand to win, you have to determine your chances of improving in comparison to your pot odds. With a flush draw or an open-ended straight draw — we'll assume the game is five-card draw poker — you would be correct to call a $10 bet when the pot is $50 since your chance of making the flush or the straight is better than 5-to-1. Specifically, the odds of making the flush are 4.22-to-1 against and the odds of making the straight, 4.88-to-1 against.

Figuring the odds for making a hand is done on the basis of the number of unseen cards and the number among them that will make the hand. In five-card draw there are 47 unseen cards — the 52 in the deck minus the five cards in your hand. If you are holding four of a suit, nine of the 47 unseen cards will give you a flush and 38 won't. Thus, the odds against making the flush are 38-to-9, which reduces to 4.22-to-1. If you are holding, say

then eight of the 47 unseen cards will make the straight — four 8s and four kings — while 39 of the cards won't help, which reduces to 4.88-to-1. When a joker or bug is used, as in public card rooms in California, you have an additional card to use to make flushes and straights, which improves the chances of making the flush to 3.8-to-1 and of making the straight to 4.33-to-1. With a joker in your hand, the chances of making a straight improve dramatically;

instead of having eight or nine cards to help your hand, you might have 12 or even 16. For example, if you are holding

any 6, 7, jack, or queen makes the straight, reducing the odds to exactly 2-to-1 against. Sixteen cards make the hand, and 32 don't.

The smaller the pot odds vis-à-vis the chances of making your hand, the more reason you have to fold. With only $30 in the pot instead of $50, calling a $10 bet for a flush draw or a straight draw (assuming you do not have a joker in your hand) becomes incorrect — that is, it becomes a wager with negative expectation — unless the implied odds are very large, as they might be in a no-limit or pot-limit game.

It is because of the pot odds that people say you need at least three other players in the pot to make it worth paying to draw to a flush in draw poker. With the antes in there, the pot odds are about 4-to-1, and when the bug is used, your chances of making the flush are 3.8-to-1. Notice, incidentally, the effect of the antes. The higher they are, the better the pot odds, and the easier it is to call with a flush draw. On the other hand, with no ante and three other players in the pot, you'd be getting only 3-to-1 if you called a bet before the draw, and so you'd have to fold a four-flush.

Exposed Cards

There is one aspect of comparing the odds of making your hand to your pot odds that is frequently overlooked in open-handed games like stud poker and razz: The effect on your play of the cards exposed in other players' hands, which of course includes cards that were folded along with those still out against you. For instance, it would be crazy to play a pair of 5s in seven-card stud with the two other 5s exposed.

Your chances of improving a hand change dramatically according to the number of needed cards that are gone and the total number of cards exposed. The second factor is important. For example, with three spades on your first three cards and *no other cards seen,* you will make a spade flush in seven cards 18 percent of the time. Now, suppose when you look around the table, you see that exactly one of your seven opponents shows a spade. What does this do to your chances of making a flush? If you say it increases them, you are right. True, one of your needed cards is gone, but so too are six unneeded cards. Therefore, there are more spades *proportionally* among the unseen cards than you would assume if you had seen no cards at all.

Generally, though, it's not so much the total number of exposed cards that people ignore but the number of cards among them that they need. It is very important to pay attention to these cards because their presence can change a playable hand into an unplayable one. Let's say you start with three spades on your first three cards in seven-card stud, and you have seen seven other cards. The following table shows the effect of the other cards on your making a flush.

Number of Spades Besides Your Own	Chances For a Flush %
0	23.6
1	19.6
2	15.8
3	12.3
4	9.1

With no spades out, you have a strong hand. With two out, your hand becomes marginally playable. With four or more out, it becomes a hand not worth a call.

Here are a few more examples from seven-card stud and seven-card razz to demonstrate the effect of exposed cards on the chances of making a hand.

You start with

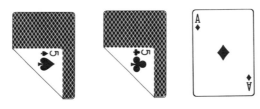

on your first three cards in seven-card stud. You have seen seven other cards.

Number of 5s and Aces Seen Besides Your Own	Chances For Aces Up Or Three-of-a-Kind (%)
0	41.0
1	34.1
2	26.5
3	18.3
4	10.5

You start with

on your first four cards in seven-card stud and have seen eight other cards.

Number of 5s and 10s Seen	Chances For a Straight (%)
0	49.8
1	44.8
2	39.4
3	33.8
4	27.8

You start with

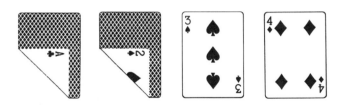

on your first four cards in seven-card razz. You have seen ten other cards.

Number of 5s, 6s, 7s, and 8s Seen	Chances For an 8 Low or Better (%)
0	81.8
2	76.0
3	72.7
4	69.2
5	65.3
6	61.2
7	56.7
8	51.9

Though you're a favorite to make an 8 low or better with as many as eight of your needed cards among the ten exposed, notice how much harder it is to make a 7 low.

Number of 5s, 6s, and 7s Seen	Chances For a 7 Low or Better (%)
0	69.2
4	51.9
8	29.1

These tables indicate the importance of taking the cards you see in other players' hands into account before you compare the pot odds you are getting to your chances of making your hand.

Position

Just as the number of needed cards you see reduces your chances of improving your hand, your position in the sequence of betting may also reduce the pot odds you are getting. If a player ahead of you bets and thère is a possible raise to your left, you must be cognizant of the fact that that possibility cuts down on your odds. If, for example, there is a $100 pot and the bet is $20, you appear to be getting 6-to-1 odds ($120 to $20). However, when there is a raiser behind you and the original bettor calls, you are really getting only 4½-to-1 if you call the raise. Although the pot has grown to $180, you must put in a total of $40. If the original bettor reraises, your odds drop to 3⅔-to-1. The pot grows to $220 (assuming the opponent behind you calls the reraise), but you have to put in $60. What's more, your chances of winning, even when you make your hand, have certainly decreased with all that raising going on between your opponents, suggesting they have pretty big hands.

How does the concept of position vis-à-vis pot odds work in practice? Let's say in seven-card stud you have a four-flush in six cards and a player to your right bets after pairing his *door card.* (The door card is the first open card the player receives. When it is paired on board, *trips,* or three-of-a-kind, is a strong possibility since the player may have started with a pair.) At the same time that the player with the open pair bets, you notice that a player to your left has caught a card that looks as if it has made him a straight. Before you call the first bet, you must be aware that the player to your left may raise if he made a straight (or even if he didn't). Furthermore, the original bettor may reraise with three-of-a-kind or, of course, a full house. So before calling the first bet, you have to assess your pot odds not just at the moment but in the event there is a raise or two behind you. You also have to decide what your chances of winning are if you do make the flush. You would, of course, beat the straight, but the question is whether the original bettor is the kind of player who would bet into a possible straight with less than a full house or at the very least three-of-a-kind.

Adjusting your pot odds before calling a bettor to your right with players behind you comes up most often in games like five-card draw, draw lowball, and hold 'em, where position is important. Let's say in hold 'em you hold the

and the flop comes

You would seem to have a strong hand with the top pair, but if you are in second position with a number of players behind you and the player in first position bets, you should probably throw away your aces. Not only has the player in first position suggested a great deal of strength with his bet, but he may get raised by such hands as an ace-king, ace-queen, and three-of-a-kind, which shortens your pot odds and further decreases the possibility of your ending up with the best hand. Additionally, the chance of calls from flush draws and straight draws behind you further diminishes the strength of your pair of aces. You face the uncomfortable double possibility of being second-best at the moment and of being outdrawn on the last two cards.

Similarly, in seven-card stud you might have to throw away a pair of jacks in the hole if the player representing queens to your immediate right bets. Not only do you figure to be second-best to the queens, but someone behind you might raise, thus reducing your pot odds and chances of winning. On the other hand, you'd probably call the bet in a late position, especially because of the deceptive value of your hidden pair, if you happen to catch another jack. (For a full discussion of the importance of position, see Chapter Seventeen.)

Extra Outs

Just as many players overlook the effects of position and exposed cards to lower the value of a hand, so too do they sometimes overlook extra outs to increase the value of a hand. An out is a way of improving your hand. With four hearts your only out is another heart. But suppose you have two pair along with the four-flush against what looks like aces up. Now you have two outs — making a flush and a full house. Suppose you have a four-flush, two pair, and an inside straight draw. Now you have three outs — that is, three ways of beating your opponent with the aces up, assuming that player doesn't fill. Each extra out increases the value of your hand, and it increases it considerably more than may at first be apparent. Starting off with a two-flush and a pair in seven-card stud is significantly better than starting with a pair and no two-flush. In hold 'em, a *back-door* straight (that is, a possible straight requiring two perfect cards at the end) or a *back-door* flush draw along with a pair may be enough to change a fold to a call.

To see how much effect these extra outs have, let's say we assess our hand as a 7-to-1 underdog. Now we notice we have an extra out that is about 20-to-1 against coming in. By itself that extra out is a long shot, but it adds tremendously to our chances of improving. Changing those 7-to-1 and 20-to-1 odds to percentages, we have a 12½ percent chance and about a 5 percent chance, which, added together, comes to approximately 17½ percent. Returning from percentages to odds, we see that the extra out has dropped us from a 7-to-1 underdog to a 4¾-to-1 underdog. With pot odds of, say, 5-to-1 or 6-to-1, a hand we would have folded now becomes one worth playing. Always be aware of extra outs. Otherwise you may fold hands with which you should have called.

Drawing to the Second-Best Hand

Equally important in determining whether a hand that needs improvement is worth a call is the question of whether the hand will win even if you do make it. Your hand might lose in a variety of ways. It can happen because you are drawing dead — that is, the hand you are looking to make is already beaten by your opponent. For example, when that open pair bet into your four-flush and a possible straight earlier in this chapter, he might have been betting a full house, which you have no way of beating. It can also happen that you make your hand and your opponent makes an even better hand even though you weren't drawing dead. Your four-flush might, for example, be up against three-of-a-kind. You may make your flush, but your opponent may very well make a full house.

In such situations you must reduce your odds of winning and sometimes throw your hand away. For instance, a four-flush against three-of-a-kind in seven-card stud is a much greater underdog than a four-flush against two pair because three-of-a-kind is more than twice as likely to improve to a full house. The ability to fold correctly when you suspect you are drawing dead or drawing with too little chance of ending up with the best hand is one attribute that distinguishes a good player from an average one. On the other hand, poor players are likely to call thoughtlessly on the come no matter what. They do not consider that they may be drawing dead; and when they're not drawing dead, they do not adjust their chances of ending up with the best hand, taking into account the possibility of an opponent's making a bigger hand than their own.

In hold 'em and other community card games, you can sometimes draw dead because the cards that will give you the hand you want will also give your opponent an even better hand. Suppose in hold 'em you are holding

your opponent is holding

and the board is

If a queen falls on the end, you make a straight, to be sure, and a straight beats three jacks. However, the queen also happens to give your opponent a full house. Similarly, if you hold

and the board is

there is no card in the deck that will make you a winner against an opponent holding the ace of hearts and another heart. A heart at the end gives you a king-high flush, but it gives your opponent an ace-high flush.

When you think your opponent might beat you even if you make your hand, you must adjust your odds of winning before comparing them to the pot odds you are getting. Let's say you are a 5-to-1 underdog to make your hand, and you are getting 7-to-1 from the pot. By itself your hand is worth a call. But suppose you feel there is a 30 percent chance your opponent will make a hand that beats the one you are trying to make. Should you still call? As a 5-to-1 underdog you are going to make your hand one-sixth of the time, which is 16⅔ percent. However, of that 16⅔ percent of the time, you will be good only 70 percent of the time. All of a sudden, instead of winning 16⅔ percent of the time, you will win only about 11⅔ percent of the time. You go from a 5-to-1 shot to just about a 7½-to-1 shot. What appeared to be an easy call has become a fold.

In general, you don't need to calculate your chances of winning so precisely; when there is a chance of drawing dead or being outdrawn after you make your hand, you had better throw away most of your close plays because they will swing into losing plays. You have to overcome the double adversity of having the worst hand in the first place and the possibility of not winning when you make the hand you are hoping to make. To call a bet in such a situation requires very good pot odds indeed.

Summary

In this chapter we have explained how to use pot odds to determine whether to call or fold with a likely second-best hand. When all the cards are out, your hand is worth a call if you think your chances of winning are better than your pot odds. Before the draw in draw poker and with exactly one card to come in stud games, your decision to call with a hand that needs to improve depends upon these factors:

1. Your chances of improving, taking into account the needed cards already out against you (in stud) and any extra outs you might have.
2. Your chances of winning if you do improve.
3. The odds you are getting on this next-to-last round of betting, taking into account the possibility of a raise behind you if you are not the last to act.

4. Your expected extra profits on the last round of betting if you do make your hand.

This last factor is what I call *implied odds*. It is the money you expect to win by betting or raising on the last round (or rounds) when you do make your hand. I will discuss implied odds in full in Chapter Seven. First we must consider how pot odds are affected when you are deciding whether to call in stud games when there is more than one card to come and you must anticipate having to call more than one round of betting. This question is the subject of the next chapter.

Chapter Six

Effective Odds

When there is only one round of betting left and only one card to come, comparing your chances of improving to the pot odds you are getting is a relatively straightforward proposition. If your chances of making a hand you know will win are, say, 4-to-1 against and you must call a $20 bet for the chance to win a $120 pot, then clearly your hand is worth a call because you're getting 6-to-1 pot odds. Those 6-to-1 odds the pot is offering you (excluding bets on the end) are greater than the 4-to-1 odds against your making your hand. However, when there is *more* than one card to come, you must be very careful in determining your real pot odds. Many players make a classic mistake: They know their chances of improving, let's say, with three cards to come, and they compare those chances to the pot odds they are getting right now. But such a comparison is completely off the mark since the players are going to have to put more money into the pot in future betting rounds, and they must take that money into account. It's true that the chances of making a hand improve greatly when there are two or three cards to come, but the odds you are getting from the pot worsen.

Reducing Your Pot Odds
With More than One Card to Come

Let's say you are playing hold 'em, and after the flop you have a four-flush that you are sure will win if you hit it. There are two cards to come, which improves your odds of making the flush to approximately 1¾-to-1. It is a $10-$20 game with $20 in the pot, and your single opponent has bet $10. You may say, "I'm getting 3-to-1 odds and my chances are 1¾-to-1. So I should call."

However, the 1¾-to-1 odds of making the flush apply only if you intend to see not just the next card, but the last card as well, and to see the last card you will probably have to call not just $10 now but also $20 on the next round of betting. Therefore, when you decide you're going to see a hand that needs improvement all the way through to the end, you can't say you are getting, as in this case, 30-to-10 odds. You have to say, "Well, if I miss my hand, I lose $10 on this round of betting and $20 on the next round. In all, I lose $30. If I make my hand, I will win the $30 in there now plus $20 on the next round for a total of $50." All of a sudden, instead of 30-to-10, you're getting only 50-to-30 odds, which reduces to 1⅔-to-1.

These are your *effective odds* — the real odds you are getting from the pot when you call a bet with more than one card to come. Since you are getting only 1⅔-to-1 by calling a $10 bet after the flop, and your chances of making the flush are 1¾-to-1, you would have to throw away the hand, because it has turned into a losing play — that is, a play with negative expectations. The only time it would be correct to play the hand in this situation is if you could count on your opponent to call a bet at the end, after your flush card hits. Then your potential $50 win increases to $70, giving you 70-to-30 odds and justifying a call.[2]

It should be clear from this example that when you compute odds on a hand you intend to play to the end, you must think not in terms of the immediate pot odds but in terms of the total amount you might lose versus the total amount you might win. You have to ask, "What do I lose if I miss my hand, and what will I gain if I make it?" The answer to this question tells you your *real* or *effective* odds.

Let's look at an interesting, more complex application of effective odds. Suppose there is $250 in the pot, you have a

---

[2] While a call on the flop might be a bad play, a semi-bluff raise could be a good play. Sometimes folding is a better alternative to calling, but raising is the best alternative of all. (See Chapters Eleven and Thirteen.)

back-door flush draw in hold 'em, and an opponent bets $10. With a back-door flush you need two in a row of a suit. To make things simple, we'll assume the chances of catching two consecutive of a particular suit are 1/5 X 1/5. That's not quite right, but it's close enough.[3] It means you'll hit a flush once in 25 tries on average, making you a 24-to-1 underdog. By calling your opponent's $10 bet, you would appear to be getting 26-to-1. So you might say, "OK, I'm getting 26-to-1, and it's only 24-to-1 against me. Therefore, I should call to try to make my flush."

Your calculations are incorrect because they do not take into account your effective odds. One out of 25 times you will win the $260 in there, plus probably another $40 on the last two rounds of betting. Twenty times you will lose only $10 when your first card does not hit, and you need not call another bet. But the remaining four times you will lose a total of $30 each time when your first card hits, you call your opponent's $20 bet, and your second card does not hit. Thus, after 25 such hands, you figure to lose $320 ($200 + $120) while winning $300 for a net loss of $20. Your effective odds reveal a call on the flop to be a play with negative expectation and hence incorrect.

Situations When Effective Odds Need Not Apply

There are a few times when you do not have to consider future bets when assessing your pot odds. The first case occurs when either you or your opponent is all-in or almost all-in. Obviously, when your opponent has no more money to bet or you have no more money to call, the last card will be free. So all you need to do is observe your immediate pot odds and compare them to your chances of winding up with the best hand. In the example

---

[3] For the finicky, the exact equation is $10/47 \times 9/46$. Ten of the 47 unseen cards make a four-flush on fourth street, and then nine of the 46 remaining cards will produce the flush at the end.

just given, if either you or your opponent were all-in when the opponent bet $10 on the flop and you called, it would be worth drawing to your back-door flush since it would now be a case of getting 26-to-1 on a 24-to-1 shot. However, you must remember that the chances of making the hand you are drawing to are not the same as your chances of winding up with the best hand. You might make your hand and still lose to a better hand.

There is a second case, similar to the first, when you might call in close situations even if your effective odds would indicate a fold. This comes up when you have good reason to think your opponent might check on the next round. If he does check, you are getting a free card just as though you or he were all-in. Once again all you need to consider are your immediate pot odds, since you expect to see two cards for the price of one. Such situations might come up when you suspect your opponent has a weak hand or when you think your opponent might fear to bet on the next round because he interprets your call to mean you're stronger than you really are, even when you don't catch the card you need.

Finally, it may sometimes be correct to call to see *one card only* when your effective odds indicate a fold. If that card does not make your hand, you should not call any further bets. These circumstances usually occur in games where there is a large increase in the bet from one round to the next. You might, for example, be playing in a $10-$50 hold 'em game and catch a four-flush on the flop. Your opponent bets $10 into a $40 pot, and you expect he'll bet $50 on the next round. To call both bets would mean you were getting effective odds of 100-to-60, too low for you to contemplate going all the way with a flush draw. However, you are getting 5-to-1 on your opponent's first bet, which is greater than the odds against hitting on the next card (not to mention your potential profits on the last two betting rounds should you hit the flush). When deciding whether to call for one card only, all you need to consider are your immediate pot odds versus your chances of hitting *on the next card only.*

In most cases, however, when you have a hand that needs to improve, you must realize that future bets cut down your apparent pot odds substantially, frequently enough to make you throw the hand away. Therefore, before deciding to go all the way with a hand, you must calculate whether the effective odds you are getting by calling several rounds of betting justify a call now.

Calculating Effective Odds

Figuring effective odds may sound complicated, but it is a simple matter of addition. You add all the calls you will have to make, assuming you play to the end, to determine the total amount you will lose if you don't make your hand. Then compare this figure to the total amount you should win if you do make the hand. This total is the money in the pot at the moment plus all future bets you can expect to win, excluding your own future bets. Thus, if there is $100 in the pot at the moment and three more $20 betting rounds, you are getting $160-to-$60 effective odds if both you and your opponent figure to call all bets. If you know you won't call on the end unless you make your hand, your effective odds become $160-to-$40. When you think your opponent won't call on the end if your card hits, your effective odds would be reduced to something like $140-to-$40. If, on early betting rounds, these odds are greater than your chances of making your hand, you are correct to see the hand through to the end. If they are not, you should fold.

Chapter Seven

Implied Odds and Reverse Implied Odds

During the early and middle rounds of betting, having to call future bets usually reduces your apparent pot odds considerably, and you have to calculate your real or effective odds. However, there are times when the existence of future bets is the very reason you play a hand. Your immediate pot odds may not seem high enough to justify calling for one more card. But if that card may give you a monster hand that figures to get you a lot of action, you frequently don't need the initial odds from the pot. You'll get them later. These odds are what I mean by *implied odds*.

Implied Odds

Implied odds are based on the possibility of winning money in later betting rounds over and above what is in the pot already. More precisely, your implied odds are the ratio of your *total expected win* when your card hits to the present cost of calling a bet. A good example of playing a hand for the implied odds occurs in hold 'em when you have a small pair in the hole. It's about 8-to-1 against flopping that card to hit three-of-a-kind, but the small pair is worth playing in most cases even getting something like 5-to-1. If there is $50 in the pot and it is $10 to you in a $10-$20 game, you are getting implied odds of about 150-to-10, or 15-to-1, since you should average about $100 further profit when you do flop a set of trips. Of course, when you don't make trips, you would normally throw away your hand rather than call a bet on the flop.

In earlier discussions we have come across other situations where implied odds were operating. In Chapter Four on ante structure, we pointed out that in games with a small ante and a small initial bet in comparison to future bets, it pays to play looser than the small ante would dictate for the *initial bet* only. The reason is that the big bets in later rounds give you good implied odds.

For instance, the $1-$3 and $1-$4 seven-card stud games which you find in every card room in Las Vegas start off with a 50-cent bet. It is *not* correct to play very tight for this initial bet, especially against the weaker players you tend to find in these games. When you can see fourth street for only 50 cents, you should, for example, call for one card with any pair, so long as your cards are *live* — that is, so long as few of the cards you need have appeared among your opponents' exposed cards. This is because your implied odds are enormous. Should you make two pair or, even better, three-of-a-kind, you figure to get a lot of action from lesser hands, especially when your initial pair is hidden.

Implied odds were operating in the example in Chapter Six on effective odds which advocated calling to see *one card only* if the immediate pot odds justify a call though your effective odds indicate a fold. The suggestion was that when your card hits, you'll probably make more money on future bets.

To take this point a step further, you might call even when the immediate pot odds do not quite justify a call if there is a large increase in the bet from one round to the next. Your possible future profits when your card hits — that is, your implied odds — will make up for the short odds you are getting at the moment. For example, if in a $10-$20 game an opponent bets $10 into a $20 pot, your pot odds are 3-to-1, which would dictate throwing away, say, an open-ended straight. However, if your hand (or your opponent) is such that should the hand improve on the next round, you figure to beat your opponent for another $40 on future betting rounds, then your implied odds are $70-to-$10 or 7-to-1, which would make a call worthwhile with an open-ender. If you miss and your opponent bets $20 on the next round, you would once again be getting 3-to-1 odds ($60-to-$20), but your implied odds would have diminished.

Implied Odds in Pot-Limit and No-Limit Games

In general, the larger the difference between future bets and the present bet you have to call, the greater your implied odds. Hence, implied odds become most significant in pot-limit games and in no-limit games, where a future bet can be as large as the amount of money a player has in front of him. In fact, in these games one is almost always considering not how much is in the pot right now, but rather how much can be won on a future round of betting.

A classic illustration of such a situation occurred in the final hand of the 1980 no-limit hold 'em championship at Binion's Horseshoe Casino in Las Vegas. Doyle Brunson, a two-time world champion, had $232,500 in front of him, and his opponent, young Stu Ungar, a gin rummy and poker whiz from New York's lower East Side, had $497,500. (These astronomical sums resulted from 73 players buying into the championship tournament for $10,000 apiece.)

In the final hand Brunson held an ace,7, and Ungar, the 4 and 5 of spades. Before the flop, $30,000 went into the pot, and then the cards came ace,2,7. Ungar checked, but looking at aces and 7s, Brunson bet $17,000, a bet intended to lure Ungar in.

"I wouldn't have called too much more than that for a gut shot," Ungar admitted. (A *gut shot* in poker parlance is a draw to an inside straight.) "But if Doyle has a hand, it's worth $17,000 because if I do catch a 3, I'm going to bust him."

Ungar's call was strictly in terms of the *implied* odds he was getting. He had no thought for the $47,000 in the pot at the moment, which gave him less than 3-to-1 odds, but rather for Brunson's entire $232,500 stake. With $15,000 of his own money also in the pot, Ungar's implied odds were approximately 14½-to-1; and with four 3s available among the 47 unseen cards, the odds against making the straight on the next card were 10¾-to-1. Hence his call.

Needless to say, a 3 fell on fourth street. Ungar bet $40,000. After some reflection, Brunson moved all-in with the remainder of his chips. Since Ungar had the nuts at that point (Brunson's only outs were an ace or a 7 on the last card to make a full house) he called gleefully and won the world championship.

At a poker seminar in Gardena, California, the following year, given by Brunson, myself, and draw poker expert Mike Caro, Brunson acknowledged he played incorrectly in betting $17,000 on the flop. He said that instead of giving Ungar the chance for a perfect card, he should have bet more than Ungar would have been able to call, in the event he did have an inside-straight draw — in other words, too much to warrant a call even in terms of implied odds.

When you estimate your implied odds, you must try to predict how much money you can win if you do make your hand. This prediction depends on three factors

1.   The size of future bets.
2.   How hidden your hand is.
3.   The ability of your opponents.

Factors in Determining Implied Odds

Obviously, the larger the size of potential bets, the greater your implied odds and the more reason you have to call with a hand that might improve to the nuts. However, the other two factors are important too.

In adding the possibility of future bets to the present pot to get your implied odds, you should take into account whether the strength of your hand is hidden. When the cards that help are obvious, you cannot expect to get as much value out of your hand if you make it, since opponents simply might not call when you bet.

When you have a close decision, you should call a bet against weaker opponents more readily than against tougher ones: You can usually assume you are getting higher implied odds from a weak player, who is more likely to call your bet or raise when you make your hand, than from a tough player, who may fold his hand and not pay you off.

Two words of caution. Implied odds obviously cannot apply when either you or your opponent is already all-in or nearly all-in. Secondly, implied odds have little meaning when there is a decent chance that you can make your hand but still wind up second best. If you are going to take a short price from the pot in hopes of winning future bets, you had better be awfully sure that your hand will hold up when you make it.

Reverse Implied Odds

Implied odds explain situations when your odds are better than they seem. There are other times when you must realize that your odds are not as good as they seem. These situations occur when you have a mediocre hand with little chance of improving, which you think is the best hand at the moment, yet your opponent keeps betting. You think he may be bluffing, and you can beat only a bluff — that is, a hand that is weaker than what your opponent is representing. However, since your opponent is controlling the betting, he will probably back off on later rounds if he doesn't have you beat. Thus, you are in the position of winning the minimum if you have the best hand but losing the maximum if you have the worst hand. The true pot odds in such situations are much worse than they seem, and so we call them *reverse implied odds.*

For instance, there is $50 in the pot, and your opponent bets $20. You think you have him beat, but you are not sure. You also have little chance of improving. You cannot say, "I'm getting 70-to-20 odds here," because your opponent may come out betting again next round if he has a better hand than yours — or if his hand improves to a better hand — but he is likely to give it up if he has a worse hand than yours. You are in a situation where, if you lose, you figure to lose not just the $20 you are calling right now but a total of $60. However, if you win, you'll probably win only the $70 in the pot right now because once your opponent sees you're committed to the pot, he won't bet further with the worst hand. All of a sudden, then, you're not getting 70-to-20 odds but closer to 70-to-60.

Actually, reverse implied odds of 70-to-60 represent the worst possible case of such situations, as they come up in practice. If, for instance, you are sure your opponent will not bet again without a good hand, then you should obviously fold if he does bet again. So you have risked only $20 and not $60 to win $70. Conversely, if there is some chance your opponent will bet once or twice more without the best hand, then when you continue calling, you are risking $40 to win $90 or $60 to win $110, depending on how many times he bets. You are risking $60 to win $70 only when you plan to call to the end if your opponent bets, even though you assume you have little chance of winning if he continues betting.

Summary

In sum, reverse implied odds describe situations in which:
1. You're not sure where you're at.
2. You have little chance of improving to beat the hand your opponent might already have or might make.
3. A call commits you to calling future bets all the way to the end.
4. Your opponent can back off at any time.

In such cases, you must not think you are getting odds according to what's in the pot and what you have to call right now. You are getting much worse odds — so much worse that it is often better to throw your hand away immediately rather than get committed. Such a situation would occur in hold 'em if you held

and the flop came

A similar situation might occur in seven-card stud if you held two black aces and an opponent with three hearts on board came out betting on fifth street.

Whereas implied odds are based on the possibility of winning more money in later betting rounds, reverse implied odds are based on the possibility of *losing* more money in later betting rounds. Put another way, when you're getting implied odds, you're glad you're not all-in, for you expect to make money on future bets if your card hits. However, when you're getting reverse implied odds, you wish you were all-in so you could see the hand to the end without having to call future bets.

Chapter Eight

The Value of Deception

One approach to poker is to raise when you have a very good hand and fold when you have a very bad hand. But what happens when you follow that approach? Let's say you have three aces rolled up on your first three cards in seven-card stud. That's the best possible hand you could have at that point. You put in a raise, and everybody folds. You have won a very small pot with a hand that potentially could have won a huge pot.

The Cost of Giving Your Hand Away

This extreme example points up a basic poker dilemma. You want to make the most of your hands by maximizing your gains and minimizing your losses, yet what are you costing yourself when you play in such a way that your opponents should know what you have? The answer to this question is contained in the Fundamental Theorem of Poker, which states that *every time opponents play a hand differently from the way they would have if they could see all your cards, you gain; and every time they play a hand the same way they would have played it if they could see all your cards, you lose.*

The Fundamental Theorem indicates that when you play in a way that lets your opponents know what you have, you may be costing yourself substantially. If opponents know exactly what you have, they will never make a mistake except on very close mathematical decisions. The more your play gives away what you have, the less likely it is that your opponents will make a mistake. Yet you want them to make mistakes. Creating mistakes is, in a sense, the whole objective of the game. Clearly you might not want to raise immediately with three aces rolled up because you don't want your opponents to know what a strong hand you have. You want to win more money from them on later betting rounds. At the same time, never raising with a big hand could be a mistake too.

An interesting example of such a mistake came up toward the end of the 1977 World Series of Poker in a hand between two world-class players, Doyle Brunson from Longworth, Texas, and Bones Berland from Gardena, California. The game was no-limit hold 'em. Brunson had about $20,000 in front of him, and Berland, about $50,000. Before the flop Berland raised in early position, a hefty raise, and Brunson called him with two queens. The flop came J,5,2. Again Berland made a pretty good bet, and Brunson called him. On fourth street came another small card, and Bones made a gigantic bet, just about enough to put Doyle all-in. Doyle thought and thought and thought, and finally he pushed in his money and called.

Many people thought Brunson played incorrectly in calling with two queens. Berland was not about to bluff in this situation. These critics felt there was a great chance that Berland had two aces or two kings, and there were other hands he could have had that Doyle's two queens couldn't beat. Given the way he played it, the only hand Bones might possibly have that Brunson could beat was an ace, jack — the top pair on board with an ace kicker.

When Bones turned over his cards in the showdown, he had precisely ace, jack. Brunson won the hand with two queens and went on to win the world championship of poker that year. I asked Doyle afterward about his risky call. "Well," he said, "Bones couldn't have two aces or two kings because he never raised in early position with these hands before the flop. He would just call, hoping to reraise, you know, on a slowplay."

Here was a case, then, where a top player was given information because another top player played properly but with too much consistency. In no-limit hold 'em it is generally correct to slowplay in early position with two aces or two kings. However, when Berland always played those pairs the same way, as he supposedly did, the information he gave away was much more costly than the money he figured to gain by playing the aces and kings properly every time.

To illustrate further the cost of giving away your hand, suppose you are playing head-up razz with no ante, no forced bet, and all the time in the world. You have decided, therefore, to play super-super-tight, folding everything except A,2,3 on your first three cards. With no ante it would seem you're a cinch to end up a winner, but the fact is a good player will slaughter you. He'll soon know you are playing only A,2,3, and he'll play his cards accordingly. He'll start off with slightly worse hands than yours, like three-card 5s and three-card 6s, but he'll wind up beating you on later plays since he'll know exactly what you have. He'll know when you pair up and when you don't, and he'll never make a mistake. On the other hand, though you start out with the better hand, you will make mistakes because you won't know what your opponent has. Thus, while in general it is correct to play very tight when there is no ante and no forced bet, by playing only A,2,3 in razz, you are giving away so much information that you don't stand a chance against a good opponent.

Deception and the Ability of Your Opponents

A question you must always address, then, is when to play a hand straightforwardly and when to use deception. The most important criterion for making this decision is the ability of your opponents. The tougher they are, the more you must consider playing a hand other than optimally to throw them off. The weaker they are, the more you can get away with optimum play. Thus, if you have a good hand on an early round, you would not put in that last raise against tough players, but with a weaker hand you might consider putting in an extra bet to make your opponents think your hand is stronger than it is. For example, with a three-flush on third street in seven-card stud you might throw in a reraise to create the wrong impression. Now if you happen to pair on board, you have the extra equity that your opponents may fold incorrectly, afraid you have three-of-a-kind or two pair.

On the other hand, if you are playing against dunces or just mediocre players, you don't gain enough in deception to justify the cost. Against such players you should put in an extra raise when you think you have the best hand, but throwing in an extra bet with a weaker hand, against someone who won't fold anyway, simply costs you extra money. In using deception, then, you must weigh the ability of your opponents against the extra cost.

Deception and the Size of the Pot

Another criterion for deciding how to play a hand is the size of the pot. As the pot grows larger and larger, it becomes less and less important to disguise your hand because good players are not likely to fold any more than bad players are. Nor will good players try to bluff as much when you show weakness, because they too recognize that the pot is so big there is almost no chance you will fold. So when the pot has become large, you usually no longer have to think about using deception.

Deception and Bet Size

There is a related concept. If early bets are much smaller than later bets, you usually shouldn't throw in a small raise with a big hand. You may put people on guard so that even if they don't fold immediately, they will when the bets increase in later rounds. You're likely to get more action on your big hands by slowplaying them. Conversely, with a large increase in bets from one round to another, you may decide to put in extra action with a weaker hand on an early, cheap betting round to create the wrong impression later when the bets are expensive. Thus, you should consider not only the amount in the pot now but also how much the bets are now compared to what they may be later. You might check a big hand early to win big bets later, and on the other hand, you might bet with a weaker hand early in hopes that your opponents will check later to give you a free card.

Obviously, you can better afford to disguise your hand in early rounds in pot-limit and no-limit games than in limit games, since both the size of the pot and the size of the bets may increase enormously from one round of betting to the next. With a big hand and a lot of money in front of you, you can check and give your opponents many more free cards. You are not so concerned about protecting the money in the pot as you are about getting paid off when you bet a much larger amount later. Furthermore, it costs too much to protect small pots, especially when you have only a fair hand. To win them, you need to make a considerably bigger bet than you would in limit games, and so in no-limit you would tend to give more free cards even when you are not altogether happy about it. (See Chapter Ten, "The Free Card.")

Deception and the Number of Opponents in the Pot

With weak players, with a large pot, and with large early bets, you need not be so concerned about disguising your hand. A corollary is that the more players in the pot, the less you gain by disguising your hand. You cost yourself too much when you do. You won't be able to make everybody fold when you bet with a weak hand, and you cost yourself too many bets when you miss a raise with a strong hand. What's more, when you let many opponents in cheaply, you increase the chances of being outdrawn. Heads-up situations require disguising your hand more than do multi-way pots.

Let's look at two early-round betting situations — one in which you don't care that you've given your hand away and the other in which you should use deception. In both situations you have a pair of aces in the hole before the flop in hold 'em. That is, you have the nuts, the best possible hand at that point.

The first game is no-limit. You've made a small raise, four or five people have called, and now someone puts in a substantial reraise. You must reraise again even if your play gives away your hand completely. It is worth dropping all disguise because as the pot gets larger and larger, what's in the pot right now counts more than potential bets on later rounds. With two aces you should put in all the bets you can.

On the other hand, with two aces against a good player in a limit hold 'em game, you should often not put in all bets. A reraise is fine because you could have a variety of hands. However, if your single opponent reraises again, you should probably just call. If you raise one more time, your opponent figures you for two aces. All you have gained is one small extra bet right there, but you may have cost yourself two or three bets later on. In this case, you have lost too much by giving your hand away. You stand to gain more by using deception.

Summary

The general rule is: The better the players and the smaller the pot, the more you disguise your hand when there are more cards to come. The worse the players and the larger the pot, the more you play your hand normally, without regard to giving anything away. Sometimes, though, playing your hand normally may be the best deception of all against very tough players who *expect* you to be deceptive. The following hand from seven-card stud will illustrate this point:

You

Opponent

If a tough opponent acts before you and raises, reraise just as you would against a sucker. A tough opponent who has two kings knows you might be reraising with a three-flush or any number of second-best hands. So you still have your deception as well as an extra bet.

It is extremely important to disguise your hand against players who put great emphasis on reading hands, though such players may not necessarily be good, and when deceptive play has gotten the super readers confused, they've got no chance. This type tends to put you on a hand early, and like a captain going down with the ship, he sticks to his opinion until the end.

There are five criteria for using deception to avoid giving your hand away.
1. You are up against good players or super readers.
2. The pot is small in comparison to future bets.
3. The present round of betting is small in comparison to future bets.
4. You have only one or two opponents against you.
5. You are slowplaying a monster hand.

The first two conditions are most significant. It is not necessary to meet all five conditions before deception is employed. Three of the five are usually sufficient so long as one or both of the first two are included.

Do not use deception against bad players, against many players, when the pot is large, or when the early bets are large. It is especially important to play a good hand strongly if the pot is large. The only exception would be when you have an unbeatable hand and figure you will gain more by waiting a round before making your move.

The basis of your decision to play normally or deceptively is simple. You should play each session and each hand of each session in the way that will win the most money and lose the least (except when you intentionally play a hand badly to create an impression for future hands). Always remember from the Fundamental Theorem of Poker that the more your opponents know about your hand, the less likely they are to make mistakes. However, there are situations when deception can be costly and straightforward play is best. We shall look at such situations in the next chapter.

Chapter Nine

Win the Big Pots Right Away

As we showed in the last chapter, it is often important to disguise your big hands so that your opponents don't know what you have because you want to get as much value for them as you can. However, there is one special application of the Fundamental Theorem of Poker, which we hinted at: As a pot gets larger and larger, you nearly always want to win it instantly. Naturally you would like your opponent to play incorrectly and throw away the best hand. But even when your hand is the best hand, you generally prefer your opponent to fold rather than call when the pot is large. The reason is that when you bet in a limit game and the pot is large, your opponent's hand, though second best, is rarely so much of an underdog that he is not getting good enough odds to chase you. Hence, his calling you with good odds is a profitable play for him in the long run. Since he is correct to take the odds, you do not gain when he calls. You gain only when he folds and turns down those odds. When he calls, you lose even if you happen to win that particular pot; for over the long run his call has positive expectation. It will end up costing you money.

Betting When Your Opponent is Correct to Call

At the same time, it would be incorrect not to bet at all with the best hand, even though you were 100 percent certain your opponent would make the correct play and call. By not betting, you are giving your opponent a *free chance* to make the best hand. Put another way, you are giving him infinite odds. Let's say the odds are 5-to-1 against your opponent making a hand that beats yours. By betting $20 into a $150 pot, you are offering that player 8½-to-1 odds ($170-to-$20), and so he is correct to call the $20. But by betting nothing, you are offering him infinite odds, in that he has to call zero dollars for the chance to win $150. Therefore, when the pot is large — even though you are offering your opponent favorable odds — it is always correct to bet with the best hand. The opponent's odds are not so favorable as they would be if you didn't bet at all. Furthermore, there is always the outside chance he might give up and fold. (See the next chapter for an extensive discussion on the free card.)

In no-limit and pot-limit games it is easier to win the big pots right away because you have the luxury of being able to bet almost any amount. So you can choose what odds to give your opponent. For example, with a $150 pot in a pot-limit game and your opponent a 5-to-1 underdog, betting the maximum $150 allows you to offer your opponent 2-to-1 odds ($300 to $150) on a 5-to-1 shot. If your opponent calls, he is taking the worst of it, and you are not unhappy with the call. Whenever possible, then, with the best hand, bet an amount large enough so that by calling, your opponent is not making the correct play. Furthermore, in no-limit and pot-limit games, you must be careful, as we saw in Chapter Seven, to bet a sufficiently large amount so that your opponent is not getting sufficiently good *implied* odds to make a call correct.

By definition, in limit games you are not free to bet whatever you want, and when the pot gets large, it's hard to make a player fold. However, unless you have the pure nuts, you should give your opponent every opportunity to fold and make it as expensive as you can for him to call, even when by calling he is still getting favorable odds.

Betting (or Raising) to Drive Opponents Out

One step toward winning a big pot is driving out as many opponents as possible. Let's say you are playing seven-card stud, and there has been a lot of raising on the first three cards, which has created a big pot. You have three-of-a-kind, a powerful hand, and now on fourth street the man to your right bets. Should you call or raise? You should definitely raise even though you are driving out all the weaker hands behind you. Indeed that is precisely the purpose of your raise. The pot has become sufficiently large for you to try to win it right now, forsaking any future bets you might win. If everybody folds after you raise, you are delighted. If your raise succeeds only in cutting down the number of opponents, that's still pretty good.

Most people don't think in terms of this special case of the Fundamental Theorem of Poker, but it is vital. Wanting to win the present pot instantly — even with the best hand — depends on your chances of winning if the hand continues and upon the pot odds you are giving your opponents. You must ask yourself whether an opponent would be correct to take those odds knowing what you had. If so, you would rather have that opponent fold. If not — that is, if the odds against your opponent's making a winning hand are greater than the pot odds he's getting — then you would rather have him call. In this case, instead of winning the pot right away, you're willing to take the tiny risk that your opponent will outdraw you and try to win at least one more bet. If, in the seven-stud example of the preceding paragraph you had four-of-a-kind instead of three-of-a-kind, you would not want to put in a raise to drive people out. Your hand is so good you'd want to collect a few more bets with it.

It's rare to catch a monster hand like four-of-a-kind in the first four or five cards. With just about anything less than that, you should try to win large pots right away instead of letting players in cheaply or free. Nor do the pots you go after have to be gigantic, just fairly large relative to the betting structure of the game you're playing. Your opponent or opponents may fold after you bet or raise, but while you might have won another bet or two, you still have the reward of having locked up a good-sized pot.

Betting (or Raising)
With the Second-Best Hand

There is a curious corollary to the principle of trying to win the big pots right away. Obviously you want to bet or raise to drive out as many players as possible when you have the best hand. But if the pot is very large, it is frequently desirable to do the same even when you suspect you have the second-best hand, especially when you believe you're not that far behind.

A good example of this concept comes up in razz:

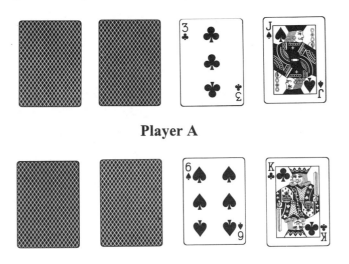

Player A

Player B

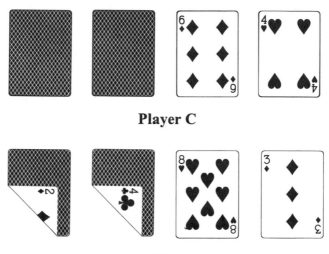

Player C

You

You have four cards to an 8, and you suspect the player to your right, Player C, has four to a 6. If there are a few raises on third street, creating a good-sized pot, it is important that you raise the 6,4 when he comes out betting, even though his hand is probably better than yours and he will probably reraise. Why should you be willing to add two bets to the pot when you suspect you don't have the best hand? The answer is that you want to force out the other two hands. With a large pot they might call a single bet, but in the face of a bet, a raise, (and a probable reraise), they should now fold. You have succeeded in reducing the opposition to one, and you now have about a 45 percent chance of winning the pot. Your underdog status is more than compensated by all that extra dead money in there. On the other hand, with the other players involved, you would have only about a 30 percent chance of winning the pot.

Let's look at a similar situation in seven-card stud. You have two queens and the raising on third street has produced a large pot. The man to your immediate right has

Your hand may or may not be the best hand. You don't think it is, but you are quite sure it is second-best and not much of an underdog. If the man to your right with the K♦9♦ comes out betting on fourth street, you should raise to drive the other players out. In the event your two queens is the best hand because the K♦9♦ is a four-flush or two 9s, you don't have to worry about any of the other players outdrawing you. On the other hand, if the K♦9♦ is in fact two kings, you have a better chance of winning the pot against him alone than you would if you let in other players who could outdraw you even if you made queens up or three queens.

The same principle comes up in hold 'em. The man to your right bets, putting you in a position to raise immediately to make other people fold. When the pot is large, you should do it with a good hand even if you suspect it might not be the best.

Delaying One Round to Drive Opponents Out

In structured games the size of the bet doubles on the third round of betting — for example, from $5 to $10 in a $5-$10 game and from $10 to $20 in a $10-$20 game. In these games you may want to wait until the bet doubles in size before putting in a raise — not as a slowplay but as a better way of driving people out. If in $10-$20, for example, you raise a $10 bet to $20 on the second round, some players behind you may be willing to call; but if you wait until the next round to raise a $20 bet to $40, these players will not be so willing to pay the price. The greater likelihood of driving opponents out with a big raise on the third round of betting offsets the cheap $10 card you allowed them on the previous round.

Summary

The basic concept set forth in this chapter is a simple one. When the pot is big, you want to win it right away. To try to win it right away, you should bet and raise as much as possible, hoping to drive everybody out, but at least reducing the opposition. You should bet and raise with the best hand, and you should frequently do the same even with a hand you think maybe second best. The fewer opponents you have in a pot, the greater your chances of winning it, even if those chances are less than 50 percent; and when the pot gets large, winning it should be your foremost concern.

Chapter Ten

The Free Card

A free card is exactly that. It is a card that does not cost a bet to receive. While players might get a free card (or cards) in draw poker if a hand is checked around before the draw, concepts about the free card apply primarily to stud and hold 'em games where there are several rounds of betting.

In general, when you have the best hand, you do not want to give opponents a free card since you are giving them a chance to outdraw you and win the pot. By the same token, when you do not have the best hand, you want to try to get a free card to get a free shot at winning the pot.

Giving a Free Card

Giving a free card means checking a hand you could have bet when there are more cards to come. Of course, when you check with the intention of raising, you are giving a free card only when your opponent is so uncooperative as not to bet into you.

When you know or are pretty sure you have the best hand, you have to decide whether or not to give your opponent a free card. We saw in the last chapter that it is almost never correct to give a free card when the pot is large. It turns out that it is rarely correct to give a free card with medium-sized pots, even when you know your opponent will fold if you bet. You simply have to be satisfied with what there is in the pot already. One reason you should bet is that generally you want your opponent to fold.

If there is, let's say, $50 in the pot and you bet $10, your opponent is getting 6-to-1 odds. As a 5-to-1 underdog, he should call. As we have seen in earlier chapters, any opponent who doesn't take the odds when he has the best of it is losing money. Therefore, you have gained when that person folds.

However, the principle of not giving a free card goes even further. If your opponent is a 9-to-1 underdog, getting 6-to-1 odds, you should still bet. In this case, you hope that opponent calls, but you don't mind when he folds. His folding is better than your giving him a free 10 percent chance to make his hand and beat you. As we saw in the last chapter, giving a free card is equivalent to giving a person infinite odds on that betting round. That person needs to make a zero investment for a chance to win whatever is in the pot.

Suppose, going into the last card in seven-card stud, you think a player has a gut-shot draw to a straight, and you have three-of-a-kind. Your opponent is at least a 10-to-1 underdog to make the straight, and even if he hits, you may make a full house. So you're a big favorite to win the hand. Nevertheless, it is still better that you bet and force your opponent to fold than that you check and he check behind you. By checking you are giving your opponent a free shot at beating you, a chance he would not have if you had bet.

When you are not so big a favorite, it is even more important to bet rather than give a free card. Let's say you have

in hold 'em, and the flop comes up three spades. With a modest pot you should come out betting even though you expect everybody will fold because you can't let somebody with, say, a lone 10♠ get a free shot at a higher flush. You might not want the person to fold when you bet, but making him fold is better than giving him a free chance to outdraw you. (The only time you might check your flush is if the pot is so small you expect to gain more through deception. Thus, if no spades fall after the flop, your profits on later bets are likely to be considerably larger than what you would gain by betting on the flop. However, if another spade does come, you have to be prepared to fold.)

When you have a chance to bet and you have a decent hand, especially a hand you think is the best one, it is almost always correct to bet. The only conditions that might make it *incorrect* to bet are the following:

1. The pot is small in comparison to what it might be in the future and you figure to gain more in future bets through deception than by giving your hand away now; this situation occurs most often in pot-limit and no-limit games.
2. You think you can get in a check-raise.
3. Your hand is so strong it's worth giving a free card even with a medium-sized pot.

Giving or Not Giving a Free Card in Practice

We'll look at two hold 'em hands to see the difference between a situation where you should bet and another where you might consider checking. In both cases there is a medium-sized pot:

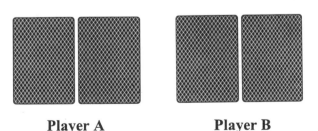

Player A   Player B

Board

You

With two jacks you should bet in an attempt to win the pot right there, even if you think only a better hand will call. If you give your opponents a free card (with what would have been the best hand) and an ace, king, or queen falls on fourth street, you are clearly in trouble. Thus, you don't want to give your opponents a free chance to draw one of those cards to make a higher pair than yours. Even if an ace, king, or queen doesn't make an opponent a higher pair, your checking on the flop gives anyone the opportunity to bluff you successfully if one of those cards falls.

Now we'll change your pair of jacks to a pair of aces:

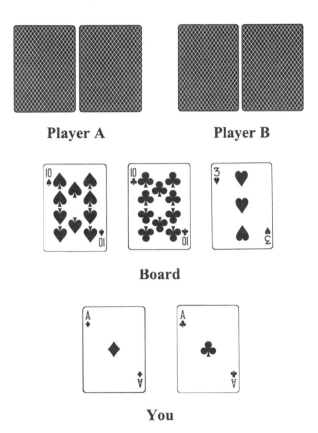

Player A   Player B

Board

You

With aces you can give serious consideration to checking on the flop. Having two aces instead of two jacks has not significantly affected your chances of having the best hand since we'll assume that in both cases there has been no reason to think you are up against two kings or two queens in the hole. With two aces, however, you are not worried about as many fourth street cards as you would be with two jacks, and so you might as well check just in case someone has made three 10s. Assuming no one has a 10 in the hole, an additional benefit of your checking your pair of aces is that you have disguised your hand. Not only do you not fear a king, queen, or ace falling on fourth street (as you would with a pair of jacks), you would welcome it, since any of those cards, as well as a jack, might give an opponent a playable second-best hand.

Of course, you should nearly always bet if you think a worse hand will call. You should also bet if the pot is large, since a large pot is worth the risk of running into three 10s in order to shut out the possibility that a miracle card will fall for an opponent on the next round. With a large pot it is also more likely that an opponent will call your bet with a bad hand like

or

Now let's suppose you are in another hold 'em hand. There is a medium-sized pot, and the flop comes:

How should you play with two jacks? How should you play with two kings?

With two jacks you would once again be more inclined to bet since there are more free cards that will beat you. But with two kings in the hole, it might be better to check in case someone has made a pair of aces. If you do have the best hand, you have less to lose by giving a free card since fewer cards will beat you than when you have two jacks.

The basic concept to be emphasized is that you do not want to give an opponent with a worse hand a free card that might make his hand better than yours. Therefore, if you expect to be called, always bet what you think is the best hand unless you figure it is better to try for a check-raise. Except when you have reason to slowplay, either because the pot is small or because you have a monster hand, always bet the best hand even if you don't expect to be called. You gain most when your opponent folds if there were sufficient pot odds for a call. However, even when your opponent isn't getting good enough pot odds to call and figures to fold, you should bet. You would prefer a call when that opponent is making a mistake by calling, but making him fold is still better than giving him a free shot to outdraw you.

Getting a Free Card

If not giving a free card is that important, it should be clear how valuable it is to get a free card when you don't have the best hand. That free card might turn a hand you would have folded into a winner or save you a bet on a hand with which you intended to call anyway. Of course, getting a free card against reasonably good players is not easy. One way is to put in a small raise on an early round in the hope that everyone still in the pot will check around to you on the next round. Then you can also check. To make this play you must be sure you will act after your opponent (or opponents) on the next round, so the play is used most commonly in a game like hold 'em where the order of betting is fixed by the position of the dealer.

Other ways of getting a free card fall under the heading of tricks and ploys. For example, you can bet out of turn to make your opponent check, which is not quite ethical but usually legal. After being reminded it's not your turn to act, you retrieve your bet, and when your opponent checks, you also check. You can take chips from your stack as though you intend to raise, and then when your opponent decides not to bet after all, you check. Sometimes just getting your chips ready to call, as though you're enthusiastic about calling, will prevent your opponent from betting. However, against top players such plays usually work only to create a bad impression, and they rarely succeed more than once or twice.

Position and the Free Card

When a hand is reduced to two opponents, the player who acts first cannot give himself a free card, but the player who acts second can. If you are second to act and your opponent has checked to you, you should bet when you are pretty sure you have the best hand; but if you suspect you have the worst hand, you can check and give yourself a free card.

When you check in first position, you are not giving yourself a free card; you are offering your opponent a free card. That player can decide whether to take it or to bet. Consequently, in first position you have to bet some hands you wouldn't bet in last position because you do not want to give your opponent the option of checking for a free card with the worst hand. With a marginal hand you should bet in first position, especially if you don't fear a raise, because if your opponent has a worse hand than yours, he will check behind you when you check, making you wish you had bet. On the other hand, if your opponent's hand is indeed better than yours, he will bet when you check. So you couldn't give yourself a free card anyway.

Giving or Not Giving a Free Card With a Marginal Hand

When you are certain you have the best hand, deciding whether to bet with more cards to come is relatively easy. However, you are frequently in a situation where you suspect you have the best hand, but you know you will be called only if you are beaten. Still, you must consider betting so that you do not give your opponent a free shot to outdraw you in the event you do have the best hand. The factors to consider when deciding to bet are:

1. Your chances of having the best hand.
2. The chances the next card will give your opponent the best hand when he would have folded had you bet.
3. The size of the pot.
4. The chances you will outdraw a better hand that might call you.

The larger the pot and the greater the chances your opponent will outdraw you on the next card, the more reason you have to bet.

Point number 4 needs some explaining. Suppose you are afraid you do not have as good a hand as your opponent. Before betting, you should take into account what your chances are of outdrawing the hand you fear your opponent might have. The higher those chances, the more reason you have to bet. The lower they are, the more reason you have to check. To take an obvious example first, if you have two pair and a four-flush in seven-card stud and you are worried that your opponent has made a straight, you should most certainly bet rather than give him a free card in the event he does not yet have the straight. Your combined chances of making either a full house or a flush to beat a straight are very good. On the other hand, if you have two pair with no four-flush and fear your opponent has made a straight, you would be inclined to check since your chances of making a full house are slim.

Here is a more subtle example of the same principle from hold 'em. The flop comes:

In one instance you are holding

and in the other you are holding

Which hand would you be more inclined to bet? It turns out you are in much better shape with the A♠7♣ (which gives you two 7s) than you are with two 8s because there are five unseen cards that will improve the A♠7♣ three aces and two 7s — while there are only two cards that will improve the pair of 8s — namely, the remaining two 8s. (You disregard pairing any card on board since the pair improves your opponent's hand as much as or perhaps even more than it does your own.) Since you have more ways of improving to beat someone with, say, two jacks, you would be more inclined to bet with an A,7.

The fewer ways you have of improving, the more convinced you have to be that you already have the best hand in order to bet. Thus, while you might check two 8s when the flop comes J♣7♠3♥, you would most definitely bet two queens even though the latter hand also has only two ways of improving (the remaining two queens). With two queens you are pretty sure you already have the best hand, yet you are not strong enough to risk giving a free card.

Summary

When you're trying to decide whether or not to bet your hand and worry about making a mistake, you should keep in mind one very important principle — a mistake that costs you the pot is a catastrophe, especially if the pot has become relatively large, while a mistake that costs you one bet is not. When in doubt, make sure you don't make a mistake that costs you the pot. Checking and giving an opponent with a worse hand a free card may cost you the pot when he outdraws you. However, betting and getting called by a better hand costs you at most just that one bet. Thus, the only time to give free cards with the probable best hand is when your hand is so strong it is in little danger of being outdrawn and your deception sets up the likelihood of larger profits in future bets in comparison to what is currently in the pot.

Chapter Eleven

The Semi-Bluff

Remember what was said toward the end of the last chapter about betting when you are afraid you do not have the best hand. The more ways you have of improving to become the best hand, the more reason you have to bet. The semi-bluff is an extension of this concept. From another point of view, it is an extension of theories of bluffing, which are discussed in Chapters Eighteen and Nineteen. I define the semi-bluff this way: A semi-bluff is a bet with a hand which, if called, does not figure to be the best hand at the moment but has a reasonable chance of outdrawing those hands that initially called it.

Obviously, then, a semi-bluff cannot occur unless there are more cards to come. When you bet as a semi-bluff, you are rooting to win right there just as you are when you make a pure bluff. However, in contrast to a pure bluff, you still retain a chance of outdrawing your opponent if you are called. Even when you bet with a legitimate hand, you are generally rooting to win instantly, but when you semi-bluff, you especially want your opponents to fold because one of them may be folding the best hand.

The semi-bluff is one of the least understood tools of poker, yet it is a very valuable and potent weapon. All professional players use it, and it may be used in any game. It may be a bet, a raise, or even a check-raise. Essentially you are representing a bigger hand than you actually have; however, in contrast to a pure bluff, your hand must have some chances of improving to the best hand.

Types of Semi-Bluffs

Betting on the come is the most commonly used form of the semi-bluff. When you raise with a four-flush in draw poker, you are using a semi-bluff. You are hoping your opponents fold right there, but if they don't, you may make your flush and beat them anyway. Raising with

in draw lowball is a semi-bluff; you'd like your opponents to fold but don't mind a call that much since you have a good chance of drawing the best low hand. In hold 'em, betting after the flop with the third pair and an ace kicker or the third pair and an inside straight draw would be a semi-bluff: In this case, you want very much to win instantly, but if you are called you still have a chance of outdrawing your opponent.

Let's say in seven-card stud a player representing kings bets on fifth street, and you hold:

You make a semi-bluff raise, representing a straight. You'd like to win right there, but you have a good chance of making the straight if you are called. Furthermore, you'll almost certainly get a free card on the next round when the king checks to you. Also if you don't make the straight, you may possibly win with two pair or three 4s.

Semi-bluffs can be much more varied and often more complex than simply betting on the come. They can range from almost pure bluffs, when your hand has little chance of catching up if your bet is called, to a bet with a hand that may possibly be the best hand. In the first case, you have to think you have almost as good a chance of getting away with the bluff as you would with a pure bluff, taking into account the pot odds you're getting. In the second case, when you may in fact have the best hand, it is essential to bet to keep from giving a worse hand a free card. Betting is particularly important when you're in first position, in which case you should apply the following rule: If your hand is worth a call or almost worth a call when someone else bets, it is better to bet yourself, especially when you have little fear of a raise and when there is some chance you will win right there by making your opponent fold.

We'll look at two examples of semi-bluffs from seven-card stud. In the first, you are making a semi-bluff bet because your hand is worth a call if you checked and your opponent bet. Let's say you have:

Right off the bat a queen raises you. You know the raiser is not a very imaginative player, but he may be raising with a three-flush or something like a pair of 7s in the hole. You call.

On the next card, you catch an ace, giving you a pair of 8s and an ace, king kicker. Your opponent catches a small card. You are high on board, and now it is very important to bet because with a pair and two overcards your hand is certainly worth a call if you check and your opponent bets. Furthermore, you have little reason to think your opponent will raise because he now fears that you have made a pair of aces or even aces up. In fact, your opponent may fear what you are representing so much that he might fold the best hand.

The added equity of possibly winning right there when your opponent folds is the primary reason to semi-bluff. If you had checked your pair of 8s with an ace, king and called your opponent's bet, you would have a reasonable chance of making kings up, aces up, or three 8s to beat his queens or queens up. By betting out instead of checking and calling, you add to these chances the possibility of winning right away. This possibility gives a semi-bluff greater mathematical expectation than checking and calling since it adds another way to win besides winding up with the best hand in the showdown.

If you know there is no chance that your opponent will fold a pair of queens, the semi-bluff becomes more debatable, for by definition a semi-bluff is a bet where there is some chance your opponent will fold a hand he should have played. However, since you would call your opponent's bet anyway, betting yourself still has certain advantages. Your bet suggests more strength than you actually have. Suppose you catch something like two running 6s. When you bet with nothing but 8s and 6s, your opponent will probably fold a hand that he shouldn't have if he knew what you had. Even when a semi-bluff has no chance of making an opponent fold immediately, it may lead him to fold later when your board appears to improve to a better hand than you actually have. This situation comes up only in stud games, both high and low, where your opponent can see you "improve." It does not occur as much in hold 'em, where everyone shares a common board, nor, of course, in draw.

In the second semi-bluff example from seven-card stud, you are more of an underdog if your opponent has the hand he is representing. Nevertheless, a semi-bluff is indisputably the correct play:

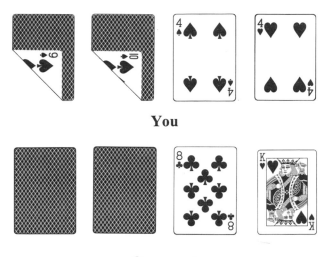

You

Opponent

Your opponent raised on the first round, and you called with a three-flush. Now when you pair fours in sight, you must bet even though you have only a small pair with no overcard and your chances of making a spade flush are about 9-to-1 against. Your opponent will fold without a pair, which is to your advantage, and he may fold a higher pair, thinking you've made three 4s, which would be great. On the other hand, if he calls your bet, you still have several ways of beating him.

Advantages of the Semi-Bluff

First, the semi-bluff tends to make your opponent play incorrectly according to the Fundamental Theorem of Poker. When you semi-bluff, you presumably do not have the best hand. If your opponent could see your cards, his correct play would be to raise. However, since you are representing something with your semi-bluff, opponents will nearly always only call. Sometimes they will make the worst play of all by folding the best hand.

Second, when the hand with which you are semi-bluffing is in fact the best hand at the moment, by betting you are not making the mistake of giving worse hands free cards. As we saw in the previous chapter, it is critical to bet the best hand with more cards to come in order to avoid giving people a free card. Not only will a worse hand usually fold, which is fine, especially if the opponent is getting proper odds to call, but a better hand might fold. If the better hand calls, which is more likely, you still have the chance of improving to the best hand. If, instead of betting, you check and a better hand bets, your hand probably justifies a call. So you have gained nothing by checking. You do not get yourself a free card. Hence, you are more likely to semi-bluff in first position than in last, where you have the option of giving yourself a free card.

A third advantage of the semi-bluff is that, used correctly, it adds an enormous amount of deceptiveness to your game. For example, suppose in seven-card stud you started with:

On fourth street an opponent with

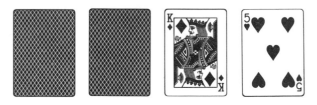

bets. You've caught the

giving you Q♠J♠ showing. This is a good spot for a semi-bluff raise even if you are almost certain your opponent will call you. Why? Well, notice what happens when you catch certain cards on fifth street. If you catch a card such as the 9♠ or for that matter any card that looks as if it's given you a straight or a flush, your opponent will very possibly fold, if not a better hand, certainly a hand that was justified in calling against a measly pair of 7s. Suppose you catch a jack or a queen, making a pair on board. Now your opponent almost has to fold because of the strength you showed by your earlier raise. However, if he in fact has two kings, he is making a mistake folding against two smaller pair. Finally, notice what happens if you catch the one card that will make you root for a call, namely a 7, which gives you three-of-a-kind. Because of your previous bet, that 7 will look completely harmless, as though it didn't help your hand one bit. Now when you bet, your opponent will keep coming just as you want him to. In sum, your semi-bluff raise on fourth street has made subsequent cards that help you only moderately look very dangerous, while it has made cards that give you a big hand look insignificant.

This last point is an additional benefit of the semi-bluff in stud games but especially in hold 'em. When you do hit the card that makes your hand, your opponent will often misread it because of your bet on the previous round (except in the cases where you were straightforwardly betting on the come with a flush or a straight draw). Thus, you may win a larger pot than you would have otherwise expected.

Both the semi-bluff and betting a marginal hand rather than risking giving a worse hand a free card are cases of the general precept that it is usually better to be betting than calling. By betting as a semi-bluff you have a chance of winning the pot right there, something you are usually hoping to do, and you have shown greater strength than you really have. If you catch scary-looking cards after you have been called, you are still likely to win pots you wouldn't otherwise have won. When you bet now, your opponent is quite likely to fold. On the other hand, when you don't improve and are caught in a semi-bluff, that can be of value as an advertisement for the future.

A final advantage of the semi-bluff, as I suggested in the previous chapter, is that you can sometimes use it to get a free card. Let's say an opponent in hold 'em bets on the flop, and you raise with a four-flush. If that player calls your raise, it is likely he will check to you on fourth street. If you haven't made the flush, you have the option of checking behind him for a free card.

Semi-Bluffs and Pure Bluffs

A pure bluff is a bet, which, if called, has no chance of winning in a showdown. A semi-bluff is a bet with more cards to come which, if called, is probably not the best hand at the moment but has a reasonable chance of becoming the best hand.

Many expert players believe their bluffs should have negative expectation. They see them as a form of advertising that will lead to their being called on other occasions when they do have the best hand. However, I believe pure bluffs should have no worse than zero expectation as I shall explain in more detail in a later chapter. At the same time, I agree that bluffs are an important part of a player's game. If you never bluff, your opponents will always know you have a legitimate hand when you bet. They will be likely to play correctly on the basis of what you have in your hand, which is to their advantage and your disadvantage, according to the Fundamental Theorem of Poker.

Since it is correct to bluff occasionally so that you don't give away too much information when you bet with a legitimate hand, the question is when to do it. Clearly, you cannot establish a regular pattern of bluffing. Observant opponents will soon pick it up, and you will be caught bluffing too often to make it profitable.

Rather than try to guess when to bluff, especially against tough players, use your cards to randomize your play. (*See* Chapter Nineteen, "Bluffing and Game Theory.*") In early betting rounds, with more cards to come, the most convenient and profitable way to use your cards is to bluff when you have the kind of semi-bluff hands I have been discussing. Then you are still bluffing occasionally, you will get all the advertising you need, but you have the extra advantage of sometimes winning even when you do get caught.

There are numerous situations where a pure bluff would not work often enough to be profitable, but where a semi-bluff is more profitable than simply checking and hoping to draw out and win in the showdown. Suppose you are playing $10-$20 hold 'em. After six cards your hand has fallen apart; you have no win. There is one more card to come and $60 in the pot. So if you bet $20 as a pure bluff against a single opponent, you are getting 3-to-1 for your bet when he folds. The key question, then, is whether that opponent will fold often enough to make a bluff profitable in terms of the pot odds you are getting. Let's say you expect he will fold 20 percent of the time. That is, he will call four times out of five and fold once. Thus, the odds against getting away with a bluff are 4-to-1, while you are getting only $60-to-$20 or 3-to-1 odds when you bet. Therefore, the play has negative expectation. In the long run it is unprofitable. (This is assuming you give up your bluff when you're called and don't bet on the end.)

Now instead of a busted hand with one more card to come, let's assume you are holding a hand that you assess as having a 30 percent chance of winding up the winner — something like, say, a four-flush and a small pair. Again there is $60 in the pot, and you figure you have a 20 percent chance of stealing that $60 right there if you come out betting against a single opponent. Readers should see intuitively that a semi-bluff bet now turns into a profitable play. In fact, it is more profitable than simply checking and hoping to win in the showdown.

To make this point absolutely clear, we'll do some arithmetic. We'll assume that if you check after six cards, your opponent will check behind you, and we'll ignore bets on the end on the assumption that you will fold when you don't make your hand and your opponent will fold when you do. We'll take 100 identical situations where you check and hope to draw out and 100 situations where you make a semi-bluff bet.

Take checking first. With $60 in the pot and a 30 percent chance of winning, you will average winning $60 30 times for a total of $1,800.

What happens when you bet? Well, since your semi-bluff has a 20 percent chance of making your opponent fold, you will average winning $60 immediately 20 out of the 100 times you try it for a total of $1,200. Of the 80 times your opponent calls your bet, you will average winning $80 (the $60 already in the pot plus the $20 called) 30 percent of the time and losing your $20 bet 70 percent of the time. That works out to an $80 win 24 times and a $20 loss 56 times for a net win of $800. So after 100 identical situations, you will average winning $1,200 when your opponent folds, plus $800 when he calls for a total of $2,000, which is $200 more than you would win by checking. That comes to only $2 per hand, but it is with such small edges that you increase your hourly rate and your profits at the end of the month and the year.

The important thing to notice from this example is that both a pure bluff by itself and a value bet by itself would be wrong. Had you bet as a pure bluff, you would be getting only 3-to-1 odds for a wager that has only one chance in five of winning. Had you bet only for value — that is, with the certainty your opponent will call — you would also be making an incorrect play since you have estimated that you are a 7-to-3 underdog. You are wagering even money (your $20 bet for a $20 call) when the odds are 2⅓-to-1 against your winning. However, the combination of the two possibilities — namely, winning with a bluff or winning by improving to the best hand — makes a semi-bluff bet not just a good play but a mandatory one.

Just as a semi-bluff bet can be profitable, so too can a semi-bluff raise. Suppose in hold 'em you start with

and the flop comes

Everybody checks. The next card is the

which gives you a flush draw and an inside-straight draw (not to mention a straight-flush draw). If someone now bets, you should raise. Even if that person folds only 20 percent of the time, the combined possibilities of winning right there and of making the best hand when he calls turns raising in this spot into a more profitable play than just calling. In general, when there is a possibility of winning the hand right there, even a slight one, it is important to bet — or raise. What's more, sometimes when you think you are semi-bluffing, you are actually betting the best hand.

Another consideration when deciding to semi-bluff is the size of the pot. The larger the pot, hence the bigger the pot odds you are getting, the smaller your chances of getting away with a semi-bluff need to be to make the play profitable. Game theory suggests the opposite — that you should bluff less with a larger pot, assuming expert opponents. However, in practice most players do not adjust their calling strategy correctly to the size of the pot, which makes both semi-bluffs and pure bluffs more profitable when the pot is large.

When Not to Semi-Bluff

As we have seen, a semi-bluff can be profitable because it sometimes works as a bluff (when your opponent folds the best hand) and sometimes lets you improve to the best hand (when your opponent calls). It is the *combination of these circumstances* that makes the semi-bluff profitable. Therefore, it is important to realize that you usually don't semi-bluff if you are sure you are going to be called. Why? Because then the bluff aspect of your bet has vanished, you are betting only for value, and it is clearly incorrect to put more money in the pot on a hand you know to be the underdog. The only exception to this principle may occur in seven-card stud and razz, as we saw earlier, when your semi-bluff confuses your opponent on later rounds as he watches your board develop into what looks like the best hand.

It is also a good idea to semi-bluff less often when you are last to act, especially if many players have checked ahead of you. Not only do you have the opportunity to give yourself a free card in last position, but it's possible that somebody ahead of you was sandbagging with a big hand and will check-raise when you bet. In contrast, when you are in first position, you would be more inclined to bet with a semi-bluffing hand. Since you can't assure yourself of a free card in first position, you might as well become the aggressor and bet when the situation warrants it.

Summary

We'll summarize this somewhat lengthy chapter point by point.

1. A semi-bluff is a bet, raise, or check-raise with a wide variety of hands which you believe are not the best at the moment. However, they may win not only right there when your opponent folds but also in a showdown when they improve to the best hand. They may also win when your opponent folds on a later round after you catch a scare card that makes your hand look like the best hand.

2. A semi-bluff may be used in any game, but it may be used only with more cards to come.

3. Sometimes a hand with which you think you are semi-bluffing is in fact the best hand. By betting, you prevent a worse hand from getting a free card.

4. If you have a hand that warrants a call when your opponent bets, it is usually correct to bet yourself, particularly in first position. You thereby gain the chance of winning the pot immediately, and you show more strength than you actually have, which can be to your advantage later.

5. Semi-bluffs allow you to be the bettor instead of the caller, which nearly always puts you in a more advantageous position.

6. Semi-bluffs are a good way to randomize your bluffs, for you have the added equity of a possible win even when you are called.

7. A semi-bluff can frequently be a profitable play in situations where a pure bluff is not. Your extra out of outdrawing your opponent can swing your mathematical expectation from the minus to the plus side.

8. You usually do not semi-bluff when you are sure your opponent will call. However, if there is a possibility that

opponent will fold, you should bet — or raise — with a semi-bluffing hand, especially as the pot gets larger.

9.   It is usually better to make a semi-bluff bet when you are first to act; when you are last, you have the opportunity of giving yourself a free card, and you may not want to risk the chance of an opponent check-raising you.

Chapter Twelve

Defense Against
the Semi-Bluff

The Power of the Semi-Bluff

Let's say you're playing seven-card stud. You have a pair of jacks, and on fifth street your opponent bets. You know he has a big hand. So your response is easy: You fold. Suppose you know your opponent is bluffing with nothing. Again your response is easy: You raise. Suppose you think he has you beat with two small pair, but you're getting sufficient pot odds for a call. So you call. Straightforward bets, straightforward responses.

But what if your opponent is not so straightforward? What if he's the kind of player who might be betting with a legitimate hand but might also be semi-bluffing? He's not always semi-bluffing, of course. That would also make it too easy to respond, because if you know an opponent is semi-bluffing when he bets, you can simply raise with anything, and he will probably fold. The problem arises when you think an opponent may be semi-bluffing but can't be sure he does not have a legitimate hand. What's more, if he doesn't have a legitimate hand now, he may get it later — or he may look like he's gotten it later.

It turns out there aren't many defenses against the semi-bluff, which is why it is such a powerful play. Frequently the best play against a possible semi-bluff is to fold, especially when the pot is small. All right, your opponent has beaten you. He may even have made you throw away the best hand. But if you call his bet, he has three other ways of beating you. He may in fact have had the best hand when he bet. He may have been semi-bluffing, but he now outdraws you. Or he may have been semi-bluffing, but he proceeds to catch scare cards that force you to fold. Therefore, though you may have thrown away what was the best hand at the moment, still your opponent had too many ways of beating you to justify your calling his bet.

Even when you think you are favored to have the best hand, it may be correct to fold. Let's say you think it's a little better than even money that your opponent is semi-bluffing. For convenience, we'll say you think there's a 52 percent chance he's semi-bluffing and a 48 percent chance he has a good hand. If he is semi-bluffing, you figure you're a 6-to-5 favorite to beat him. However, if he isn't semi-bluffing and has the hand he's representing, you're virtually locked out. Thus, 52 percent of the time you're a favorite to win. Should you call his bet? Many professionals as well as amateurs make the mistake of calling in such situations, but unless the pot is large, the correct play is to fold.

Let's work it out mathematically. You lose almost automatically 48 percent of the time. Of the remaining 52 percent, you'll win an average of six out of 11 hands (since you estimate yourself to be a 6-to-5 favorite). In other words, you'll lose almost half the time when you're a slight favorite and virtually all of the time when you're a big underdog. You stand to win the hand only 29 percent of the time in all. To call the bet then, you would need to be getting at least 7-to-3 *effective* odds from the pot, which is not very likely in an early betting round. Hence, the correct play would normally be to fold.

The Difficulty of Defending Against the Semi-Bluff

To illustrate the difficulty of defending against the semi-bluff, we'll take a seven-card stud hand from our discussion of semi-bluffing in the preceding chapter and reverse roles:

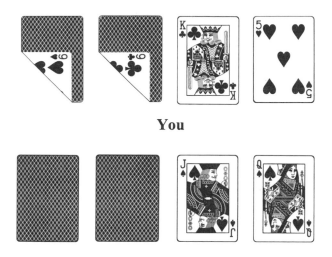

You

Opponent

Suppose you bet on fourth street, and your opponent raises. Knowing your opponent is fully capable of semi-bluffing in this spot with something like a pair of 7s in the hole, you still should probably not call with a pair of 9s. He may in fact have a pair of queens or jacks. Or he may be semi-bluffing with a four-flush. The problem is that your pair of 9s is no favorite over a four-flush with a jack and a queen. Thus, if your opponent has a pair of jacks, a pair of queens, or two pair, you may lose because he already has you beat; and if he has a four-flush, you may lose because he outdraws you (which with his overcards as well, he's a favorite to do). Even if your opponent has nothing better than a gut-shot straight draw, your two 9s with a king kicker are not a hand to be excited about. Consequently, even though you suspect this opponent is semi-bluffing, it doesn't do you much good to call with a poor hand because you have two ways of losing: You may lose to a legitimate hand or by being outdrawn.

Suppose you grit your teeth, close your eyes, and call your opponent's bet. The dealer raps on the table and deals the next card:

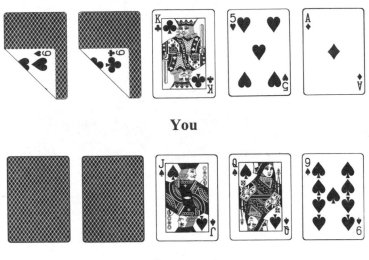

You

Opponent

What in the world do you do now? That nine of spades your opponent caught is a very scary-looking card. It might have made your opponent a flush. It might have made him a straight. If it didn't help him at all, well, then he was probably betting on fourth street with jacks or queens so that now he has a big pair and at least a three-flush — maybe a four-flush. All you can do is check, and when your opponent bets, as he surely will, you will probably throw away your hand, perhaps cursing the poker gods for delivering the 9 to your opponent and not to you. So here is a third way a semi-bluffer can beat you — namely, by catching scare cards that force you to fold.

(If you don't remember the exact hand from the previous chapter, all your opponent has in the hole, it turns out, is 7♠7♣. Knowing that, it would of course be incorrect to fold at this point with two 9s and an ace, king kicker. Your opponent's semi-bluff on fourth street, followed by his semi-bluff on fifth street, caused you to make a mistake, according to the Fundamental Theorem of Poker, in contrast to what you would have done if you could see your opponent's hand. Your opponent gained, and you lost. However, not knowing what your opponent had, you did make the only sensible play.)

The Semi-Bluff Raise as a Defense Against the Semi-Bluff

While the confrontation just described shows the difficulty of defending against the semi-bluff, it also demonstrates one of the best defensive counter-strategies against it — the *semi-bluff raise*. Notice that when you bet into a Q♠J♠ with a pair of 9s in the hole and K,5 showing, you were semi-bluffing yourself. You were trying to represent kings in the hope that your opponent would fold with a pair of queens, a pair of jacks, or a worse hand. It turns out your opponent did have a worse hand — a pair of 7s and a three-flush. But what did he do instead of folding? He raised. He made a semi-bluff raise into a possible pair of kings with a three-flush and a small pair. Of course, if you had really had two kings, he'd be in trouble. But since you were semi-bluffing yourself, as your opponent suspected, his semi-bluff raise turned the tables on you. It put you on the defensive and him in the driver's seat.

To elucidate the effect of this type of play further, we'll talk about stealing the antes. Stealing antes is one form of the semi-bluff. A player raises immediately, representing a strong hand, and makes it too expensive, given the size of the pot, for a mediocre hand to continue. A simple example would be from seven-card razz, where the high card typically has to make a small bet to start the action and a low card usually raises.

Let's say I have a low card showing, with a second low card and a king in the hole. One player behind me also has a low card showing. With a two-card low, I do not have a legitimate hand, but nevertheless, I'm in a profitable semi-bluffing situation because I suspect that if I raise, one of two things can happen. The low card might fold behind me, in which case I win the antes immediately since the high cards will also fold. Or the low card might call, in which case I'm in trouble.

However, all is not lost because my bet was not a pure bluff but a semi-bluff. I have an extra chance to win if I catch a little card on the next round and my opponent catches a big card.

When I bet at that point, my opponent is likely to fold. If he calls, well, we both presumably have three-card lows, so I can't be too much of an underdog. I may still make the best low hand and win in the showdown.

When you semi-bluff, then, you are looking to win in one of three ways — by making your opponents fold, by catching a scare card on the next round to make them fold, or by drawing out on them and producing the best hand in the showdown. This combination of possibilities makes you the favorite when you raise.

But what happens when, instead of calling my raise, that low card behind me reraises? Suddenly my semi-bluff has been shattered.

When you reraise a possible semi-bluff in such situations, your opponent is pretty much forced to fold when you've caught him without a legitimate hand. For instance, in seven-card stud a player with

may raise against a jack showing in an attempt to steal the antes. Even if the jack calls, the semi-bluffer may catch an ace or a king on the next card, giving him the best hand against two jacks, or he may catch a scare card like a queen suited with the king. Therefore, you should usually reraise with a decent hand like two jacks. If the king is semi-bluffing and doesn't have two jacks beat, you are applying pressure on him to fold or call with the worst hand. Of course, we can take this situation a step further. The original semi-bluffer could make a semi-bluff reraise if he thinks there's a reasonable chance the obvious pair of jacks will give up and fold.

Observe, though, that in none of these instances is a simple call any kind of a defense when you suspect you're up against a possible semi-bluff. You should not say to yourself, "This may be a semi-bluff, and I may have the best hand. Therefore, I'll call." When you call, you are faced with the problem that your opponent may subsequently make the best hand if he doesn't have it already or he may look like he's made it. However, when you raise, you probably take away these latter two possibilities. An opponent will call — or perhaps reraise — with a legitimate hand, but he will very possibly fold if he was semi-bluffing. Even if he does call, it is with the worse hand. Another advantage to your raise is that it will deter your opponent from semi-bluffing against you in the future, and still another is that you are getting more money in the pot when an opponent calls with a worse hand.

To repeat, when you suspect an opponent may be semi-bluffing, you still have to fold most of your hands — like that pair of 9s earlier in the chapter. However, when you have a hand that is worth a call, in most cases you should raise. This is just one of many situations in poker where, when folding is not the best play, raising is, and calling is the worst of the three alternatives.

There is a situation that frequently comes up in hold 'em which calls for a semi-bluff raise. You're in last position, and you pick up something like a pretty fair starting hand. Suddenly the man to your right raises, and you suspect he's using his late position to try to steal the antes. Since your hand is too good to fold, you must reraise. You must not let the first raiser have that extra double chance of winning on a semi-bluff. Similarly, as we saw earlier, if you're the last low card in razz and the next-to-last low card raises, very possibly as a semi-bluff, you cannot simply call with a decent hand and give your opponent two extra ways of winning. Even with a hand as marginal as

you must reraise to make that player fold or pay with his poor hands.

You gain another advantage when you make this kind of response. You do not want to have an opponent who is semi-bluffing with the correct frequency. By picking off his semi-bluffs, you reduce the times he'll try it on those occasions when he ought to. Your reraise has forced him to think twice about semi-bluffing in the future. (See Chapters Eighteen and Nineteen.)

When to Fold and When to Raise

We have said, up to this point, that the two main defenses against the semi-bluff are simply giving up and folding, or raising. (In all cases we are assuming the pot is relatively small.) The question now is when to do the one and when to do the other. That is, when do you fold, and when do you raise?

Obviously when you have a very poor hand, you fold. When you have a big hand, you raise unless it's so big you want to slowplay and trap your opponent later. The difficult decisions occur when you have a medium-value hand. There are three principle criteria you should use in deciding whether to raise or fold:

1. The chances your opponent is bluffing or semi-bluffing.
2. The chances that opponent will outdraw you if he is betting with the worst hand.
3. The chances you will outdraw that opponent if he is betting the best hand.

The more you believe your opponent is bluffing or semi-bluffing, and the greater your chances of outdrawing him if he does have a legitimate hand, the more you will tend to raise. On the other hand, the smaller these chances are and the greater the chances your opponent will outdraw you if he is betting the worst hand, the more you would tend to fold. Recall an example earlier in this chapter. The chances that your opponent had the best hand were quite high (48 percent); the chances of your outdrawing him were so low as to be virtually nonexistent. At the same time the chances of your opponent outdrawing you were very high (you were only a 6-to-5 favorite if he didn't already have you beat). It was the combination of all these chances that dictated a fold.

Exceptions When Calling is Correct

We have said that either folding or raising is the correct play against a possible semi-bluff *most of the time*. There are three situations in which just calling would be correct.

Calling a Possible Semi-Bluff When the Pot is Large

First, you would call when the pot is large, even if there's a chance your opponent is semi-bluffing. Possessing any kind of competitive hand yourself, you certainly don't want to give away a big pot to a possible semi-bluff. So you can't fold. At the same time, there is no point in risking a raise since, because of the size of the pot, your opponent will call even if he is semi-bluffing. And if he's not semi-bluffing but has the best hand, he may reraise you. Therefore, the only play is to call.

Calling a Possible Bet On the Come

Secondly, in stud and hold 'em games, it is usually a mistake to raise with a good but not a great hand when you think your opponent — particularly a very tough opponent — has bet or raised on the come for a flush or a straight. If his bet was legitimate, he probably has you beat, so you're simply donating money to the pot. If he was on the come, he has an easy call of your raise, which eliminates most of the reasons for you to make it. Thus, even if you were quite sure that the Q♠J♠9♠ earlier in this chapter had only a four-flush, you would not be correct in raising. You would only call.

However, when you call an opponent who you think is on the come, you usually do so with the intention of *betting right out* on the next round any time that opponent draws a blank card that would not make his hand if he was in fact on the come. You now become the favorite if your opponent was on the come, and you don't want to give him a free card.

There is a mathematical reason for you to play your hand this way. Let's say you bet with two cards to come, and someone raises you. You estimate that there is a one-third chance that player has you beat and a two-thirds chance he is on a draw. Nevertheless in most cases he is still a mathematical favorite. So you can only call the raise since you're the underdog. However, when the next card cannot have made his flush or straight if he was drawing to it, now, with only one card to come, you have reverted to being the favorite. So you should usually bet. On the other hand, if that card makes the possible flush or straight, you should usually check and fold if your opponent bets, unless you are getting good enough pot odds to chase. Your opponent almost certainly has you beat, whether he was originally betting a legitimate hand or betting on the come.

Here is an example of this calling defense against a possible semi-bluff that came up when I was playing recently in a seven-stud game. I started with a three-flush and a 10 showing and was lucky enough to make three 8s on fifth street. I bet, and a good player who caught a K♥ with the J♥ as his door card raised. I reasoned the raise meant one of three things. Either my opponent had started with kings in the hole, in which case he was raising with the best hand; or he had started with two jacks, made kings up, and raised, figuring I was betting 10s and 8s; or he had a flush or a straight draw. I called the raise. When no heart, ace, or 9 fell on sixth street, which might make a straight or flush, I bet right out, much to my opponent's surprise, for my opponent had been expecting to get a free card. It turned out the opponent was in fact on a flush draw with a small pair, and the three 8s held up. (Of course, if a heart, ace, or 9 had fallen, the play in this instance would have been to check and call since there was a reasonable chance for me to make a full house on the last card.)

The Delayed Semi-Bluff Raise

A third case in which calling against a possible semi-bluff might be a good play is what I might call the *delayed semi-bluff raise*. It's a play I make against very tough players who frequently semi-bluff and who are thoroughly familiar with the ordinary semi-bluff raise as a response to their semi-bluffs.

Here's how it works. In seven-card stud I might have a queen showing and a queen in the hole, giving me a pair of queens, and an opponent with a king showing raises. I suspect this person might be semi-bluffing with maybe a small pair or even less, but I just call. On the next card we both catch blanks, and the opponent comes out firing. What I do now is raise! I raise with a pair of queens into a possible pair of kings. It may seem like a strange play, but it adds a confusing twist to the ordinary semi-bluff raise. When I called the first bet, my opponent suspected I had queens though I could have had something like a three-flush. Now when I raise him on fourth street, my opponent has to wonder whether I've made queens up. Unless he really does have two kings, he can't conceivably call with something like ace, king high. And I want him to fold even if my pair of queens is the best hand. I want him to make a mistake according to the Fundamental Theorem of Poker, because with a couple of overcards or with, say, a small pair and one overcard, he is getting sufficient odds for a call.

Suppose, though, my opponent really does have kings. Well, I'm not in the best of shape, but my opponent most likely won't reraise, fearing I have queens up. Furthermore, he'll check to me on the next round if his hand hasn't improved, and I can get myself a free card. Should this card happen to give me an open pair, it would be very difficult even for a pair of kings to call my bet since it looks as if there's a good chance I've now made a full house.

Summary

While calling may be a good defense against the semi-bluff in situations similar to the three described, remember that normally the correct play is to fold with marginal hands, and if folding isn't correct, then you should raise. We'll conclude this chapter with an example of each response to the possible semi-bluff:

Seven-Card Stud
(Small Pot)

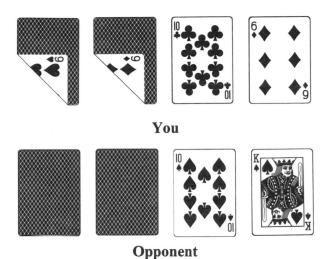

You

Opponent

Your opponent bets. How should you play?

You should fold without hesitation. Even though your opponent may be betting a four-flush or a straight draw, you have too many ways to lose. Your opponent might not even get the flush or straight but make a pair of 10s or kings to beat you:

Seven-Card Stud
(Medium-Sized Pot)

You

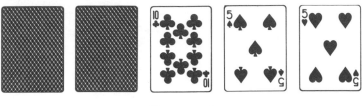

Opponent

Your opponent bets when he pairs the 5s. How should you play?

Your should raise. If your opponent has only one pair, you want to make it expensive for him to draw another card, perhaps even forcing him to fold. If he does have two pair smaller than your kings, you're not that much of an underdog. He may even fold two small pair. If he does call with them, he figures to check to you on the next round, giving you a chance to take a free card. The only hands he might have that are real trouble for you are aces up and three 5s, but there is no reason to think he has them:

Hold 'em
(Medium-Sized Pot)

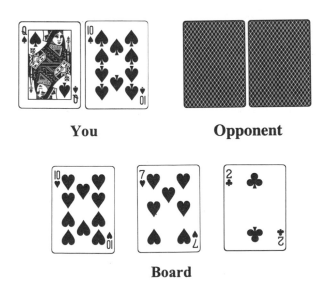

You   **Opponent**

Board

You bet, and your opponent raises. How should you play?

The question you are facing here is whether your opponent has a flush draw, an open-ended straight draw, or something like 10,9 — or whether he has a better hand than yours, something like an A,10, a K,10, two pair, or three-of-a-kind. Since the combined chances of your being beat already or being outdrawn make your opponent the favorite at this point, you should call rather than raise. But on the next card you should come right out betting, unless a heart, 6, 9, or jack falls. If your opponent raises again, you should usually fold; most players won't bluff or semi-bluff a second time in this spot.

When someone bets or raises but may be semi-bluffing, your decision is one of the trickiest in poker. You must choose whether to fold; raise; reraise; call and bet on the next round; call and check-raise on the next round; call and then check and call on the next round; or call and fold on the next round if the card your opponent catches would make the hand with which he might have been semi-bluffing. Making the correct decision consistently separates the true champion from the merely good player.

Chapter Thirteen

Raising

According to the Fundamental Theorem of Poker, you gain when your opponents play a hand differently from the way they would if they knew what you had. Any time you raise, for whatever specific tactical reason, you are doing so to avoid making a mistake yourself, according to the Fundamental Theorem, and to cause your opponents to make mistakes. There are numerous reasons for raising. Many have been discussed in various contexts in earlier chapters. In this chapter we will review all these reasons and explain several of them in more detail. We will also explain how raising is an extension of the Fundamental Theorem of Poker.

We reduce the principal reasons for raising to seven:
1. To get more money in the pot when you have the best hand.
2. To drive out opponents when you have the best hand.
3. To bluff or semi-bluff.
4. To get a free card.
5. To gain information.
6. To drive out worse hands when your own hand may be second best.
7. To drive out better hands when a come hand bets.

Now let's look at each of these reasons individually.

Raising to Get More Money in the Pot

Getting more money in the pot is the primary reason to raise when you think you have the best hand. Clearly you would raise a single opponent on the end with what you think is the best hand,

121

but on earlier rounds you must always decide whether it's worth giving your hand away to get another bet or two in the pot. (See Chapter Eight, "The Value of Deception," and Chapter Fifteen, "Slowplaying.") Essentially, the decision to raise on an early round depends upon the size of the pot and how big a favorite you think your hand is.

Ironically, the better your hand, the more reason you would have for not raising on an early round. If you think opponents will call another player's bet but fold if you raise, and if at the same time you figure they aren't getting sufficient pot odds to call a bet if they knew what you had, then you should not raise. You should give them the opportunity to make the mistake of calling. However, if they are getting correct pot odds to call a single bet, which is most often the case, you should raise even if they are still getting sufficient pot odds to call both the bet and the raise. In this instance, you're rooting for them to fold, but when they do call, you're at least getting more money in a pot you expect to win most of the time. Then again, by all means raise if you expect an opponent who shouldn't even call a single bet to call a raise. You might as well get as much money from a hopeless chaser as you possibly can. Similarly, when you get heads-up with one opponent in a limit game, it is generally correct to raise if you think you have the best hand to make your opponent fold hands with which he might outdraw you.

As the pot gets larger and larger, it becomes less and less important to disguise your big hands and more and more important to get even more money in the pot. Often with a large pot, you're rooting for opponents to fold when you raise, for they're probably getting sufficient pot odds to call. However, whether you hope they fold or hope they call, the size of the pot is likely to keep them around to see another card. Therefore, it is usually correct to raise with what you think is the best hand and get more money into a large pot even if it tends to give your hand away.

Getting More Money
In the Pot By Not Raising

Sometimes — even with no more cards to come — you can get more money or at least as much money into a multi-way pot by calling instead of raising, and at the same time avoid the risk of a reraise from the original bettor. You *go for the overcall.* That is, you call instead of raising in order to extract money from one or more of the players still in the pot behind you.

Suppose, after all the cards are out, the bettor to your right appears to have a hand you can beat. If you raise, that player will probably call, but if he reraises, you're in trouble. At the same time, there are two players to your left whom you know you have beat. You also know they will call if you call, but they will fold if you raise. In such a situation it becomes absolutely incorrect to raise. You should only call. By calling you figure to win two extra bets from the players behind you, but by raising you will win only one extra bet at most when the original bettor calls your raise, which he may not even do. What's more, your raise could cost you two bets if the original bettor reraises and you fold, or three bets if he reraises and you call with the second best hand. It could also cost you two bets if the original bettor calls your raise and turns out to have the best hand.

The situation at the end need not be so extreme as the one just described to make a flat call correct. Let's look at the following hands:

Seven-Card Stud

Bettor

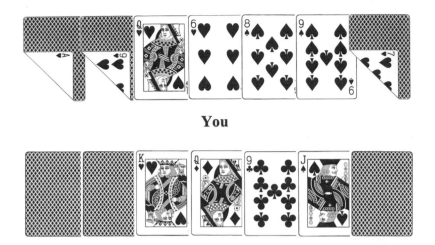

You

Player Behind You

If you raise with your A,Q high-heart flush, the third player will probably fold, and the original bettor may throw away a small straight and not pay you off either. So you may not gain a thing by raising; at most you'll win one extra bet. And what if the original bettor reraises, which he will do if he has, for example, an A,K high flush, especially since he knows you cannot have the king of hearts? (It's in the third player's hand.) By raising you lose two or three bets instead of the one you would have lost by calling. Furthermore, by just calling, you figure to win one bet from the player behind you when he calls too. So you gain exactly as much as you could have gained by raising, while you risk nothing.

In general, you should not usually raise but try for the overcall whenever all the cards are out and your hand is clearly better than any hand that might overcall behind you but not clearly better than the bettor's.

However, you must realize that to go for the overcall, you must be sure you have the player or players to your left beat. If there is some chance one of them has a better hand than yours but might not call your raise, it is critical that you *do* raise when you have a decent chance of having the original bettor beaten. You certainly don't want an overcall if it will cost you the pot.

Raising to Drive Out Opponents

When you raise to get people out, what you are really doing is raising to cut down their odds. In fact, you may sometimes cut their odds so severely that you hope they will call rather than fold after you raise.

By cutting down a person's odds, we mean reducing the amount of money he may win per dollar invested. For example, if there is a $100 pot, someone bets $10, and you call the $10, the player behind you gets 12-to-1 odds on a call. That is, that player hopes to win $120 from his $10 call, or $12 per $1 invested. But suppose you raise the initial bettor, making it $20 for the player behind you to call. Now there's $130 in the pot instead of $120, but the player behind you must invest twice as much — $20 — for a chance to win it. You have thus cut his odds almost in half — from $120-to-$10 to $130-to-$20, or from 12-to-1 to 6½-to-1. In so doing, you have created a situation where the player may make a mistake, according to the Fundamental Theorem of Poker, by either calling or folding. Even when he folds correctly after you raise because he is getting insufficient pot odds to call a double bet, you certainly prefer that to his calling an unraised bet correctly and proceeding to outdraw you and win the pot.

Raising as a Means of Cutting Down Opponents' Odds

To illustrate this important point, we'll examine a hand from five card draw poker. You have a pat flush; the player to your right has nothing at all, and the player to your left has two pair. For the purposes of this illustration, we'll assume you know exactly what both opponents have. We'll also assume the betting limit is a flat $10 but that somehow a $100 pot has been created before betting gets under way. With the cards out, we'll say the chances of the two pair improving to a full house are 9-to-1 against. In other words, the player behind you will improve to the best hand one out of ten times on average.

With absolutely nothing, the player to your right bets $10 in an attempt to steal that big pot. You know this player will fold instantly if you raise, and you are fairly sure the player behind you will fold too. However, if you just call the $10, the player behind you will also call. Consequently, you may win $120 plus perhaps another bet at the end if you call, whereas if you raise you'll most likely have to make do with the $110 already in the pot. Should you call or raise?

The answer, of course, is you should raise, but let's look at the problem logically. The opponent with two pair is a 9-to-1 underdog. If you call, there is $120 in the pot. He would be getting 12-to-1 from the pot for his call when the odds against his making the best hand are only 9-to-1. Therefore, if you call and he calls behind you, he is making the correct play, the play with positive expectation. He will lose $10 in nine hands out of ten on average, for a total loss of $90, but he will win $120 in one hand out of ten for a net profit of $30. He gains on the play, and according to the Fundamental Theorem of Poker, any time your opponent gains, you are costing yourself money.

On the other hand, when you raise, making it $20 for the two pair to call, you are cutting that player's pot odds from $120-to-$10, or 12-to-1, to $130-to-$20, or 6½-to-1. Since the two pair is a 9-to-1 underdog and is now getting only 6½-to-1 from the pot, you have made it correct for the two pair to fold. If he plays correctly and does fold, you do better, as we shall see presently, than if you had played incorrectly and allowed him sufficient odds for a call. However, if the two pair plays incorrectly and calls after you raise, you do *best of all,* because when an opponent makes a mistake, you gain. What your raise did was to reduce correct odds for a call into incorrect odds for a call. The curious effect of this turnabout is that although you raised to drive the two pair out, you are rooting for him to call after you raise.

To prove this point, let's see what happens over ten average hands if:
1.   You call, and the two pair calls behind you.
2.   You raise, and the two pair folds.
3.   You raise, and the two pair calls your raise.

If you call and the two pair calls, you will win nine out of ten hands. Assuming you check after the draw and don't pay your opponent off the one time he makes a full house, you will win $120 (the $110 already in the pot — not counting your own $10 call — plus the two pair's $10 call) nine times for a total of $1,080, and you will lose $10 once. Your net profit is $1,070.

If you raise and the two pair folds, you will win all ten hands, which at $110 per hand comes to $1,100. You win $30 more than you would if you called and the two pair overcalled.

If you raise and the two pair calls, you win $130 (the $110 already in the pot plus the two pair's $20 call of a double bet) nine times for a total of $1,170 and lose $20 once for a net profit of $1,150. You win $80 more than you do when you call and the two pair overcalls and $50 more than when you raise and your opponent folds.

Taking the $1,100 profit as the norm (since both you and your opponent play correctly in that case), we can say you lose $30 over ten hands or $3 per hand when you play incorrectly and only call, and you win $50 over ten hands or $5 per hand when your opponent plays incorrectly and calls your raise. To repeat, when you raise to drive people out, you are actually raising to cut down their odds. If they fold, that's fine, but sometimes you have cut their odds to a point where you are rooting for them to call after you raise. In no-limit games you can control the odds you are giving your opponents by the amount you bet, and you frequently find yourself rooting for them to call your raise even though you would be rooting for them to fold if you had just called.

Of course, it is correct just to call, as I did in the no-limit hold 'em hand of Chapter Three, when you know your opponent will fold if you raise but would make a mistake by overcalling if he knew what your cards were. You want to give your opponent every opportunity to make a mistake since that mistake is your gain even if he happens to get lucky and win an individual hand *because* of that mistake. In poker as in any game of skill with an element of chance, you cannot play results. That is, you cannot judge the value of a play because of the way it works out in a specific instance. In backgammon, for example, it's possible for a player to make a mistake or a series of mistakes that results in a hopeless position from which he can extricate himself only by rolling double six. The odds against rolling a double six are 35-to-1. If the hapless player happens to roll that double six and go on to victory, you cannot say he played the game correctly, anymore than you can say a person who puts his money on number 20 on the roulette layout plays correctly when number 20 happens to come up. Both players were just very, very lucky.

To summarize this section, when you raise to drive people out, you are really cutting down their odds. So you should raise with what you think is the best hand only when opponents are getting good enough odds to overcall or when you think an opponent will call a double bet even though he shouldn't even call a single bet.

Raising to Bluff or Semi-Bluff

Raising as a pure bluff with a hand that has no chance of winning if called is a tricky play, too risky to be attempted often. It is usually done only when there are no more cards to come, often when you didn't make the hand you were hoping to make but are trying to convince your opponent you did. Presumably your opponent has a decent hand to bet into you and is reluctant to throw it away when you raise. In limit poker, raising as a pure bluff can succeed often enough to be profitable only against a very tough player who is capable of making super-tough folds. The weaker the player, the more likely he is to call your raise with any kind of hand.

Pure bluff raises are a more important part of no-limit poker. Indeed some world-class no-limit players, like 1982 poker champion Jack Straus, are famous for their ability to bluff raise successfully. However, the fact that bluff raises are more important in no-limit than in limit doesn't make them any less difficult or tricky to use; it only makes them more costly when they are misused. (See Chapters Eighteen and Nineteen for a further discussion of bluff raises and bluffing in general.)

The semi-bluff raise is a more significant and frequently used part of a good poker player's arsenal. As with the pure bluff, you make a semi-bluff raise in the hope of winning the pot right there, but in contrast to the pure bluff, you always semi-bluff with more cards to come and with a hand that can improve, so there is a reasonable chance you will outdraw your opponent and win the pot even when you are called.

As we observed in the last chapter, the semi-bluff raise can also be a good defense against someone else who may be semi-bluffing. When you raise a possible semi-bluffer, that player usually has to throw away a semi-bluff hand. When he calls your raise, you can be pretty sure he has what he's representing. So an added benefit to your semi-bluff raise is that you have gained a bit of information. Furthermore, your opponent may fear you have the best hand, and check to you on the next round, giving you the chance to take a free card.

Thus, even though you may not achieve your primary goal when you raise — in this instance, making your opponent fold a semi-bluff hand — you often achieve secondary goals — such as gaining information and getting a free card. Similarly, when you raise to drive worse hands out but one of your opponents calls (and is getting proper odds for the call), you have at least achieved the secondary goal of getting more money in a pot you think you are the favorite to win.

Raising to Get a Free Card

As we just noted, when your semi-bluff raise is called, it may have allowed you the opportunity to get a free card on the next round. However, when you're thinking of raising specifically to get a free card, you should keep in mind two considerations — your position and the cost of the raise.

To get a free card, you must be last to act; if you are not last and you check, you will have shown weakness. A player behind you with a better hand than yours will probably bet, denying you the chance for a free card. In hold 'em, you can always be sure of your position since it's fixed throughout a hand, but in games like seven-card stud and razz, you often have no guarantee you will be last to act from one round to the next. In seven stud, for instance, the player to your left may have a king high to start the betting, but on the next card the player to your right or you yourself catch an ace. Now you must lead off, which you certainly do not want to do if you're still banking on a free card. So if you have some doubt about securing last position on the next round, raising to get a free card can just cost you money needlessly when it turns out you're not last after all.

Which brings up the second consideration when you're thinking of raising to get a free card — namely, that that free card is not free at all. It costs you the price of your raise. So unless you have other reasons for raising, you would make the play only when the cost of the raise now is cheaper than what you'd have to pay for a call on the next round. In a $10-$20 hold 'em game, for example, in which the bet doubles on fourth street, you might raise $10 after the flop to avoid paying $20 to call a bet on the next round.

Of course, you need not take advantage of the free card option. You certainly wouldn't when you catch the card that makes your hand. Nor would you when you catch a card that looks as if it makes your hand. For example, the holder of the pair of black 7s with Q♠J♠9♠ showing, a hand we discussed in the preceding two chapters, probably knew he had the worst hand and might have taken a free card in the hope of making a flush, but he found it much more profitable to continue the semi-bluff and bet after the 9♠ hit, since only an opponent with a very strong hand could risk a call.

Raising to Gain Information

Raising simply to gain information is a tricky play and shouldn't be done often. Generally you should consider any information gained as an extra benefit of a raise you are making for other reasons.

There are occasions, though, when you cost yourself less by raising to gain information early than you would if you had not led your opponent into giving his hand away. These occasions usually occur in heads-up situations and only in early betting rounds. Furthermore, your opponent should be the type of player whose response to your raise is likely to reflect the hand he is holding. Otherwise your raise could very well give you wrong information.

What can you learn by raising? Well, if your opponent calls, he probably has a good hand. If he reraises, he probably has a very good hand. (It's for this reason you cannot raise to gain information when your opponent is the sort of player who is capable of a semi-bluff reraise.) If your opponent folds, that, of course, tells you he's weak, and you take down the money. An added benefit to raising to gain information is that sometimes your opponent may fold marginal hands that he shouldn't have folded.

You invest in an early raise to gain information in order to save yourself money later. If, for example, you call on fourth street in seven stud, you may continue to call three more bets only to discover in the showdown that you didn't have a chance from the beginning. But a raise on fourth street followed by a call or a reraise from your opponent allows you to play your hand knowing you're up against considerable strength. Depending upon your own strength, you can then decide whether and how long it's worth continuing in the hand.

Let's say with a pair of kings on fourth street in seven-card stud you raise an open pair of 9s. Your opponent reraises. You decide that opponent has three 9s and fold. By risking one bet (your raise), you save as many as three bets you might otherwise have called on fifth street, sixth street, and on the end. Your savings is even greater when the bet doubles after fourth street. A trial-balloon raise on a $10 round could save you three $20 calls later.

Nevertheless, raising just to gain information is tricky. For example, if that open pair of 9s just calls your raise, can you be sure that opponent doesn't have three 9s? What to do on the next round may still not be clear to you. That is why you should generally reserve your raises for other purposes and consider whatever information you gain from your opponents' responses as an added benefit.

Raising to Drive Out Worse Hands When Your Own May Be Second Best

Depending on the size of the pot and your assessment of your own and your opponents' hands, it may be correct to raise with what you believe may be the second-best hand if you can get the third-, fourth- and fifth-best hands out. The reasons for this play were suggested in an earlier chapter. If, for instance, the bettor has a 50 percent chance of winning the pot, you have a 30 percent chance, and two other hands each have a 10 percent chance, you improve your chances by driving those two worst hands out with a raise. Now the best hand may have a 60 percent chance of winning, but you've improved your own chances to 40 percent. In seven stud you may, for instance, have two kings against a probable two small pair. Two other players behind you appear to be drawing to straights. By raising them out, you almost surely win when you improve to kings up and may win when it turns out your single opponent had only one pair and, say, a flush draw.

However, if the straight draws stay in, you may lose with kings up against an unimproved two pair when one of the straights gets there.

Raising to Drive Out Better Hands When a Come Hand Bets

Let's say on fifth street in seven stud you have two 10s, and the player to your right bets with an obvious flush draw. You know there are a couple of players behind you with higher pairs than yours. Nevertheless, you may be in a position to raise if you think the better hands will fold rather than call a double bet. When they do fold, you become the favorite heads-up against the come hand, and if that player misses his flush, your raise on fifth street has won you the pot. The player betting on the come was expecting at least two callers in order to get proper odds for his bet. Your raise turns that bet into a mistake since he is not getting a proper return for his investment. At the same time, when the players behind you fold after you raise, they too are making a mistake since their hands are better than yours.

On the other hand, if you suspect one or both of the higher pairs behind you will call your raise, not only should you not raise, you should not even call the original bet since you are beat in two places and may get beat in a third. This somewhat rare situation is one of those times when your only alternatives are to raise or fold. It is a time when a call is patently incorrect.

Raising Versus Folding or Calling

Raising is often a better alternative than folding, with calling the worst of the three. Such situations occur frequently when there are several players in the pot. Thus, when you raise with two 10s against someone betting on the come and succeed in driving better hands out, you show a profit on the hand in the long run. However, when you don't want to try this play, calling cannot be profitable because you are too big an underdog.

Similarly, we have noted it may be correct to raise with what is possibly the second-best hand if your raise will drive third-, fourth-, and fifth-best hands out — usually straight and/or flush draws. However, if you know those players are not going to get out when you raise, all of a sudden your hand might not be worth even a call. Not only is there a good chance you're already beat by the bettor, but frequently you'll get caught from behind by one of the drawing hands. When you cannot get the drawing hands out by raising, you have so many ways of losing that your best alternative is to fold.

Let's say in five-card draw you have two 3s and two 2s before the draw. You are in a game where people are going to come in behind you with medium-sized pairs. If you want to play the hand, you must raise to drive all medium-sized pairs out. In this case you're not interested in cutting down your opponents' odds, because you can never cut them down sufficiently as far as your hand is concerned. You want them out of the hand, pure and simple. If they stay, you have too many ways to lose since any two pair beat you unless you hit a lucky 11-to-1 shot and make a full house. Therefore, if for some reason you choose not to raise or if you think raising will not drive out the people with the medium pairs, then your only alternative is to throw away your two tiny pair. They simply have too little chance of winning in a multi-way pot to make it worth calling. You must either raise or fold.

As we discussed previously, raising is better than calling against a possible semi-bluff when your hand is too good to fold. It is better for a variety of reasons. It gives you control of the hand. It sometimes allows you to win the pot right there. It allows you to take a free card on the next round when you need to. It prevents your opponent from getting a cheap card that will beat you when he is on a semi-bluff. It disguises your hand so that you might very well win when a worthless scare card falls. Raising against a possible semi-bluff is so much better than calling (except in the three situations described at the end of the last chapter) that unless you can raise, you're usually better off folding.

Frequently a semi-bluff raise is indicated even though a call would be clearly unprofitable. Let's say you have a four-flush with one card to come. You know the odds against making the flush are 4-to-1, and your opponent bets $20 into a $40 pot. That is, he's offering you 3-to-1 odds on a 4-to-1 shot. You cannot usually call the bet since a call has negative expectation unless you are almost sure of winning a double bet on the end when you hit the flush. In 100 identical situations you will win only 20 times on average and lose 80 times. That is, you will win $60 20 times for a total of $1,200, and you will lose $20 80 times for a total of $1,600. Your net loss will be $400 or $4 per hand. So the decision is clear. People who make such calls are perennial losers.

Of course, if you fold, you lose nothing beyond the money you put into the pot in earlier betting rounds. But suppose you read your opponent to be weak — to have, say, only one pair, and you figure there's a 25 percent chance that opponent will fold instantly if you raise. Now, although a call has negative expectation, a semi-bluff raise becomes a profitable play. We'll work it out over 100 average hands, discounting any bets on the end. Your opponent will fold 25 times, and you steal $60 for a total of $1,500. He will call you 75 times, but one-fifth of those times you'll make the flush to beat him. Thus, 15 times you'll win $80 (the $60 in the pot plus your opponent's call of your $20 raise) for a total of $1,200. The remaining 60 times you'll lose $40 (your $20 call and $20 raise) for a total loss of $2,400. After 100 such plays, then, you figure to win $2,700 ($1,500 plus $1,200) and lose $2,400 for an average net profit of $300 and a mathematical expectation of $3 per play. The difference between calling incorrectly and raising correctly is a swing of $7 — from a $4 loss per play to a $3 profit.[4] What's more, if the bets you might win on the last round when you make the flush were included, your expectation would be even greater.

Summary

Some players are wary of raising, especially in situations like the one just described. However, raising should not be a rare play in your arsenal. Whether to get more money in the pot, to drive players out, to semi-bluff, or for any other reason, you should not hesitate to raise when strategic, financial, or mathematical considerations demand it. Furthermore, raising may often be the best alternative to folding, while calling is altogether incorrect. A lot of average players find this concept hard to believe, yet as we have seen, it is indisputably true. It further emphasizes the adage that a caller in poker is a loser in poker.

---

[4] Mathematically your semi-bluff raise would still be a profitable play as long as your opponent were to fold more than four times out of nineteen.

Chapter Fourteen

Check-Raising

Check-raising and slowplaying are two ways of playing a strong hand weakly to trap your opponents and win more money from them. However, they are not identical. Check-raising is checking your hand with the intention of raising on the same round after an opponent bets. Slowplaying, which we discuss in more detail in the next chapter, is playing your hand in a way that gives your opponents no idea of its strength. It may be checking and then just calling an opponent who bets, or it may be calling a person who bets ahead of you. When you slowplay a hand, you are using deception to keep people in for a while in order to make your move in a later round. Clearly, then, a hand you slowplay has to be much stronger than a hand with which you check-raise. Check-raising can drive opponents out and may even win the pot right there, while slowplaying gives opponents either a free card or a relatively cheap card.

The Ethics of Check-Raising

There are some amateur poker players who find something reprehensible about check-raising. They find it devious and deceitful and consider people who use it to be less than well-bred. Well, check-raising is devious and it is deceitful, but being devious and deceitful is precisely what one wants to be in a poker game, as is implied by the Fundamental Theorem of Poker.

Checking with the intention of raising is one way to do that. In a sense, check-raising and slowplaying are the opposites of bluffing, in which you play a weak hand strongly. If check-raising and slowplaying were not permitted, the game of poker would lose just about as much as it would if bluffing and semi-bluffing

137

were not permitted. Indeed the two types of play complement one another, and a good player should be adept at both of them. The check-raise is a powerful weapon. It is simply another tool with which a poker player practices his art. Not allowing check-raising in your home game is something like not allowing, say, the hit and run in a baseball game or the option pass in a football game. Without it poker loses a significant portion of its strategy, which, apart from winning money, is what makes the game fun. I'm much more willing to congratulate an opponent for trapping me in a check-raise than for drawing out on me on a call he shouldn't have made in the first place — and if I am angry at anyone, it is at myself for falling into the trap.

Necessary Conditions for Check-Raising

Two conditions are needed to check-raise for value — that is, when you expect you might be called by a worse hand. First, you must think you have the best hand, but not such a great hand that a slowplay would be proper. Second, you must be quite sure someone behind you will bet if you check. Let's say on fourth street in seven-card stud someone bets with

showing, and with

you're getting sufficient pot odds to call. Now on fifth street you catch a king to make kings up. Here you might check-raise if you are pretty sure the player representing queens will bet.

This second condition — namely, that someone behind you will bet after you check — is very important. When you plan to check-raise, you should always keep in mind that you could be making a serious, double-edged mistake if you check and no one bets behind you. You are giving a free card to opponents who would have folded your bet, and in addition you are losing a bet from those who would have called. So you had better be very sure the check-raise will work before you try it.

Check-Raising and Position

When you plan to check-raise with several players still in the pot, you need to consider the position of the player you expect will bet because that position determines the kind of hand you check-raise with, to a large extent. Let's say you have made hidden kings up on fifth street, and the player representing queens is to your *right*. Kings up is a fairly good hand but not a great hand, and you'd like to get everybody out so they don't draw out on your two pair. You check, and when the player with queens bets, you raise. You are forcing everyone else in the hand to call a double bet, the original bet and your immediate raise, and they will almost certainly fold. You don't mind the queens calling your raise, for you're a big favorite over that player. However, if he folds, that's fine too.

Now we'll place the player representing queens to your left instead of to your right. In this case you should bet with kings up even though you know the player with queens will bet if you check and even though you think you have the best hand. When you bet in this spot, you are *hoping the queens will raise* so that the double bet will drive out the other players in the pot, just as your check-raise was meant to do in the other instance. And if that opponent does raise, you can now reraise.

Suppose that instead of kings up, the king on fifth street gives you three kings. Now you are much stronger than you were with two pair, and your hand can tolerate callers. Therefore, you would use the opposite strategy you employed with kings up. With the probable bettor to your right, you should bet, and after everyone calls, you hope that bettor raises so that people will be calling a single bet twice (which they are much more likely to do than to call a double bet once).[5] On the other hand, if the probable bettor is to your left, then you check the three kings, and after that player bets and everyone calls, you raise. Once again, you are inviting your opponents to call a single bet twice and not a double bet once.

In sum, the way you bet or check-raise depends on the strength of your hand in relation to what you can see of the other hands and the position of the player you expect to bet or raise behind you when you check or bet. With a fairly good hand, like kings up or aces up in seven stud, you try to make opponents call a double bet because you'd like to drive them out. With a very good hand like three kings or three aces you play to induce your opponents to call a single bet; then you confront them with having to call another single bet. In this case, you don't mind their staying in since you're a big favorite over them.

----

[5] This situation occurs when you only call the raiser. Often the better play is to reraise.

Check-Raising With a Second-Best Hand

While you generally check-raise because you think you have the best hand, it is frequently correct to check-raise with a second-best hand if the play will drive other opponents out. The principle here is identical to the principle of raising with what you think is the second-best hand as it was explained in Chapter Nine and Chapter Thirteen. If the probable best hand is to your immediate right, you can check, wait for that player to bet, then raise so that the rest of the table will fold rather than call a double bet. While you may not be the favorite, you have still increased your chances of winning the pot, and you have the extra equity of whatever dead money is in the pot from earlier betting rounds.

Sometimes you can check-raise with a come hand like a four-flush if there are many people in the pot already and you don't expect a reraise, for you are getting good enough odds, especially if you have a couple of cards to come. This play should usually be made only when the probable bettor is to your immediate left; then the other players will call that bettor before they realize you are putting in a raise. You do not want to drive players out because you want to get the correct odds for your raise.

Summary

The factors you must consider when you plan to check-raise are:
1. The strength of your hand.
2. Whether someone behind you will bet after you check.
3. The position of the probable bettor.

To check-raise with a hand with which you want to thin out the field, you want the probable bettor to your right so that people will have to call a double bet to stay in. With a very strong hand and with most come hands, you want the probable bettor to your left so the other players in the hand might call that bettor's single bet and then be invited to call your raise.[6]

---

[6] For a discussion of check-raising when you are heads-up on the end, see pages 206-208.

Chapter Fifteen

Slowplaying

As we saw in the last chapter, check-raising is playing a hand weakly in order to raise later in the same round of betting. It is possible that you will win the pot right there when you check-raise. At the very least, you will probably reduce the opposition to one or two players, which is what you usually want.

Slowplaying Versus Check-Raising

Slowplaying is not the same thing. It is playing a hand weakly on one round of betting in order to suck people in for later bets. Typical slowplays are to check if there has been no bet or just call a bet rather than raise. In other words, you take no action beyond what is necessary to stay in the pot. You give nothing away about the strength of your hand.

When you check-raise you usually want to reduce the number of your opponents, but when you slowplay you are trying to keep as many players in the pot as you can, expecting to collect later bets from them as a result of your early deception. Obviously, since you are not worried about having many players in the pot and are not particularly concerned about giving them free cards, you must have a very strong hand to slowplay — much stronger than a hand with which you would check-raise. In seven-card stud it might be three-of-a-kind on the first three cards or a flush or full house against one pair. In hold 'em it might be the top set of trips after the flop with no possible straight or flush draw showing. In draw lowball it might be something like a pat

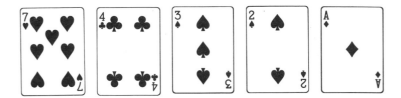

Requirements for Slowplaying

In most cases, for a slowplay to be correct, all of the following must be true.

1. You must have a very strong hand.
2. The free card or cheap card you are allowing other players to get must have good possibilities of making them a second-best hand.
3. That same free card must have little chance of making someone a better hand than yours or even giving that person a draw to a better hand than yours on the next round with sufficient odds to justify a call.
4. You must be sure you will drive other players out by showing aggression, but you have a good chance of winning a big pot if you don't.
5. The pot must not yet be very large.

Point 1, having a strong hand, needs to be true for points 2 and 3 to be true. Suppose in seven-card stud you have made a full house in five cards, and it looks as if your opponents are on flush draws and straight draws. When you slowplay and give them a free card, you would like all of them to make their hands so that you will get more action when you bet. At the same time, you are not worried that a free card will give them better hands than yours or draws to better hands with proper odds to chase. (However, you should not slowplay against these come hands if you think they would call when you bet.) In contrast, with three-of-a-kind in this situation, you should probably bet right out since there is a good chance a free card will allow one or more of your opponents to draw out on you when you don't make a full house.

Points 4 and 5 are also related. Opponents are much less likely to call a bet when the pot is small than when it is fairly large. As the pot gets larger, it becomes less and less likely that a slowplay is the correct play. The reason is that your opponents are getting larger and larger pot odds, and it is less and less likely that you could actually want them to get these odds. Therefore, when the pot becomes large, you are less inclined to slowplay because the odds you are giving opponents are so great that they can probably take them and not make much of a mistake, if any mistake at all. Furthermore, since opponents are unlikely to fold when the pot is large, it is not necessary to slowplay to keep them from folding.

Nor should you slowplay when you are showing obvious strength on board. Most players will know what you are doing, and they will not pay you off when you bet later. Players who don't know what you are doing, despite the strength of your board, will call an early bet anyway if they have any kind of hand.

When you are slowplaying, you are giving your opponents free cards or cheap cards. The Fundamental Theorem of Poker suggests such a play is incorrect unless your expectation is to show on a later round a larger profit than you would expect if you bet early. In other words, your deception has to have more implied value than what you would gain by betting immediately. At the same time, it is important that when your opponent calls on a later round, after getting a free or a cheap card, he is still not getting proper odds. Otherwise, it cannot be right to give him that free or cheap card, for you have given him the opportunity to develop a hand he is justified in playing even if it is not yet the best hand. Before slowplaying, then, you should make sure there is little chance you will be outdrawn. In seven stud and hold 'em games, you must be especially careful that you are not up against a possible straight draw or a flush draw unless, as we noted earlier, you have a straight or a flush beat already.

Ironically, you would tend to slowplay with excellent hands but not with the pure nuts. With the pure nuts you should bet and raise immediately in case someone else has a strong hand too. Don't make the mistake made by a friend of mine who flopped a straight flush in hold 'em. He kept checking it on a slowplay only to find someone else was doing the same with an ace-high flush.

To elucidate this point further, let's take two situations from draw lowball. If the player to your right raises the blind, you should just call in middle position with a pat

You have a strong hand and hope other players will call the original raiser and stay around for the draw. At the same time, there is the slim possibility that the original raiser has you beat. However, with a pat bicycle — A,2,3,4,5 — you'd like to win some money from the first raiser. So you should reraise in the hope he has a monster and is happy to reraise you. The other players will probably fold, but you might beat the original raiser out of many bets before he discovers you have the pure nuts.

Summary

Slowplaying is an extremely effective way to get good value for your strong hands, but since you are giving weaker hands free or cheap cards, you must slowplay with caution. You must have a very strong hand. You shouldn't slowplay when your strength is obvious or when the pot is large. Nor should you slowplay when a cheap or free card has a fair chance of giving an opponent a better hand than yours or a justifiable draw. For example, in seven-card stud an obvious straight bets into your hidden ace-king-high flush. You might just call if there are other flush draws around. But if you have only a king-high flush, you should raise to make it as costly as possible for higher flush draws to call and possibly draw out on you. Ideally a good slowplay occurs when, by making the hand they are hoping to make, opponents still end up second-best — i.e., when they are drawing dead. However, so long as your opponents will still not be getting proper odds after receiving a free card or a cheap card, a slowplay is worth considering.

Chapter Sixteen

Loose and Tight Play

Loose poker players play a large percentage of hands. They have relatively low starting requirements, and they continue in the pot with relatively weak hands. Tight players play a small percentage of hands. Their starting requirements are high, and they are quick to throw away weak hands that don't develop into big hands. Some players always play loose. Others always play tight. Good players adjust their play to the game.

In Chapter Four we saw how the size of the ante relative to later bets is a primary consideration in deciding how loose or tight you should play. The higher the ante, the looser you play. The smaller the ante, the tighter you play. With a high ante, there is more money in the pot from the start; and the more money there is in the pot, the better pot odds you are getting to play hands that might not be worth playing were the ante very small. With a small ante, on the other hand, there's no point in gambling with marginal hands, especially when you know other players in the game are likely to be betting and calling only with big hands.

Which brings us to a second consideration in deciding how loose or tight to play — namely, the way in which the other players in the game play. Assuming a normal ante — about 10 percent of the average future bets — it is commonly believed that when the players in the game play loose, you should play tight, and when the players in the game play tight, you should play loose. There is some truth to this principle. For example, you can steal antes with anything (a loose play) much more successfully against tight players, who will fold their marginal hands, than you can against loose players, who are likely to call you with those same hands. However, the principle of playing loose against tight players and tight against loose players is in need of refinement.

Loose Games

Semi-Bluffs in Loose Games

Remember that in a normal game, semi-bluffs have three ways of winning — by making the best hand later, by catching a scare card to make opponents fold later, or by making opponents fold immediately. It is these three possible ways of winning that make semi-bluffs profitable plays. But what is likely to happen in a loose game? First, loose players don't fold easily, so your semi-bluffs will rarely win immediately. Second, when you catch a scare card that doesn't really help your hand, loose players are more likely to want to "keep you honest" with a call than are average and tight players. Consequently, one of the ways a semi-bluff can win — when opponents fold immediately — has been all but completely eliminated; and a second way — when you catch scare cards — becomes doubtful. Without these two extra ways of winning, semi-bluffs no longer have positive expectation. Therefore, you must abandon most semi-bluffs when there's a high probability that the only way they can win is by improving to the best hand. With respect to semi-bluffing, then, it's true that you must play much tighter in a loose game.

Legitimate Hands in Loose Games

What about legitimate hands? In a loose game people are willing to play a hand that is relatively lower in value than the average. Therefore, your own legitimate hands don't need to be quite as good as in a normal game since your opponents are likely to be staying with you with even worse hands. This becomes especially true when you get heads-up against one opponent.

However, because of the action and the participants' style of play, loose games frequently tend to have multi-way pots. With many players staying in, you would be wrong to loosen up with hands like two small pair or one medium pair. Even though these marginal hands might be favorites to hold up against each of several loose opponents individually, chances are they will lose when there are several opponents in the pot. By the same token, if you bet with these hands, you are much less likely to get two, three, or four opponents to fold, particularly when they are loose players, than you are to get one opponent to fold.[7]

Come Hands in Loose Games

In contrast to other semi-bluff hands and small pairs, come hands increase in value with many players in the pot because you are usually getting excellent pot odds to draw to them. Furthermore, when the game is loose, you figure to get paid off well once you've made a straight or a flush. Therefore, in a loose game with several players in the pot, you should play more drawing hands, such as big three-flushes on fourth street in seven-card stud, than you would usually play.

In loose games, then, you should tighten up considerably on semi-bluffs but loosen up with legitimate hands. However, you would not play loose with marginal hands like two small pair or one medium pair when several opponents are in the pot.

Tight Games

In a tight game semi-bluffs increase in value, and even pure bluffs can be profitable since tight players are more likely to fold. Paradoxically, though, legitimate hands don't have nearly the value in a tight game that they would have in an average or loose game. The reason should be obvious. When you bet a legitimate hand for value in a tight game, you will be called only by players who have strong hands themselves because tight players' starting

---

[7] The mathematical principle here is the same as the principle that governs bluffing against more than one opponent. See Chapter Eighteen.

requirements are higher. In a loose game an opponent with two small pair at the end will probably call your bet with aces up. But when you bet that same hand in a tight game — especially if both of your aces are showing — and you get called, you cannot feel too comfortable. The caller probably has you beat.

Many aggressive players fail to devaluate their legitimate hands when they sit down in a tight game. They steal money with bluffs and semi-bluffs, but when they get a decent hand, they wind up losing. Then they mumble to themselves, "If I just never got a hand, I'd be doing great because it's with my good hands that I lose." What they fail to realize is that in a tight game the value of a hand goes down because players who stay in the pot will have good hands themselves — better hands on average than players in a regular game would have.

In a tight game, then, you loosen up on bluffs and semi-bluffs, but you tighten up on your legitimate hands. Nor would you play as many drawing hands in a tight game, since you'd be getting pot odds sufficient to make it worthwhile less often, and when you did hit, you wouldn't get paid off as much as you would in an average or in a loose game.

Summary

Scrap the general notion that you play tight in a loose game and loose in a tight game and use the following guidelines instead. In a loose game you must tighten up on your bluffs and semi-bluffs, but loosen up on your legitimate hands. You bluff less, but you bet for value more. You also call with more hands and play more drawing hands. In a tight game you loosen up on your bluffs and semi-bluffs, but you must tighten up your legitimate hand requirements. You bluff more, but you bet for value less. You also call less and give up more quickly with drawing hands.

These guidelines can also be applied to individual players, as well as to games. When a very tight player with raises in a small-ante seven stud game and everyone ahead of you folds, you would probably throw away a pair of jacks. You've tightened up your requirements because the chances are good your opponent already has you beat with a pair of kings. But when a very loose player raises in the same spot and everyone ahead of you folds, you might reraise with jacks, not as a semi-bluff but as a bet for value.

On the other hand, if you had

you might semi-bluff raise the very tight player who's betting a pair of kings since there's a decent chance that player will throw away the best hand, fearing you have aces. You wouldn't try that play against a very loose player, who is sure to call with kings.

To use all the poker tools at your disposal, you need to adjust your play according to the game and according to the individual players in the game.

Chapter Seventeen

Position

A player's position in the betting sequence is an important, yet underrated aspect of poker. In our discussion of raising, check-raising, and the free card, we have shown how position affects the way you play a hand. Indeed it can be said that position is one of the key elements affecting virtually every play in poker.

In games like five-card draw, draw lowball, and hold 'em, you know your position in advance of each deal since the person to the left of the dealer, the man *under the gun* as he's described, always acts first, and the dealer acts last. However, in stud games, both high and low, you can rarely be sure where you'll be in the betting sequence from one round to the next, as we have noted.

Position is more important in some games than in others; it is particularly critical in hold 'em and in five-card draw and draw lowball. However, in all poker games it is far better to be last to act, primarily because it is generally easier to decide what to do after you have seen what your opponents have done. Logically, then, the worst position is to be first since you must act before you know what any of your opponents are going to do. You might, for instance, have a hand that's worth a call if there are two or three other callers, but in first or early position you cannot be sure there will be any other callers. In last position you could know for sure whether you were getting favorable pot odds for a call, and if you weren't, you could save a bet and fold. When you are neither first nor last, the closer you are to last position the better, since you have fewer unknown quantities behind you and more relatively known quantities in front of you.

Advantages of Last Position

To suggest how important it is to be last, let's take a situation from seven-card razz. Suppose you started off with a good three-card low, and you think your opponent did, too. Now you catch a king or even a queen, and your opponent pairs up on board. Without a pair, you clearly have the best low hand if play were to stop immediately, yet you should *not* bet. The open pair makes it likely that your opponent will be last to act on every betting round, and that fact more than makes up for your slightly better first four cards.

Why is it so much better to be last? For a variety of reasons. If you are in last position with only a fair-to-good hand and the first player bets, you can call without having to fear a raise behind you. Players in early or middle position have no such comfort. If they call with a fair hand, they risk having to throw it away or pay a big price to continue when there's a raise behind them.

If you have a big hand in last position, your advantage is even greater. To see how much so, compare it to being first. In first position with a big hand, you might try to check-raise. But if no one bets behind you, you have lost a few bets from players who would have called a bet from you, while you have given a free card to players who wouldn't have called.

On the other hand, if you come right out betting in first position, you cost yourself money when a check-raise would have worked. Even in middle position with a big hand, you have difficult tactical decisions. If no one has yet bet and it's up to you, you must decide whether to bet or risk sandbagging. If someone has bet in front of you, you must decide whether it is more profitable and tactically correct to raise, inevitably driving out some players behind you, or to call in the hope of some overcalls behind you. In last position, you have no such problems. If no one has bet, you can, and if someone has bet ahead of you, you are at liberty to raise or to slowplay after knowing how many players are likely to remain in the pot.

If your hand is mediocre, it is still advantageous to be last. On the first round you can call the small opening bet without fear of a raise. On later rounds players ahead of you may check better hands than yours, which allows you to check behind them and get a free card. However, if you checked that same mediocre hand in an early position, an opponent might bet a fair hand behind you, denying you a free card and probably forcing you to fold.

When the pot is down to two players, positional considerations still apply, perhaps more than when there are several players in the pot. In last position you can bet a big hand when your opponent doesn't and raise when he does. With the same hand in first position, you'd have to decide whether to try a check-raise or bet; when you check with the intention of raising and your opponent checks behind you, you cost yourself a bet; if you bet when a check-raise would have worked, you also cost yourself a bet.

With a mediocre hand against one player, it's also advantageous to be last. If you can't call a bet, you still may get a free card when your opponent checks. In first position, as we saw in Chapter Ten, you are not at liberty to give yourself a free card. Finally, if your hand is somewhere in the middle — good but not great — it is better to be last. It's true you will bet in either position, but in last position you have the edge of being able to call when your opponent bets. In first position you might bet what is a *calling hand* and find yourself raised by your opponent in last position.

The only real threat to a player in last position is the possibility of a check-raise. Consequently, in games where check-raising is not allowed, being last is even more advantageous. Once players ahead of you have checked, you can feel reasonably confident they are not sandbagging with a big hand.

Advantages of First Position

However, this point does bring out the fact that there are a few situations where it's advantageous to be first. In first or early position you get more check-raising opportunities. Furthermore, with a lock in first position you might win three bets by betting and reraising. Finally, you sometimes want to drive players out to make your hand stand up; only raising in early position, before opponents have had the opportunity to call the first bet, can succeed in doing this. Nevertheless, these first and early position advantages are minimal in comparison to the many advantages of being last.

Adjusting Play to Position

There are times when your positional advantage allows you to win a pot you would not otherwise have won. Most of the time, though, the best hand wins, whether it happens to be first or last. So what we really mean by positional advantage is the extra bets that may be saved or gained by your being in late position — a check after your opponent checks, a raise after your opponent bets, and so on. The importance of these extra bets cannot be overemphasized. Never forget that in poker we are trying to win money, not pots. Every decent player wins a fair share of pots, but it is the extra bets you can get into the pots you win and those you can save from the pots you lose that increase your hourly rate and the money won in the long run.

There is little you can do to secure last position from one deal to the next, but when you have it, you should make the most of it. In seven-card stud, for example, you should anticipate the position you will be in from one round to the next. If an ace or an open pair is to your immediate left, that figures to make you last in the next round. You may play your hand a little differently, a little more aggressively, a little more loosely, than you would if you were expecting to be first.

In contrast, when the bettor is to your immediate right, forcing you to act ahead of everyone else, you must tighten up considerably. It is extremely important that you fold almost all marginal hands in this position. The possibility of a raise behind you plus the chance of a reraise from the original bettor is devastating. Furthermore, you can frequently count on being in the same unpleasant position — not accidentally called *under the gun* — for the remainder of the hand. If you constantly call bets with marginal hands in this position, you will have to fold so many of them — either later in the same round when the bet is raised or on the next round when the bet is repeated — that you will lose an enormous amount relative to the occasional pots you might win by staying in.

Thus, in five-card draw, if a player to your immediate right in early position opens, you should throw away two aces in most cases. In the same position in lowball, you'd usually have to throw away a one-card draw to a 7,6 and possibly a 7,5, even though these are hands you'd gladly play if you were sure there would be no raises behind you. In seven-card stud if the player to your right raises the opener on third street, you should fold most middle-sized pairs when there are several people behind you who might reraise.

With any of these hands you'd almost certainly call in last position, a fact that underlines another of that position's advantages: You can play more hands. You no longer need to fear a raise from players who have not acted, and in most instances you will probably remain last on future betting rounds as well. Even in seven-card stud, when the bettor to your left happens not to be high on board and thus first to act, the other players will usually check around to that bettor on the following round.

Strong Hand, Bettor to the Left

Another significant advantage to last position is that when you make a strong hand, you have more opportunity to win a big pot. You can sit there innocently with your monster hand and let the bettor to your left drive the other players around to you. That opponent bets, two or three players ahead of you call, and now bang, you raise. You get at least a single bet from opponents who fold after you raise, and you get a double bet from those who call. You're also making it more expensive for them to try to draw out on you when there are more cards to come. (Notice, in this situation, the problems faced by players in first and middle positions. Those callers in the middle always risk a raise from a player behind them.)

Strong Hand, Bettor to the Right

If you had the same strong hand but the bettor were to your right, you would not be able to play the hand in the same way. If you raised, you would be requiring players behind you to call a double bet to continue. Thus, you'd get fewer callers (if any) than you would if you raised in last position after they had committed themselves by calling the first bet. On the other hand, by just calling in first position, the best you can hope for is to collect some single bets from players behind you. At the same time, when there are more cards to come, you're making it relatively cheap for the callers to draw out on you. So with more cards to come, you have to decide whether your hand can stand competition or whether you should raise to drive players out.

How Position Affects Play

To show how differently you have to play in first and last positions, let's say I'm dealt

in no-limit hold 'em (where position remains fixed throughout the hand). If the opponent on my left raised a moderate amount and got three calls, I would also call as long as most of the players had a decent amount of money in front of them. Were I to flop three

6s (the odds against it are about 8-to-1), I'd anticipate winning a big pot. However, were the player on my *right* to raise the same amount, I'd have to fold my pair of 6s even if I thought there would be some calls but no raises behind me.

My bad position is what makes the difference. It changes things enough on future rounds to turn a call into a fold. If I were to flop three 6s in last position, that 6 on board would look pretty innocuous. The original bettor would probably bet again, maybe get called, and then I could put in a big raise — or perhaps slowplay and wait to raise on fourth street. However, if the bettor were to my right, I couldn't immediately raise with three 6s and hope to be called by players behind me whether on the flop or on fourth street. Thus, when I'm directly behind the bettor, my implied odds are reduced so much that it's not worth calling that bettor's first raise before the flop.

Position Vis-À-Vis Other Players in the Game

Position is important in relation to the playing style of the other players in the game. You prefer having the loose, aggressive player in the game sitting to your right and the tight, conservative player to your left. Then you can usually decide how to play your hand after the aggressive player has acted, while you don't have to worry about many surprises from the conservative player behind you. You are also in a better position to control the aggressive player and indeed to trap him into mistakes. Similarly, if there are players in the game who tip off whether or not they are playing a hand, you'd like them to your left so you can use that information when deciding whether to call the first bet yourself.

Summary

In sum, while in a horse race you like being first, in a poker game you like being last.

Chapter Eighteen

Bluffing

The 1978 no-limit hold 'em world championship at the Horseshoe in Las Vegas came down to a battle between owlish Bobby Baldwin of Tulsa, Oklahoma, and sartorial real-estate magnate Crandall Addington of San Antonio, Texas. An hour before the championship ended. Addington had $275,000, and Baldwin, about half as much — $145,000. Among the gamblers along the rail Addington was the clear favorite, but then came the hand that turned everything around. Acting first, Baldwin bet before the flop, and Addington called. The flop came:

Baldwin pushed in another $30,000 worth of chips, perhaps chasing a straight or a diamond flush. Then again he might have had a pair of queens. But Addington promptly called the $30,000. Obviously he had a good hand himself.

On fourth street the ace of diamonds fell — a scary-looking card — and by that time there was $92,000 in the pot. Slowly and deliberately Baldwin pushed in one $10,000 stack of chips, then another and another, until there were nine stacks in the center of the table. Finally, with something of a flourish, Baldwin placed a short stack of $5,000 on top of the others. He was making a $95,000 bet, leaving himself almost broke.

Addington deliberated for a long time. He glanced at the stack of chips, and then at Baldwin for some clue. Was the kid bluffing? If Addington called the bet and won, Baldwin would be just about tapped out. If he called the bet and lost, Baldwin would take a commanding lead. Was the kid bluffing or not? Addington decided he wasn't and threw away his hand. As Baldwin raked in the $92,000 pot, he made sure to flash his two hole cards in Addington's direction. They were the:

Worthless. Baldwin had indeed been bluffing. Addington seemed to get rattled, and an hour later Baldwin won all the chips and became the 1978 poker champion of the world.

The Myth of Bluffing

Successful bluffs, particularly in a high-stakes game, have great drama. Furthermore, people who do not play much poker often think that bluffing is the central element of the game. When Stu Ungar appeared on the Merv Griffin Show the day after he won the 1980 world poker championship, the first question Griffin asked him was, "Did you bluff very much?" Many occasional players who visit Las Vegas are constantly bluffing in the small $1-$3 and $1-$4 games, and they pay dearly for their foolishness.

It's true bluffing is an important aspect of poker, but it is only one part of the game, certainly no more important than playing your legitimate hands correctly. Though a player who never bluffs cannot expect to win as much money as someone who bluffs with the proper frequency, most average players tend to bluff too much, particularly in limit games. When it costs an opponent only one more bet to see your hand, it is difficult to get away with a bluff, for with any kind of hand your opponent is usually getting sufficient pot odds to call your bet — especially if he has seen you trying to bluff several times already.

The Reality of Bluffing

With this proviso, it must be repeated that from a theoretical point of view, bluffing is an extremely important aspect of poker. As a deceptive weapon, it is at least as important as slowplaying. Whereas slowplaying suggests weakness when you have strength, bluffing announces strength when you are weak. Recollect the Fundamental Theorem of Poker: Any time an opponent plays his hand incorrectly based on what you have, you have gained; and any time he plays his hand correctly based on what you have, you have lost. An opponent who knows you never bluff is much less likely to play his hand incorrectly. Any time you bet, he will know you are betting for value. He will play only when he figures he has a better hand than yours or when he is getting sufficient pot odds to call with more cards to come. Bluffing, then, or the possibility that you might be bluffing, is another way of keeping your opponents guessing. Your occasional bluffs disguise not just the hands with which you are in fact bluffing but also your legitimate hands, with which your opponents know you *might* be bluffing.

To see how important bluffing is, imagine that you are up against an opponent who on the last round bets $20 into a $100 pot. You are getting 6-to-1 from the pot if you call. However, you know you can only win, as is often the case, if your opponent is bluffing. Let's say you know three opponents well. The first never bluffs in this spot, so your response to that player's bet is easy: You fold with the full knowledge that you have not cost yourself any money. The second opponent frequently bluffs. Once again your response is easy: You call, knowing you are going to win that last bet so often that calling must result in a long-run profit. The third player is the problem. He bets in such a way that the odds are about 6-to-1 against his bluffing. In fact, he can tell you in advance that if he bets, he will be bluffing once in seven times.

Now you have a tough decision. You must choose between two equally upsetting alternatives. You are getting 6-to-1 from a pot you can win only if your opponent is bluffing, and the odds against your opponent's bluffing are 6-to-1. If you fold, you know there's a chance your opponent stole the pot from you; but if you call, you know that six times out of seven you are simply donating your money to your opponent. Thus, a person who bluffs with approximately the right frequency — and also, of course, in a random way — is a much better poker player and will win much more money in the long run than a person who virtually never bluffs or a person who bluffs too much. The person who never bluffs will never get much action. The person who always bluffs will get all the action he wants until he runs out of money. But the person who bluffs correctly keeps his true holdings disguised and is constantly forcing his opponents into tough decisions, some of which are bound to be wrong.

Optimum Bluffing Frequency

What is the right bluffing frequency? It is a frequency that makes it impossible for your opponents to know whether to call or fold. Mathematically, optimal bluffing strategy is to bluff in such a way that the chances against your bluffing are identical to the pot odds your opponent is getting. Thus, if, as in the example just given, an opponent is getting 6-to-1 from the pot, the chances against your bluffing should be 6-to-1. Then that opponent would break even on the last bet by calling every time and also by folding every time. If he called, he would lose $20 six times and win $120 once; if he folded, he would win nothing and lose nothing. Regardless of what your opponent does, you average winning an extra $100 every seven hands. However, mathematically optimal bluffing strategy isn't necessarily the best strategy. It is much better if you are able to judge when to try a bluff and when not to in order to show a bigger overall profit.

To make sure we agree on what is meant by a bluff, we will define it as a bet or a raise with a hand which you do not think is the best hand. Bluffing can be separated into a couple of different categories. There is bluffing when there are more cards to come and when there are no more cards to come. Secondly, within each of these categories, there is intuitive bluffing, which is the subject of this chapter, and mathematical bluffing, which will be discussed in the next chapter.

Bluffs When There are More Cards to Come

When there are more cards to come, your bluffs should rarely be pure bluffs — that is to say, bets or raises that have little or no chance of winning if you are called, even taking into account the cards you may get on future rounds. Instead your early-round bets should be semi-bluffs, those powerful, deceptive plays we looked at in detail in Chapters Eleven and Twelve. It is important to bluff occasionally on early rounds to keep your opponents off-balance. But why do it when you have only one or two ways of winning? For a pure bluff to work, your opponent or opponents must generally fold immediately. However, as we saw in Chapter Eleven, a semi-bluff has three ways of winning. It may win because your opponent folds immediately, and it may also win either because you catch a scare card that causes your opponent to fold on a later round or because you make the best hand.

Nevertheless, while you should usually restrict your early-round bluffs to semi-bluffs, there is still nothing to prevent you from trying a pure bluff if you feel there's a good chance of getting away with it. If you think your chances of getting away with it are greater than the pot odds you are getting, then you should go ahead and try it. You may recall in the chapter on ante structure we mentioned playing in a game where certain players played too tight for the ante. There was $10 in antes, and if these players were the only ones in the pot, I knew I could bet $7 with absolutely nothing and have a good chance of stealing that $10. My pot odds in that instance were less than 1½-to-1, but I knew I could get away with the bluff about 60 percent of the time. So it was a profitable play.

If you do make a pure bluff on an early round and someone raises you, don't try to tough it out. You've been caught. Since you have no out, you don't even have to think about continuing. Give it up, and get on with the next hand.

When you bluff with more cards to come, you often get called, and then you are faced with deciding whether or not to continue the bluff on the next round. Thus, when you bluff with a hand that probably can't improve to the best hand, you need to compare your chances of getting away with it to your effective odds if you are planning to continue betting on future rounds even when you don't improve.

For instance, if there is $100 in the pot in a $10-$20 game with two cards to come, you may have to bluff twice. If you think you will bluff twice, you are risking $40 to win $120 — the $100 in the pot plus the $20 your opponent calls on the first round. So when you make that first $20 bet, you cannot think you are getting 5-to-1 from the pot. Rather you are getting 3-to-1 ($120-to-$40). For the play to be profitable, there must be a better than 3-to-1 chance your opponent will fold after the second bet. This is especially true of pure bluffs where you have no way of winning by improving to the best hand.

Deciding whether to continue with a semi-bluff really depends on how the next card affects your chances and how your opponent's card seems to have affected his. Each individual round should be evaluated separately. Suppose you make a semi-bluff raise in seven-card stud with:

You get called by a 9. Whether you should give up the bluff on the next round depends on what you catch, what your opponent catches, and also what kind of player your opponent is. If with your A,K,5 you proceed to catch a queen suited with the king and your opponent catches a deuce, you ought to bet again; but if your opponent catches, let's say, an 8 suited with the 9 and you catch a 3, give it up. Check, and if your opponent bets, throw the hand away. Your chances have not improved, and it looks as if your opponent's have. He may have a flush draw, a straight draw, or simply a pair of 9s, but whatever he has, he looks like too much of a favorite for you to call when he bets.

It takes experience to know when to give up on a bluff and when to pursue it. When your first bet is called, presumably your opponent has something. If you sense he's getting stronger and you don't improve, give it up. If you sense he's weak and staying weak and if you think he thinks you're strong, continue the bluff and hope to drive him out.

Bluffs When All the Cards are Out

When all the cards are out, you obviously can no longer semi-bluff. You have either made your hand or you haven't. So all bluffs on the end are pure bluffs. They are bets or raises that you do not expect to win if you are called.

When you are sitting there knowing you have the worst hand, knowing you cannot win by checking, knowing you cannot win by calling your opponent's bet, the only question is whether or not to try to bluff. You should not if you think the chances your opponent will call are too great in relation to the pot odds you are getting. You should if you think your opponent will fold often enough for a bluff to show a profit. If there is $100 in the pot, you should make a $20 bluff if you think your opponent will fold more than once in six times. If there is $60 in the pot, you must assume your opponent will fold more than once in four times before you try to bluff. If there is $140 in the pot, your opponent needs to fold more than once in eight times. But, of course, the larger the pot, the better pot odds your opponent is getting to call your bet and the more likely it is he will call with any kind of a fair hand.

Accurate assessment of your chances of pulling off a bluff comes, like so many advanced poker plays, only with experience. You must first be able to read hands. You are obviously not going to bluff out an opponent with a lock or any sort of big hand. In general, the weaker you think your opponent's hand is, the higher the chances your bluff will succeed.

Second, you must be able to read opponents. It's generally easier to bluff out a timid opponent than a loose opponent, and it's generally easier to bluff out a tough opponent than a weak one who looks for any reason to call, including the possibility that you might be bluffing. In essence, you must consider your specific opponent in each situation before deciding whether to try a bluff. Even the way in which play developed in previous hands can have a bearing on whether a bluff is now right or not.

Bluffing and Position

Your position can also affect the chances of a bluff's success. In most games with tough players, I've found it easier to bluff if I'm first than if I'm second and my opponent has checked. There are two reasons for this. If my opponent has checked to me, he knows he has shown weakness with his check, and when I bet, he suspects I am trying to take advantage of his weakness. So he's likely to call with any kind of hand. And, if he has a really bad hand, he might very well have tried to bluff himself. Since he checked instead, the chances are good he has a calling hand, and when I bet out on a bluff, he's likely to call, even if he thinks he's a small underdog. So in situations on the end where your hand can't win by checking but where you have reason to believe your opponent may be weak, a bluff in first position is more likely to succeed than a bluff in second position.

Bluffing Against Come Hands

Sometimes both you and your opponent have been drawing to a flush or a straight. You don't make your hand, but there's a good chance your opponent didn't make his either. Because of earlier bets on the come, there may be a fair amount in the pot — say, $100 in a $10-$20 game. Now let's say you are first, and you end up with an AJ high. You think there's a 55 percent chance your opponent made a legitimate hand, and there's a 15 percent chance he has you beat "by mistake" with something like an A,K or an A,Q high. In this spot you should bet because by betting you are likely to make your opponent throw away the A,K and A,Q high, thus improving your chances of winning from 30 percent to 45 percent.

In contrast, when you have a busted hand and you suspect your opponent does, too, you may not want to bluff if you end up making something like a small pair. If you bet, your opponent will call with a legitimate hand, and he will fold without one. But if you check and then call, your opponent may bet his busted hands as well as his legitimate ones. Thus, with your small pair you beat his bluffs, which you could not do if you came out betting yourself. Either way, of course, you lose to his legitimate hands.

Bluffing Against Two or More Opponents

It is rarely correct to try to bluff out two or more people when all the cards are out; your chances of success decrease geometrically with each additional player in the pot. Paradoxically you might have a profitable bluffing opportunity against each of two opponents individually, but not against both of them as a group. Suppose, for example, you are heads-up on the end in a $10-$20 game. There is $80 in the pot, and you think you can get away with a bluff one out of three times. Clearly this is an extremely profitable bluffing situation. Once you will win $80, and twice you will lose $20 for a net profit of $40 or an average profit of $13.33 per bet.

Now suppose you are in the identical situation except that you are up against two players instead of one. We'll assume each player has put $40 in the pot to expand it to $120, and you think, as in the former case, that each opponent will fold one time out of three. You are now getting 6-to-1 instead of 4-to-1 from the pot. Nevertheless, an attempt at a bluff is no longer profitable because the probability that both of your opponents will fold is ⅓ X ⅓, which equals 1/9. In other words, eight times out of nine one or the other of your opponents will call on average. So you stand to lose $20 eight times for a total of $160 and to win $120 once. Your net loss is $40 or $4.44 per bet. Thus, opposing each individual player by himself results in a profitable bluffing situation, but if they're both in against you, you have gone from a profitable situation to an unprofitable one.

(It should be pointed out that in most bluffing situations against more than one player the probabilities that each player will fold are not independent. The player in the middle will frequently fold a hand that he would call with if he was last, and sometimes the player who is last will call with a hand he would have folded without hesitation had he been in the middle, expecting the player behind him to call. Nevertheless, the general principle still holds that it is usually more profitable to try to bluff one player out of a pot containing 2X dollars than to bluff two players out of a pot containing 3X dollars.)

Bluffing and Betting for Value

The number of poker hands anyone can have is comparatively limited, but in addition to the hands themselves there are so many other variables that rarely if ever is a particular play always right or always wrong. Your play is affected by the size of the pot, your position, the opponent or opponents you are facing, the way they have been playing, the amount of money they have and you have, the flow of the game, and other, more subtle factors. This point is particularly applicable to questions of bluffing and betting fair hands for value on the end. Here are some general principles that usually apply.

When you bluff, you are rooting for your opponent to fold because that is the only way you can win the pot. When you bet for value, you are rooting for your opponent to call because you want your legitimate hand to win one more bet from him. It is important to realize that it may be right to bet a fair hand for value, and it may also be right to bluff, but it is almost never right to do neither. If you decide you can't get away with a bluff on the end when you miss your hand, then you should bet for value when you do make your hand. (The only exception to this principle would occur in games like hold 'em and five-card stud, where your opponent can see your last card and might often have a good sense of whether it made your hand. In those cases, if you bet a hand for value, you are likely to get called — or raised — only by a hand that has you beat.)

Similarly, when you don't think a value bet is justified with a fair hand, since your opponent will only call if he has you beat, then if you miss your hand, you should usually bluff. For when you bluff, it is possible your opponent will throw away his fair hands.

Sometimes it may be correct both to bluff and to bet a fair hand for value on the end. Suppose you are up against one player and decide, before you see your last card, that you will come out betting if you don't improve. In seven-card stud, let's say on sixth street you have:

Notice that in addition to your A,Q high four-flush you hold a small pair. When you pick up your last card, you find that you didn't make the flush, but you don't have a bad hand either. You caught another queen and so now have queens up. Should you bet this hand for value?

Many professional players say no. They contend that if you were so sure you should bluff if you missed, then you should not bet a fair hand for value since you will only be called if your opponent has you beat. However, both plays may be right, especially if the pot is large. Let's say there's an 80 percent chance your queens up are the best hand, and there's a 30 percent chance your opponent will fold if you bet. That means that if you bet your queens up for value, 30 percent of the time your opponent will fold and not pay you off. Nevertheless, you are still a 5-to-2 favorite when that player calls your bet. You will win that extra bet 50 percent of the time, while you will lose it only the 20 percent of the time your opponent has your queens up beat. Clearly, then, you should bet with your two pair since you have a 5/7 chance of winning if you are called. On the other hand, if you miss making even two pair, there is still a 30 percent chance your opponent will fold what may be the best hand if you bet. Therefore, a bluff will also be profitable in the long run, so long as your bet is less than 3/7 of the pot.

A similar situation comes up in hold 'em when I am heads-up against a good player. I raise before the flop in last position, and my opponent calls. The flop comes something like:

My opponent checks. I check. He now suspects I have A,K; A,Q; or K,Q; and he is right. He is ready to call with any pair if a high card doesn't come, but if one does, he will consider folding. I know all this. Therefore, I am going to bet when an ace, king, or queen comes, even though only two of those cards pair me. My opponent should call me often enough with the worst hand to make a value bet correct, yet I suspect he will fold with enough frequency to make a bluff profitable too.

Bluffing According to Your Opponent

You must, of course, consider your opponent when deciding whether to bet a fair hand for value or to bluff. Against a perpetual caller, obviously you should rarely bluff. However, against such a player you should bet any hand that you figure is a reasonable favorite to be the best hand. In contrast, against a tough player capable of tough folds, you can get away with bluffs more often, but you should be more reluctant to bet your fair hands for value. A tough opponent is not likely to pay you off with his worse hands, and when he does call, he's likely to show down a hand that beats you.

Here is a typical situation showing when a bluff is right and when it is not. Let's say in draw poker you draw three cards to a pair of jacks, and your opponent draws three to what you suspect is a pair of aces. First, we'll assume your opponent is the type of player who will almost always fold if his hand doesn't improve. In this instance, your play is to bluff if you don't improve since you may make your opponent throw away his pair of aces. However, if you make jacks up, you should check rather than bet for value since you are a big underdog if you bet and get called. If your opponent calls, he is likely to have made aces up.

Now let's assume your opponent is the type who almost never folds. Against this player you cannot bluff with one pair because he will almost certainly call you with his bigger pair. However, if you make jacks up against him, then you should bet for value since your two pair are almost a 5-to-2 favorite to be the best hand when you get called. The difference is that this opponent will call with one pair of aces as well as with aces up, whereas the first opponent would most likely not have called with only a pair of aces.

Bluffing as Advertising

When you get caught bluffing, you of course lose. However, you may not mind being caught and losing early in a session because you are considering your image for future hands. You may even make an ill advised bluff early so that you will get a lot more calls on your legitimate hands the rest of the night. (Similarly, an early ill-advised call against tough players may keep them from bluffing against you the rest of the night because they fear you're likely to call their bluffs.)

Creating an image that you almost never bluff can also be advantageous. I am generally considered a tight player, and I sometimes pass up an early, marginally profitable bluffing situation to enhance this image. What that does is allow me to steal some pots in the future with complete impunity. No one imagines I am daring to bluff.

When you are up against even average players, they are constantly studying the way you play. So considering the effect of any play on future hands should be an important part of your game, especially in no-limit and pot-limit poker and especially when you are playing against the same people all night or from one night to the next or one week to the next.

Some players go so far as to argue that bluffs should show a loss because those losses will be repaid with interest when they get a lot of action on their legitimate hands. Game theory, as we shall see in the next chapter, suggests that when you employ optimal bluffing strategy, you should break even on your bluffs. However, there is no reason not to develop a sense of your opponents and of betting situations so your bluffs show a profit. A successful bluff wins the whole pot, and it takes a lot of extra calls of your legitimate hands to make up for one pot. Therefore, against all but very tight players, you should bluff slightly less than optimally so your bluffs show a profit. The greater your reputation as a tight player, the more you will be able to get away with bluffs. At the same time, you will still get caught often enough to get paid off when you do have a good hand.

Summary

A bluff is a bet or raise with a hand you do not think is the best hand. With more cards to come, you should generally restrict yourself to semi-bluffs with hands that may become the best hand.

When deciding whether to make a pure bluff, you estimate whether your chances of getting away with it are better than the pot odds you are getting. However, if there are more cards to come and you plan to continue to bluff, you must take into account your effective odds.

On the end you should usually bluff with a busted hand when you think your opponent is weak. Against a tough player, the bluff tends to work more often in first position. However, if you have a hand with some value, don't bet when you are first so that you can snap off your opponent's bluffs. If you are in second position and your opponent checks, show down these same hands since they have little chance of winning if you bet and get called.

The odds against a bluff's working increase almost geometrically with each extra person in a pot. Therefore, it is rarely correct to try to bluff out two or more players, especially on the end.

When to bluff and when to bet a fair hand for value is a difficult problem of judgment and experience. In general, if you do not think you could get away with a bluff, you should bet your fair hands for value; if a fair hand cannot be a profitable bet, then a bluff should be.

Bluffs are another tool of the well-rounded poker player. In my opinion, they should show a long-run profit the same as any other poker play. Even if you get caught only occasionally, you can still expect to get paid off when you do have a hand.

Chapter Nineteen

Game Theory and Bluffing

Game theory sounds like a theory about games, but it is actually a branch of mathematics dealing with the decision-making process. While it applies to games, as we shall see, it also applies to such disciplines as economics, international relations, social science, and military science. Essentially game theory attempts to discover mathematically the best strategies against someone also using the best strategies. Against an opponent you think is weaker than you are — and it can be in any game whatsoever — you would usually rely on your judgment rather than on game theory. However, against an opponent you think is better than you or against an opponent you don't know, game theory can sometimes enable you to overcome the other's judgmental edge.

To show how game theory can work in this regard, we'll employ the children's game of odds and evens. Each of two players puts out one or two fingers. If the total is even, one player wins; if the total is odd, his opponent wins. Now mathematically this is an absolutely even game. However, over a long series it is possible for one person to gain an edge by outwitting the other, by deciding whether to put out one or two fingers on the basis of what the other person put out in the previous round or rounds, by picking up patterns — in a word, by figuring out what his opponent is thinking and then putting out one or two fingers in order to foil him.[8]

---

[8] Figuring out what the other person is thinking is, of course, a crucial aspect of poker. See Chapter Twenty-three, "The Psychology of Poker."

179

Suppose someone challenges you to this game. Feeling confident about his judgment and ability to outguess you, he is willing to lay you $101 to $100 per play. We'll assume you too feel your challenger has the best of it in terms of judgment. Nevertheless, by employing game theory, you can gladly accept the proposition with the assurance that you have the best of it. All you have to do is flip a coin to decide whether to put out one or two fingers.

If the coin comes up say, heads, you put out one finger; if it comes up tails, you put out two fingers. What has this procedure done? It has completely destroyed your opponent's ability to outguess you. The chances of your putting out one or two fingers are 50-50. The chances of a coin coming up heads or tails are 50-50. However, instead of your thinking about whether to put out one or two fingers, the coin is making the decisions for you, and most importantly it is *randomizing* the decisions. Your opponent might be able to outguess you, but you are forcing him to outguess an inanimate object, which is impossible. One might as well try to guess whether a roulette ball is going to land on the red or the black.

Since your opponent is laying you $101 to $100, by using game theory you have assured yourself of an 0.5 percent mathematical advantage (or a 50-cent positive expectation per bet). You have removed whatever advantage your opponent might have had in out-thinking you and given yourself an insuperable edge over the long run. Only if you thought you could out think your opponent would you be better off using your judgment instead of a coin flip.

Using Game Theory to Bluff

In this chapter we are mainly concerned with how game theory can be applied to the art of bluffing and calling possible bluffs in poker. For this purpose we will talk about mixed strategy, a strategy in which you make a certain play — specifically a bluff or a call of a possible bluff — a predetermined percentage of the time, but you introduce a random element so that your opponent cannot know when you are making the play and when you are not.

You will recall from the last chapter that, everything else being equal, the player who never bluffs and the player who bluffs too much are at a decided disadvantage against a player who bluffs correctly. To illustrate this point and to show how game theory can be used to decide correctly when to bluff, we'll set up a proposition.

We are playing draw lowball with no joker, and I give you a pat:

I take a:

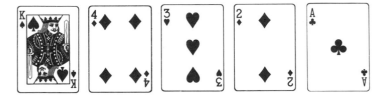

You stand pat, and I must draw one card. If I catch a five, a six, a seven, an eight, or a nine, I beat you with a better low than yours. If I catch any other card, you win. That means that of the 42 cards remaining in the deck, I have 18 winners (4 fives, 4 sixes, 4 sevens, 3 eights, and 3 nines) and 24 losers, which makes me a 24-to-18 or 4-to-3 underdog. We each ante $100, but after the draw — which you do not see — I can bet $100.

Suppose I said I'm going to bet $100 every time. Clearly you would call every time because you would stand to win $200 the 24 times I'm bluffing and lose $200 the 18 times I have the best hand for a net profit of $1,200. On the other hand, suppose I said I will never bluff; I will only bet when I have your 9,8 low beat. Then you would fold every time I bet, and once again you would win 24 times (when I don't bet) and lose 18 times (when I do) for a net profit of $600 since you win or lose $100 in each of these hands. So with either of these variations of the proposition, you definitely have the best of it.

However, if I only bluff some of the time, the situation is much different. Suppose I were to bluff only when I caught the king of spades. In other words, I would bet whenever I caught any of my 18 good cards and also when I caught the king of spades. If I bluffed this infrequently, your proper play would still be to fold when I bet because the odds against my bluffing are 18-to-1. But notice how this improves my position. Bluffing when I catch the king of spades still doesn't give me a profit, but it allows me to win 19 times instead of 18 and lose only 23 times instead of 24. That single bluff once out of 19 times has begun to close the gap between your status as a favorite and mine as an underdog. Notice too that you have no way of knowing when I am bluffing since I am randomizing my bluffs by using a card, an object as inanimate as the coin in the odds-evens game, to make my bluffing decision for me.

If bluffing with one card makes me less of an underdog than never bluffing at all, suppose I choose two — say, the king of spades and the jack of spades. Once again your correct play is to fold when I bet. But now you win only 22 times when I don't bet, and I win 20 times when I do. Assuming you have no way of knowing when I'm bluffing and when I'm not, my using just two key cards to bluff, in addition to my 18 good cards, has reduced you from 24-to-18 favorite to a 22-to-20 favorite — that is, from a 4-to-3 favorite to an 11-to-10 favorite.

This bluffing seems to have possibilities. Suppose instead of two cards, I picked *five* key cards — the king of spades and all four jacks. That means I would be betting 23 times — 18 times with the best hand and five times on a bluff. Now all of a sudden you are in a bad situation with your pat 9,8 because you have to guess whether I'm bluffing when I bet. I could even tell you precisely the strategy I am using, but *you would still have to lose your money.*

What would happen? You know there are 18 cards that will make me my hand and five other cards I will bluff with. Thus, the odds are 18-to-5 or 3.6-to-1 against my bluffing. With the $200 in antes and my $100 bet, the pot is $300. So you are getting 3-to-1 odds from the pot. You cannot profitably call a 3.6-to-1 shot when you stand to win only 3-to-1 for your money. Lo and behold, by using five cards to bluff with, I win that pot from you 23 out of 42 times, and you win it only 19 times. I make a profit of $400. Thus, my occasional random bluffing has swung a hand that is a 24-to-18 underdog into a 23-to-19 favorite.

To assure yourself there is no arithmetical sleight of hand here, you can work out what happens if you call every time I bet. You will win $200 from me the five times I am bluffing and $100 from me the 19 times I don't bet, for a total of $2,900. But you will lose $200 to me the 18 times I have the best hand for a total of $3,600. Your net loss when you call is $700, which is $300 more than you lose if you simply fold when I bet.

Had I picked seven cards to bluff with instead of five, the odds would then be 18-to-7 against my bluffing, and since the pot odds you're getting are 3-to-1, you would be forced to call when I bet. However, you would still end up losing! Seven times, when I'm bluffing, you would win $200 from me for a total of $1,400 and the 17 times I don't bet at all you would win $100 from me for a total of $1,700. Your wins after 42 hands would total $3,100. But I would win $200 from you the 18 times I bet with my good cards for a total of $3,600, giving me a net profit and you a net loss of $500 after 42 hands.

It should be pointed out — once again to make it clear there are no tricks to this arithmetic — that you would lose even more money if you folded every time I bet with my 18 good cards and seven bluffing cards. You would win $100 from me the 17 times I don't bet, while I would win $100 from you the 25 times I do. Your net loss would now be $800 instead of $500.

Optimum Bluffing Strategy

Let's say I choose specifically 6 key cards to bluff with. That means I will bet 24 times. 18 of those times I have the best hand, and 6 of those times I am bluffing. Therefore, the odds against my bluffing are exactly 3-to-1. The pot is $200, and when I bet, there is $300 in the pot. Thus, your pot odds are also 3-to-1. You are calling $100 to win $300. Now when the odds against my bluffing are identical to the odds you are getting from the pot, it makes absolutely no difference whether you call or fold. Furthermore, whatever you do, you will still lose exactly $600 after 42 hands. If you were to fold every time I bet, I would beat you out of $100 24 times when I bet and lose $100 to you 18 times, when I don't bet, for a profit of $600. If you were to call me every time, you would beat me out of $200 six times when I'm bluffing and $100 18 times, when I don't bet, for a total of $3,000; but I would beat you out of $200 18 times when I bet with my good hands for a total of $3,600. Once again my profit is $600. So other than being a psychic, there is no way in the world you can prevent me from winning that $600 per 42 hands, giving me a positive expectation of $14.29 per hand. Bluffing exactly 6 times out of 24 has turned a hand that was a 4-to-3 underdog when I didn't bluff at all into a 4-to-3 favorite — no matter what strategy you use against me.

We can now move to the heart of game theory and bluffing. Notice first that the percentage of bluffing I did was predetermined — one time every 19 bets or 5 times every 23 bets or 7 times every 25 bets. Notice secondly that my bluffing was completely random; it was based on certain key cards I caught, which my opponent could never see. He could never know whether the card I drew was one of my 18 good cards or a bluff card. Finally, notice what happened when I bluffed with precisely six cards — which made the odds against my bluffing in this particular instance identical to the pot odds my opponent was getting. In this unique case my opponent stood to lose exactly the same amount by calling or folding.

This is optimum bluffing strategy — it makes no difference how your opponent plays. We can say, then, that if you come up with a bluffing strategy that makes your opponent do equally badly no matter how he plays, then you have an optimum strategy. And this optimum strategy is to bluff in such a way that the odds against your bluffing are identical to the odds your opponent is getting from the pot. In the situation we have been discussing, I had 18 good cards, and when I bet my $100, creating a $300 pot, my opponent was getting 3-to-1 odds from the pot. Therefore, my optimum strategy was to bluff with six additional cards, making the odds against my bluffing 3-to-1, identical to the pot odds my opponent was getting.

Let's say the pot was $500 instead of $200 before I bet. Once again I had 18 winning cards, and my opponent could only beat a bluff. The bet is $100, and so my opponent would be getting $600-to-$100 pot odds when he called. Now my optimum strategy would be to bluff with *3* cards. With 18 good cards and 3 bluffing cards, the odds against my bluffing would be 6-to-1, identical to the pot odds my opponent would be getting to call my bet. If the pot were $100 and I bet $100, I'd have to bluff with 9 cards when I had 18 good cards, making the odds against my bluffing identical to the 2-to-1 odds my opponent would be getting from the pot.

It is important to realize that when the results are the same whether your opponent calls or folds, you will still average the same no matter how that opponent mixes up his calls and folds. Returning to the initial optimum strategy example, where I make a $100 bluff with 6 cards and bet 18 good cards into a $200 pot, I will still average $600 in profits per 42 hands in the long run whether my opponent calls 12 times and folds 12 times or calls 6 times and folds 18 times, or whatever. The inability of a player to find any response to offset his disadvantage is the key to game theory problems, though most game theory books don't put it in this form.

Bluffing on the basis of game theory can also be described in terms of percentages. Suppose you have a 25 percent chance of making your hand, the pot is $100, and the bet is $100. Thus, if you bet, your opponent is getting 2-to-1 odds from the pot. Since there is a 25 percent chance of making your hand, there should be a 12½ percent chance you are bluffing to create the 2-to-1 odds against your bluffing, which is the optimum strategy. For example, in draw lowball there are 48 cards you do not see when you draw one card, and we'll assume 12 of them (25 percent) will make your hand. So you should pick 6 other cards (12½ percent) out of the 48 to use for a bluff.

You pick cards, of course, to randomize your bets. Without the random factor, the good opponents against whom you use game theory to bluff would quickly pick up your pattern and destroy you. The beautiful thing about game theory is that even if your opponent knows you are using it, there is nothing he can do about it.

Game Theory and Bluffing Frequency According to Your Opponents

In actual poker situations, optimum strategy based on game theory is not always the best strategy. Obviously if you are up against an opponent who almost always calls you, then you shouldn't bluff at all. By the same token, if you are up against someone who folds too much, you should bluff with some frequency.

Game theory bears out these shifts in strategy. Notice in the first part of this chapter that if you bluffed with five cards instead of six — that is, slightly less than optimally — you would win $300 more per 42 hands if your opponent called rather than folded every time. However, if you bluffed with seven cards instead of six, you would win $300 more if your opponent folded rather than called every time. Here is where a player's judgment supersedes optimum game theory strategy: He would bluff a little less against opponents who call too much and a little more against opponents who fold too much.

Good, intuitive players understand this concept. If they notice they have folded on the end a few hands in a row, they are ready to call next time. Otherwise players will start bluffing them. And they use similar considerations in deciding whether to bluff themselves. It is against such expert players, whose calling and folding are right on target, or whose judgment is as good as or better than yours, that game theory becomes the perfect tool. When you use it, there is no way they can outplay you.

Summary of Game Theory as a Tool for Bluffing

When using game theory to decide whether to bluff, you must first determine your chances of making your hand. You must then determine the odds your opponent is getting on that bet. Then you must randomly bluff in such a way that the odds against your bluffing are identical to your opponent's pot odds.

Here's one more example. Suppose you have a 20 percent chance of making your hand, there's $100 in the pot, and the bet is $25. Your opponent is then getting $125-to-$25 or 5-to-1 odds if you bet. The ratio of your good hands to your bluffs should, therefore, be 5-to-1. Since you have a 20 percent chance of making your hand, you should randomly bluff 4 percent of the time. (20 percent-to-4 percent equals 5-to-1.) When you bluff in this fashion, you take optimum advantage of the situation.

A good, convenient way to randomize your bluffs, as we have seen, is to pick cards from among those you haven't seen. If, for example, ten cards make your hand and you need a 5-to-1 bluffing ratio, then you should pick two additional cards to bluff with.

Here is another example. You draw one card to a spade flush in draw poker, and your opponent draws three cards. Therefore, the chances are enormous that your opponent will not be able to beat a flush, only a bluff. The pot contains $20. The bet is $10. If you bet, your opponent is getting $30-to-$10 or 9-to-3 odds from the pot. Since nine unseen spades make your flush, you should pick three additional cards to bluff with, such as the two red 4s and the 4 of clubs. You now bet with twelve cards creating a 9-to-3 ratio between your good hands and your bluffs.

It is not always possible to use cards to arrive at exactly the ratio you need to bluff optimally. However, as long as you are close, you can still expect to gain. You recall that choosing six cards to bluff with in the draw lowball example created exactly the right proportion vis-à-vis the pot odds my opponent was getting; nevertheless, I still ended up with a profit when I bluffed with five or with seven cards whether my opponent called or folded. Of course, the closer you are to the exact ratio, the better, in terms of game theory.

Using Game Theory to Call Possible Bluffs

Just as you can use game theory to bluff, you can also use it to call possible bluffs. Usually when your hand can beat only a bluff, you use your experience and judgment to determine the chances your opponent is bluffing. If your hand can beat some of your opponent's legitimate hands, then you do a standard comparison of your chances of having the best hand plus the chances your opponent is bluffing against the pot odds you are getting. However, against an opponent whose judgment is as good as or better than yours, or one who is capable of using game theory to bluff, you in your turn can use game theory to thwart that player or at least minimize his profits.

Suppose the pot is $100, and your opponent assumes you will fold one out of three times rather than call a $20 bet. It then becomes profitable for that opponent to come out bluffing $20 to win $100 because he figures to lose $20 twice but steal $100 once for a net profit of $60 and an expectation of $20 per bet. By the same token, if your opponent thinks you will never fold in this situation, he will never bluff. Therefore, it behooves you to have an opponent think you might sometimes fold, but you should call sufficiently often to catch his bluffs.

When you use game theory to decide whether to call a possible bluff, you make calculations similar to those you make when deciding whether to employ a bluff yourself — and you randomize your calls just as you randomize your bluffs. You figure out what odds your opponent is getting on his possible bluff, and you make the ratio of your calls to your folds exactly the same as the ratio of the pot to your opponent's bet. If your opponent bets $20 to win $100, he is getting 5-to-1 on a bluff. Therefore, you make the odds 5-to-1 against your folding. That is, you must call five times and fold once. You can use key cards to randomize again — for example, if you catch certain unseen cards, you fold. Otherwise, you call.

In contrast to using game theory to bluff, using game theory to decide whether to call doesn't turn an unprofitable situation into a profitable one. All it does is prevent your opponent from outwitting you — just as using a coin in the odds-evens game prevents your opponent from outwitting you there. If your opponent is using optimum game theory strategy to bluff, there is still nothing you can do to get the best of him.

Summary

Game theory cannot replace sound judgment. It should only be used when you think your opponent's judgment is as good as or better than yours or when you simply don't know your opponent. Furthermore, game theory can be used accurately to bluff or call a possible bluff only in a situation where the bettor obviously either has the best hand or is bluffing — for example, a player in seven-card stud betting into your pair of aces with an obvious flush draw. However, if the bettor may be betting a legitimate hand that is not the best hand, then the concepts in Chapter Twenty-one, "Heads-Up On The End," would apply.

When using game theory to decide whether to bluff, you must determine the pot odds your opponent is getting if you bet and then *randomly* bluff in such a way that the odds against your bluffing are identical to or almost identical to your opponent's pot odds. If your opponent is getting 5-to-1, the odds against your bluffing should be 5-to-1. By playing this way, you give your opponent no correct decision. He does just as well — or badly — in the long run by calling or folding.

When using game theory to decide whether to call a possible bluff — assuming your hand can beat only a bluff and assuming your judgment doesn't give you a hint — you must determine the odds your opponent is getting on a bluff. Make the ratio of your calls to your folds the same as those odds. If your opponent is getting 4-to-1 odds on a bluff, you must call randomly four out of five times to make that bluffing unprofitable.

Chapter Twenty

Inducing and Stopping Bluffs

The two preceding chapters demonstrated how, with sound judgment or game theory, a player who bluffs correctly gains a tremendous edge over his opponents. In fact, given two games — one with otherwise poor players who bluff approximately correctly and another with solid players who do not bluff — you do better to play in the solid game. When I started playing draw poker for a living in Gardena, California, I intuitively suspected I was better off playing in games with the typically tight Gardena players than in the looser games with players who played too many hands. I realize now what the difference was. The tight players never bluffed, which was profitable for me, whereas in the looser games players were bluffing more or less correctly — and that hurt me.

Good bluffing strategy is such a powerful weapon that it is important to develop tactics to keep your opponents from bluffing correctly. Naturally you are not concerned about changing the habits of opponents who almost never bluff or bluff far too much. But when you find yourself up against a player whose occasional bluffing keeps you on the defensive, you want to try to lead that opponent away from correct bluffing strategy. You want to induce him to bluff more than he should or stop him from bluffing as often as he should.

Whether you try to induce a bluff or to stop a bluff depends upon your opponent. If you are playing against a relatively tight player who nevertheless seems to be winning too many hands without getting called, suggesting he may be stealing some pots, you want to stop him from bluffing. That is, you want to push him away from optimum bluffing strategy to the point where he is afraid to bluff you at all. On the other hand, you want to push an aggressive player who may be bluffing slightly more than optimally into bluffing even more. In other words, against an opponent who seems to bluff a little more than is correct, induce a bluff and make that player bluff more. Against an opponent who tends to bluff less than is correct, stop him and make him bluff even less. In either case, you are stopping bluffs or inducing bluffs to make your opponents bluff incorrectly.

Most professional players are aware of the power of correct bluffing strategy, so they often try to induce bluffs or stop bluffs. However, they sometimes forget an important principle: If you are trying to induce a player to bluff and that player bets, then you must call. This principle is obvious, yet many go against it. If you try to induce a bluff and still fold when your opponent bets, all you may have succeeded in doing is helping that player bluff you out of even more pots than he otherwise would have.

Similarly, if you do something to stop a bluff and then call when your opponent bets, you would do better and catch more bluffs if you didn't try to stop his bluffing in the first place. In other words, if you think your hand is worth a call after having tried to stop a bluff, it is crazy to have tried to stop the bluff. You simply reduce the possible hands your opponent might have bet with and therefore the number of hands he might have that you can beat when you call.

These two principles regarding inducing and stopping bluffs should be self-evident. When you try to induce a bluff, you will always call if your opponent bets. When you try to stop a bluff, you will always fold if your opponent bets. To do otherwise is completely counterproductive, and it would be better not to try to induce or stop a bluff in the first place.

Artificial Techniques

There are two basic kinds of techniques to induce and stop bluffs — strategic techniques and artificial techniques. Artificial techniques are easier to understand. They can be used only against average to slightly-above-average players, for they rarely work against tough opponents, who are likely to see through them fast.

An obvious ploy to stop a bluff is to reach for your chips as though you're anxious to call. If your opponent still comes out betting, fully expecting you to call, you throw away your hand. Of course, you have to use this play against the right player. An experienced player who sees you reaching for chips and suspects what you are up to is all the more likely to come out bluffing, fully expecting you to fold.

A ploy to induce a bluff is to give the impression you intend to fold your hand. Now if your opponent bets, you call. But once again an experienced player who sees through the ploy might not bet without a good hand; realizing a bluff won't work, that player saves money when he or she has nothing.

There are several other artificial ploys — feigning disinterest in the hand to induce a bluff, feigning tremendous interest to stop a bluff — but they will not succeed often against top players. Against such players you must use strategic tactics.

Strategic Techniques

Stopping Bluffs

Essentially the strategy to stop bluffs is to represent more strength than you actually have. Your opponent will not try to bluff, thinking you have at least a calling hand and perhaps better.

Let's say you are playing draw poker, jacks or better to open, against someone you want to stop from bluffing. As the dealer in last position, you open with a pair of aces. After having originally checked in a very deep position, the potential bluffer now calls you. There is no chance that player has something like two pair, since in that case he would have opened himself. Instead he must be on the come. Drawing first, he takes one card, which either makes his hand or doesn't. Now you stand pat! Even when you check after the draw, your opponent will almost never bet unless he actually made his hand. He certainly will not try a bluff in the hope that you will throw away a pat hand. He probably won't even bet a small straight. If he does bet, he's made his hand, and you fold, knowing you have not cost yourself any money — that is, knowing your opponent did not steal the pot from you.

To stop a bluff in this spot, some players would draw one card, representing two pair, and many players would draw two, representing three-of-a-kind. But in either case, their opponent may still bluff, and he will probably be bluffing approximately correctly. By standing pat, you are stopping the bluff almost completely at almost no cost to yourself. Since you have two aces, there is no chance your opponent can catch a bigger pair than yours, and the odds are approximately 500-to-1 that you would make a full house by drawing three cards at the same time that your opponent makes a straight or flush.

By stopping a bluff in this fashion, you have reduced your opponent's chances of winning money from you to a minimum. Let's assume the opponent who draws one card makes the hand 20 percent of the time. When that opponent never bluffs — and by standing pat you have pretty well forced him not to bluff — you win the pot 80 percent of the time. Given the pot's size, your opponent's proper bluffing frequency, according to game theory, is about 7 percent. However, as long as your opponent bluffs anywhere from 1 percent to 20 percent of the time, he does better than if he doesn't bluff at all. If, for instance, he bluffs only 2 percent of the time, you still shouldn't call when he bets, and now he wins 22 percent of the pots rather than 20 percent. If he bluffs 10 percent of the time, he is still a 2-to-1 favorite to have his hand made when he bets. Since the pot is giving you better than 3-to-1 odds with the antes, you are forced to call, but you will lose that last bet two times out of three. So you clearly fare better when this opponent never bluffs (or, of course, bluffs way too much) than when he bluffs anywhere near correctly.

Suppose you are up against an opponent who usually bluffs correctly in hold 'em, and the following hand develops:

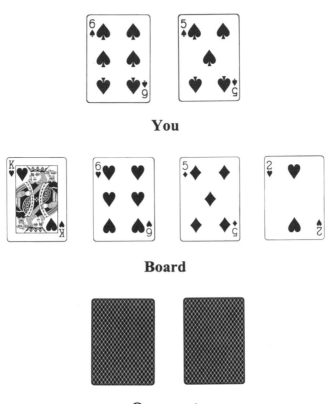

You

Board

Opponent

Your opponent is first to act and he bets. You are worried about a flush or a straight, as well as other hands, but you are also worried about a possible bluff. Therefore, after he bets, you should raise with your two small pair. If he calls with, say, a pair of kings or a four-flush, he will certainly not try to bluff you out on the end. On the other hand, if he reraises or calls and then bets on the end, you should usually throw your hand away. You know you are beat since your opponent would be afraid to bluff you after you have suggested so much strength.

Inducing Bluffs

When you are up against a player who bluffs too much, rather than stop his bluffs, you should usually induce one. Let's take an example similar to the draw poker example earlier. Once again as the dealer you open with two aces or even two queens, and an aggressive player who originally checked now calls. This player takes one card, and you're sure he's on the come. Since you want this player to bluff, you should go out of your way to take three cards, making it clear you're starting off with only one pair. Now if he bets, you call. Even if you've succeeded in increasing the player's tendency to bluff only slightly, you have gained by inducing a bluff. You have given yourself more winning chances when you call that last bet than you would have otherwise had.

Just as you try to stop a bluff by representing strength, you try to induce a bluff by representing weakness. Let's say you have a high pair in the hole in hold 'em, and on fourth street the board is something like:

You should check behind an opponent who checks if you want to induce him to bluff on the end. The only dangerous thing about this play is that you are giving your opponent a free card. If he has an ace, any ace on the end gives him the best hand. However, if he has a small pair, the odds are a long 21-to-1 that he will improve to three-of-a-kind. Of course, if your opponent is slowplaying three 9s, you are already beat, and you save a bet. The question you must ask yourself is whether you want to bet on fourth street to avoid giving a free card or whether it's worth trying to induce a bluff on the end.

Sometimes inducing a bluff is nearly the same as slowplaying. Take this hand from seven-card razz:

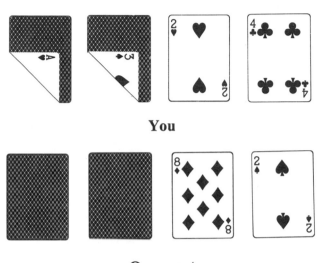

You

Opponent

You have the best possible first four cards. Yet you should frequently check and call if your opponent bets. Besides disguising your hand, you are inducing a bluff on a future betting round.

When you are inducing opponents to bluff, it isn't necessary to lure them so far away from correct bluffing strategy that they are favorites to be bluffing when they bet. All you want to do is lead them to bluff significantly more than the correct frequency. Clearly you should never stop bluffs by people who bluff way too much. However, it may be correct to induce bluffs from people who rarely bluff if you can induce them to bluff more often than their chances of making the hand.

Summary

Players who bluff with approximately the correct frequency are dangerous opponents because they often force you into the position of making an incorrect play. Therefore, it is important to try to stop or induce bluffs to lead opponents away from correct bluffing strategy.

You should normally induce a bluff against players who already bluff too much and stop bluffs against players who already bluff too little.

In the first case, you are in a situation where you would have to call if your opponent bets. By inducing a bluff, you increase your chances of winning that last bet since your opponent will bet more hands — including his bluffs — that you can beat than he otherwise would.

In the second case, against someone who bluffs too little, you feel you would have to fold if that opponent bets, even though there is some chance he might be bluffing. By stopping his bluffs, you reduce the opponent's chances of winning since he will bet only when he has made his hand, and you can comfortably fold.

Besides artificial means, you try to induce a bluff by showing weakness on an earlier round; you stop a bluff by showing strength on an earlier round. Thus, inducing a bluff is something akin to slowplaying, and stopping a bluff is something akin to semi-bluffing.

When you induce a bluff, you plan to call if your opponent bets since you have increased the chances he is bluffing. When you stop a bluff, you plan to fold if your opponent bets since you have reduced or even completely eliminated the chances he is bluffing.

Chapter Twenty-one

Heads-Up On The End

Most of the concepts we have discussed up to now apply to situations in which there are more cards to come and in which there may be more than two players in the pot. However, if the war that is a poker hand continues from the struggle for the antes to the final showdown, it eventually reaches a last round of betting, most often between two players. And in this last round, after all the cards are out, you must sometimes apply concepts totally different from those that were operative in earlier betting rounds. In this chapter we will discuss these concepts. They apply to any one-winner limit game (thus excluding high-low split) when two players are heads-up on the end.

Bluffing On The End

There are two basic conditions that determine how you act when you are heads-up on the end — whether or not you have made a legitimate hand and whether you are in first position or last position. Without a legitimate hand against an opponent with a legitimate hand, you cannot win except on a bluff — a bet or a raise that causes your opponent to fold. You cannot hope to win by checking or by calling. Determining whether or not to try a bluff on the end is based on the same logic as any other bet. You have to decide whether the attempt has positive expectation. If the pot is $100 and you bet $20 with nothing, you have to believe your opponent will fold more than once in six times in order to expect a profit. Thus, if your opponent folds once in five times, you will lose $20 four times, but you will win $100 once on average for a net profit of $20 or an average profit of $4 per hand. However, if your opponent folds once in seven times, you will lose $20 six times and win $100 once for a net loss of $20 or an average loss of $2.86 per hand. Whether a bluff works often enough to be profitable depends, like most plays on the end, upon an accurate assessment of what your opponent is likely to do.

While it's tough to get away with a bluff on the end, it's much tougher to get away with a bluff raise. Your opponent needs to fold more often for a bluff raise to show a profit because you are putting in a double bet. Suppose, as in the last case, there is $100 in the pot, and your opponent bets $20. You now call his $20 and raise another $20 on a bluff. With your opponent's $20 bet, the pot has increased to $120, but you are making a $40 investment in the hope your opponent will fold. Since you are now getting only 3-to-1 for your money, your opponent must no longer fold more than once in six times but more than once in four times for you to show a profit. Yet when calling your bluff raise, your opponent is getting 8-to-1 for his money. The $100 already in the pot, plus your opponent's original $20 bet, plus your $40 call and raise adds up to a total of $160 in exchange for the opponent's $20. So as we noted in the chapter on raising, it takes a very tough opponent, capable of super-tough folds, to throw away a legitimate hand in this situation. Average players will almost always call. The only time a bluff raise might work against them is when you suspect correctly that they have nothing themselves. Most of the time, though, when your opponent bets and you have nothing, your best play is to fold.

Let us now consider betting strategy heads-up on the end when you have a legitimate hand. You are going to be either first or last to act, and as we have noted, strategy changes according to your position. We'll begin by looking at strategy in last position, which is not quite so tricky as in first position.

Last Position Play

Last Position Play After Your Opponent Has Checked

When you are in last position, your opponent will have either checked or bet. First, what should you do when your opponent checks? Some might reply that you should bet if you think you have the best hand. But this is not at all the case. Your chances of having the best hand might be as high as 90 percent or better, but still you should not necessarily bet. Take the following hand from seven-card stud:[9]

You

Opponent

With four jacks your chances of having the best hand are enormous, but in either first or second position you cannot

---

[9] Though you are not in last position in this example, I use it because it illustrates the principle so succinctly.

possibly bet the hand on the end for the simple reason that your bet has absolutely no positive expectation. Since your four jacks are exposed for the world to see, your opponent will fold every hand he can have except four queens or a straight flush in hearts. With either of those hands, he will raise. So your bet has nothing to gain and everything to lose.

This very obvious situation points toward the key distinction between play in the final round of betting and in earlier rounds. With one card to come, you would most certainly bet the four jacks to avoid giving your opponent a free card to outdraw you. Your bet forces him either to fold and thus give up any chance to outdraw you or to call and pay for that slim chance. However, when all the cards are out, betting to avoid giving a free card no longer applies. So if you now still decide to bet your hand, you no longer ask what your chances are of having the best hand but rather what the chances are of winning the last bet *when you are called.*

This distinction may seem like hair-splitting, but it is most assuredly not. In fact, it is crucial to successful play — that is, to winning or saving extra bets — when you are heads-up on the end. To take a very common situation, let's say you have three-of-a-kind in seven-card stud, and you know your opponent is drawing to a flush and has nothing else. The odds against that opponent's making the flush on the last card are, we'll assume, 4-to-1, which means you are an 80 percent favorite to have the best hand. However, if your opponent checks, you certainly should not bet because, as in the case of the four open jacks, a bet has no positive expectation. Your opponent will fold if he didn't make the flush, and he will call or possibly raise if he did. So even though you are an 80 percent favorite to have the best hand, you become an underdog if you bet and get called. To repeat, then, the decision to bet a legitimate hand for value on the end should be based not on your chances of having the best hand but on your chances of winning the last bet when you are called.

When you bet for value on the end after your opponent has checked, you must figure your hand has better than a 50-50 chance of winning when you are called. In fact, you have to figure it has at least about a 55 percent chance of winning to compensate for those times when your opponent is planning to check-raise. With three-of-a-kind against a flush draw, you are certainly the favorite, but you are not the favorite if your opponent calls. Yet to show a profit on your last round bets, clearly you must be the favorite even when your opponent calls.

At the same time, you should not carry this principle to such an extreme that you bet only when you have a lock, because then you will not win a lot of final bets you should win. To bet on the end after your opponent has checked, it is only necessary that you are the favorite when your opponent calls. Thus, if you figure you are only a 60 percent favorite when called, you should certainly bet even though you know there's a 40 percent chance your opponent will beat you if he calls. Your bet still has positive expectation. After ten such bets you will have won six and lost four on average for a net profit of two bets. Even if one of those four losses is a check-raise which you call, you still win six bets while losing five for a one-bet profit.

To give a concrete example of such relatively close decisions, let's say you are playing draw poker, and your opponent stands pat and then checks to you when you draw one. Since your opponent stood pat, you are quite sure you are facing a straight, a flush, or a full house. Yet your opponent checked to you. You know he will call with just about any of his hands. Therefore, you should bet an ace-high straight or even a queen-high straight, because your opponent probably would have come out betting himself with a tiny flush or better. Chances are, then, he has a straight smaller than yours. It's true you may lose in the showdown, but you are enough of a favorite with a queen-high straight to warrant a bet.

Last Position Play After Your Opponent Has Bet

Let us now consider your options in last position when your opponent does not give you a free call but comes out betting. When he bets, you can either fold, call, or raise.

Deciding whether to fold or call is relatively straightforward. The question is: Are your chances of winning the pot better than the odds you are getting from the pot, either because your hand is better than your opponent's or because your opponent is bluffing? If you think your chances are better, you call. If not, you fold.

If you are thinking of raising after your opponent bets, you must ask the same question you would have asked before betting had your opponent checked: What are the chances of winning that extra bet when you are called? You should not raise unless you figure you are at least a 55 percent favorite, since you also face the possibility of a reraise. In fact, one way of looking at raising an opponent on the end without the nuts is that you are laying almost 2-to-1 odds on that last bet, especially if your opponent is capable of bluffing on a reraise. When you raise and your opponent raises back, you usually lose two bets, but if he calls, you only gain one bet. Of course, this consideration does not apply against a player who will never bluff on a reraise. If such a player raises you back, you can just throw your hand away, knowing you are beat.

Before raising on the end, you must also consider the overall ability of your opponent. Once he puts in an initial bet, an average player will call your raise almost every time. Therefore, you certainly should not try a bluff raise. However, you should raise with any hand you consider a reasonable favorite to win the last bet because you can be pretty sure of getting paid off. Tough players, on the other hand, will frequently come out betting, but they are capable of folding and not paying you off if you raise. Therefore, a bluff raise has some chance against them. However, when you are raising for value against tough players, you should have a better hand than you need against average players, because when the former are willing to call your raise and thus pay you off, they are likely to show down a strong hand. On close decisions you should not raise tough players on the end as often as you would weak or average players because you don't win that extra bet often enough to make the play profitable. Tough players either throw away a hand you would beat or call with a hand you might not be able to beat.

Ironically, though, a raise may sometimes be correct against a world-class player when you have a hand that is only fairly good. The key factor is whether a raise will make your opponent throw away some hands that are better than yours. Let's say you have a hand that you figure has a 52 percent chance of winning if you call, but little chance of winning if you raise and get called. Nevertheless, it would be correct to raise if you think your opponent will then throw away some hands that beat you. If your analysis is correct, a raise might lift you from a 52 percent favorite to a 65-70 percent favorite, and if the pot is big enough, that added 13-18 percent gives the raise positive expectation. Remember, though, that this play is worth considering only against superstars. Against average and good players — and also against superstars most of the time — the basic formula for raising on the end remains the same: Raise only if you are favored to win that extra bet when your opponent calls.

To summarize play in last position after your opponent has bet, you have three options — fold, call, or raise. You should generally fold when the chances of winning are less than the pot odds you are getting. Thus, if your hand has only a 15 percent chance of winning and the pot is $80, you cannot call a $20 bet. However, your chances of winning do not have to be over 50 percent to justify a call. All that's necessary is that the pot odds you're getting are better than your chances of winning in the showdown. Thus, if you think you have a 30 percent chance and the pot is $80, you would be right to call a $20 bet because the pot odds you're getting are greater than the odds against your showing down the best hand. Even when you decide you can or cannot call with your underdog hand, you have not necessarily eliminated the option of raising. Against a very, very good player, you might consider raising with some mediocre hands if a raise has greater expectation than a fold or a call — that is, if it will make your opponent throw away enough hands that would be better than yours. Anytime you are last and your opponent bets, you always have the three alternatives of folding, calling, or raising. The one that becomes right is the one that gives you the highest mathematical expectation.

First Position Play

When you are first to act with a legitimate hand, you have four options. One is to check with the intention of raising if your opponent bets. Another is to come out betting. The third is to check with the intention of calling if your opponent bets. And the fourth is to check and fold if your opponent bets.

Check-Raising in First Position

With very strong hands your options are to try a check-raise or to come out betting. The key factors in deciding whether to check-raise are:
1.   The chances your opponent will bet if you check.
2.   The chances your opponent will call your raise.

The second factor is just as important as the first, because if there were no chance your opponent would call your raise, it would usually be wrong to check since you'd risk not winning even a single bet when your opponent checks behind you. However, all but very tough players will generally call your raise after you have checked and they have put in an initial bet. They might grumble as they do it, but they'll do it.

In limit games the decision to check-raise or come out betting can be determined by a precise formula. To simplify, we'll assume you know for sure you have the best hand. First, determine what percentage of times your opponent will call if you bet. That's one side of the equation. Next determine what percentage of times your opponent will bet if you check but then fold when you raise. Finally, determine what percentage of times your opponent will bet if you check and then call your raise. Now double this last percentage. If the sum of the last two percentages is greater than the first, it is correct to try a check-raise.

This formula may sound overly complicated, but it really is not. Let's say you think there is a 70 percent chance your opponent will call if you bet. But you also think there is a 40 percent chance he will bet if you check and call your raise, thus rewarding you with a double bet; and perhaps there's another 10 percent chance he'll bet if you check but fold when you raise. Because you'll win two bets 40 percent of the times that you check, you double that figure to 80 and add the remaining 10 percent chance your opponent will bet and fold when you raise. That adds up to 90, and since 90 is greater than the 70 percent chance that your opponent will call your bet, it is right to check-raise.

Another way of looking at the problem is in terms of expectation. Let's say you bet 100 times, and you check with the intention of raising 100 times. In the former case, you'll win 70 bets; in the latter you'll win 80 bets when your opponent bets and calls your raise and 10 more when he bets and folds, for a total of 90 bets. You win 20 bets more by check-raising, and so check-raising has greater expectation than betting out.

Most players do not check-raise enough on the end. They'd rather go for the single bet in the hopes of getting called. However, it is worth taking a little chance of losing one bet if there is a good chance of gaining two bets. Since most players will automatically call a raise when you check-raise, you can simplify the above formula. In general, you should check with the intention of raising if you believe the chances of your opponent's betting when you check are at least half as good as the chances of his calling when you bet. Nor should you get discouraged if you occasionally check and your opponent checks behind you. Check-raising is a long-run gamble like everything else in poker. If you know you should win two bets in a particular situation more than half as often as you would win one bet, then you made the right play by checking even if it didn't happen to work. Sometimes you also gain an added benefit when a check-raise doesn't work. Since your opponents noticed you checked a good hand once, they may become a little timid about betting behind you on future hands, thus saving you some bets on second-best hands with which you were planning to call if they bet.

Check-raising on the end works best against average-to-good players. You should try it less often against weak players and tough players. Weak players tend to call so much on the end when you bet that you have to be pretty certain they will bet for a check-raise to be profitable. If, for example, you are sure your opponent will call if you come out betting, you have to be over 50 percent sure he will bet if you chèck before you consider check-raising. Even 50 percent isn't good enough unless you are also sure your opponent will call when you raise (which, of course, a weak player will most likely do).

Against tough players you would check-raise less often because tough players tend not to bet as many hands on the end as they call you with, and they frequently throw away their hands when you raise. Thus, the chances of winning a double bet with a check-raise decrease.

There is one major time to deviate from the general check-raise formula, and that is when you think you can win three bets by betting, getting raised, and then reraising. A classic example of such a situation against an average player in seven-card stud occurs when you look like a straight on board but have a hidden full house, and your opponent may have a flush. You bet your apparent straight, your opponent raises with his flush, and you lift him out of his seat by reraising.

Playing Fair-to-Good Hands in First Position as a Favorite

In first position, with fair-to-good hands that are not strong enough to try a check-raise, you have three options — to bet, to check and call when your opponent bets, and to check and fold when your opponent bets. Which play you try in any given situation depends not so much upon the strength of your hand but upon your mathematical expectation for each play. And your expectation depends upon your ability to assess your opponent's style of play and what he is likely to do in a given situation. Some players bet with more hands than they call with; others call with more hands than they bet with; and still other, very tight players bet only when they are sure they have you beat. Thus, how you act in first position depends upon your knowledge of your opponent.

Here are the general rules for each play.

If your hand is worth a call or almost worth a call had you checked and your opponent bet, you should *bet* when your opponent is one who will call with more hands than he will bet, a habit which is typical of the majority of players.[10]

If your hand is worth a call, you should check and call when your opponent is one who will bet with more hands than he will call. As we shall see, this player is usually the type who may try to bluff after you have checked in first position.

You should *check and fold* when you are not the favorite if called and when your opponent is one who will almost always bet only with a hand that beats yours. This player may call with a few hands worse than yours. However, since this type will only bet with a hand that clearly beats you, the bets you save by folding after he bets are greater than the few bets you might pick up by betting and getting called by his worse hands.

The key factor in deciding whether to check-raise, bet, check and call, or check and fold in first position is, as we have seen,

---

[10] See pages 213-214 for an exception to the rule.

which of the plays has the greatest positive expectation or the least negative expectation.

Let's say that on a scale of 0 to 100 you have hand 80, a good hand but not a great hand. Your opponent could have anything from 0 to 100, with each hand equally likely. That would seem to make you a 4-to-1 favorite if you bet, but that's not at all the case. The question is, which hands will your opponent call with? If he will call only with hands 75 and upward, you are clearly an underdog if you bet — specifically a 4-to-1 underdog since you will lose to 20 of your opponent's hands and beat only five.

We'll assume you know your opponent will call with hands 57 and upward. (We are, of course, being very hypothetical here since no player could know his opponent so precisely.) If your opponent will call with hands 57 and upward, that means that if you bet, you will win 23 times — when your opponent has hands 57-79 — and lose 20 times — when he has hands 81-100. Thus you are a 23-to-20 favorite when you bet.

However, that does not mean the correct play is to bet. You still do not have enough information. You must also know what hands your opponent will bet if you check. Suppose your opponent will bet hands 62 and up if you check (which means you blow a bet if he has hands 57-61), but he will also bet with hands 0-10. That is, there are eleven hands your opponent will bluff with. Once again there are 20 hands you will lose to (hands 81-100), but now, instead of 23, there are 29 hands you will beat — hands 0-10 and hands 62-79. Thus, if you check and call when your opponent bets, you are a 29-to-20 favorite to show down the best hand. Clearly it is better to play the last round of betting as a 29-to-20 favorite than as a 23-to-20 favorite, and so the correct play here is to check and call. This is the point of the rule: Check and call when your opponent will bet with more hands than he will call. By checking against such an opponent, you increase your chances of winning one last bet.

Suppose you are still a small favorite if you bet. Once again you have hand 80, and your new opponent will call with hands 57 and up. But this opponent is much more timid than the other, and you know he will bet only with hands 81 and upward. How should you play? It might at first seem correct to check and fold if your opponent bets, since any time he bets behind you he has you beat. However, when you check, you give up an even-money bet as a 23-to-20 favorite, which cannot be correct. That's more than the vigorish that keeps bookmakers in business. After making that bet 43 times, you will be ahead 3 units on average. Under no circumstances, then, can it be correct to check and fold if you are favored to win when your opponent calls you. As a 23-to-20 favorite, the correct play here is to bet. The only time it might be correct to check is when you're not sure whether you're the favorite and when you're also worried about a raise that you will have to call.

Playing Fair-to-Good Hands in First Position as an Underdog

In cases where you think you're the underdog if called, the decision to bet or check becomes even more ticklish. Let's say there's $60 in the pot in a $10-$20 game, and again you have hand 80. But this time you know your opponent will call only with hands 65 and up. Thus, you are a 20-to-15 underdog if your opponent calls. You also know that if you check, your opponent will bet with hands 70 and up. How should you play?

As an underdog, you might think you should check. But what will you do if your opponent bets after you check? Since there's $60 in the pot plus your opponent's $20, you're getting $80-to-$20 or 4-to-1 odds from the pot, and we said your opponent will bet with hands 70-100. You have hand 80, and so you'll lose to 20 hands and beat 10 hands. Since you are getting 4-to-1 from the pot and are only a 2-to-1 underdog, clearly you must call when your opponent bets.

Look again at what happens when you bet. Your opponent will call with hands 65-100. By betting you've added five wins — when your opponent has hands 65-69 — to your possibilities.

Instead of going in as a 20-to-10 underdog, which you would be doing if you checked, you're going in as a 20-to-15 underdog since you'll still lose to 20 hands, but now you will beat 15 hands instead of 10. So the correct play is to bet because betting here makes you less of an underdog than checking. Your hand is worth a call, and your opponent will call with more hands than he'll bet. (This play is something like splitting 8s in blackjack against the dealer's 10. You are still an underdog, but you are less of an underdog than if you had simply hit.)

Suppose with $60 in the pot you again have hand 80, and your opponent will again call with hands 65 and up. But this opponent will bet only with hands 82 and up. How should you play?

In the previous case you really didn't like your situation. You bet as a 20-to-15 underdog only because you would have had to call as a 20-to-10 underdog. But in the present case, in which you are still a 20-to-15 underdog if you bet, you don't have to worry about calling. Any time your opponent bets, you know he has you beat since he will only bet with hands 82 and up. You certainly don't want to bet as an underdog when you don't have to, so the correct play in this instance is to check and fold if your opponent bets. You blow a bet 15 times, when your opponent has hands 65-79 and checks behind you, but you save a bet 20 times, when he has hands 81-100. You save more bets than you sacrifice. Checking and folding has greater expectation than betting as a 20-to-15 underdog.

A curious situation develops, though, when you are an underdog when called and your opponent will bet if you check with only a few hands you can beat. It would seem that the correct play is to check and fold if your opponent bets. However, it often works out that the play with the greatest expectation is to bet your own underdog hands even though, if you checked, you could not call when your opponent bet. Depending upon the size of the pot, this situation occurs when your opponent will call with many hands you can beat but will bet with only a few hands you can beat.

Let's say there's $60 in the pot, and you have hand 80. You know your opponent will call with hands 65 and up (remember, we are being completely hypothetical here for the purposes of illustration), but he will bet only with hands 76 and up. Thus, if you check with hand 80 and your opponent bets, you will be a 20-to-4 or a 5-to-1 underdog. Since you're only getting $80-to-$20 or 4-to-1 odds from the pot, you cannot call. However, when you yourself bet, you add 11 wins to your possibilities — when your opponent has hands 65-75 — thus creating a situation where you are getting favorable odds from the pot.

Here's how this situation works out mathematically. Remember that we know your opponent will call with hands 65 and up but he will bet only with hands 76 and up. All the hands are equally likely. Thus if you check and fold when he bets then in 100 times you will win $60 76 times when he has hands 0-75) for a total of $4,560. However if you bet you will win $60 65 times and $80 15 times while losing $20 20 times. This works out to $4,700 which is $140 more than you would have won by checking and folding if your opponent bet. Consequently, even though as an underdog you would not call if your opponent bet on the end, it may sometimes be right for you to bet, depending upon the size of the pot and the number of second-best hands you think your opponent will call with.

Finally, there are some unusual situations, when the pot is fairly large and your opponent is somewhat timid, where it may be correct to *check and call* even though your opponent would call you with more hands than he would bet himself. This is the exception we referred to earlier to the general rule that you should *bet* when your opponent will call with more hands than he would bet.

Suppose you have hand 80. You're playing in a $10-$20 game, and there's $200 in the pot. You know your opponent will call only with hands 75 and up; so you're a 4-to-1 underdog if you bet. But you'd be getting at least 10-to-1 from the pot, so a bet could be right. However, you also know your opponent is afraid to bet for value on many hands that beat you — say, hands 81-90.

This opponent will bet hands 91-100 and he may occasionally bluff — say, with hands 1-4. Even though this opponent will bet with fewer hands than he would call with, and even though the pot odds you're getting make your hand worth a call, it nevertheless becomes correct to check in this instance. The reason is that ten times — in the cases where your opponent has hands 81-90 — you save $20 when he checks the best hand behind you. Furthermore, when your opponent does bet and you call, you're only a 10-to-4 or 2½-to-1 underdog instead of the 20-to-5 or 4-to-1 underdog you would be if you came out betting. You've also eliminated the possibility of getting raised in a situation where, given the size of the pot, you would almost have to call.

It becomes correct to check and call, though you know your opponent would call with more hands than he would bet, if when you are an underdog you think your opponent will check some better hands behind you and if you fear a raise.

Remember, though, that the last two situations we have described are unusual. The general rules still apply the majority of the time. If your hand is worth a call, you should bet when your opponent will call with more hands than he will bet, and you should check and call when your opponent will bet with more hands than he will check. In other words, you should make the play that gives you the greatest number of wins and the smallest number of losses.

First Position Play in Practice

Let us now see how first-position play heads-up on the end works in practice.

Suppose in draw poker you draw three cards in first position and make aces up. Your opponent draws one card. He may have two pair, or he may be drawing to a straight or a flush. You feel that this type of player will call with two pair if you bet but will bet them for value if you check. How should you play?

There's no mystery here. Clearly you should check and call. By checking and calling, you may save a bet in one situation and gain a bet in another. With two pair, your opponent will call if you bet and bet if you check. So you win either way. If your opponent was drawing to a flush or a straight and makes it, he will of course bet if you check, but he will call, or probably raise, if you bet — which will cost you an extra bet if you call the raise. With a busted hand, your opponent will not call if you bet, so you gain nothing by betting. However, your opponent might bet on a bluff if you check. In this single instance you win an extra bet by checking and calling. So checking and calling has greater expectation than betting. And to repeat: The object of poker is not to win pots but to win money; it is with these extra bets won or saved that you win money.

Here is another draw poker situation. You draw one card to two small pair, and your opponent draws three. You don't improve. You know your opponent suspects you were drawing to a flush or a straight, and you also know this player's a *pay station,* the type who will call "to keep you honest." How should you play?

You should bet. Assuming your opponent was drawing three to a big pair, you're about a 71 percent favorite to have the best hand. Any time you're even a small favorite against someone you know is going to call virtually every time, you should bet. In this case you're wagering even money as a 71 percent or 5-to-2 favorite. Clearly that's a wager with positive expectation even though you expect to lose 29 percent of the time.

Suppose in hold 'em you have

and the board at the end is

(Notice that there is no flush possibility.) You are first to act. How should you play?

You should probably come out betting. If you are up against something like A,10 or K,10 or J,10, you lose either way. If you check, your opponent will surely bet, and you will call. If your opponent has Q,10, you may lose a double bet by betting out since your opponent will raise. On the other hand, if your opponent has hands like 10,8 or 10,7 or 10,6, you win either way; if you check, your opponent will most likely bet. However, two very possible hands your opponent might have are A,Q and K,Q which he may very well not bet if you check but with which he will probably call if you bet. Since you are likely to gain a bet more frequently than you lose one (when your opponent raises), betting has greater expectation than checking and calling. Put in terms of the rules given earlier, in this situation your opponent will call with more hands than he will bet.

A final set of examples from draw lowball should demonstrate how your play on the end in first position varies directly in terms of your opponent. Both players in the pot draw one card, and you are first to act:

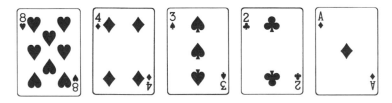

You

You are up against a player who doesn't bluff but is always afraid everyone else does. How should you act?

You should bet. Your opponent will probably call with a queen-low or better, while only a seven-low or better will beat you. Therefore your opponent will call with many hands that you will beat and a relative few that will beat you. On the other hand, if you checked, your opponent would not bet most of those losing hands. Thus, you stand to win more often by betting than by checking.

Suppose you have the same hand in draw lowball against an aggressive, tough player, and you're first. How should you play?

In this case, you should check and call because your opponent is likely to bet more hands than he calls with. Besides beating your opponent's rough 8s, you also snap off his bluffs, which you could not do if you came out betting. Ordinarily, if you bet, your opponent would give up the idea of bluffing. In general, a player who bets with more hands than he calls with is the type of player who not only bets for value but also bluffs perhaps more often than is correct. Thus, when you check, your opponent's bluffing hands are added to those he bets for value.

Now suppose instead of a perfect eight-low, you have the following hand:

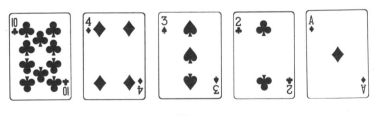

You

Once again you're up against that player who never bluffs but worries that everyone else does. You're first. How should you play?

Here you should check and fold if your opponent bets. Since your hand beats only queen-, jack-, and ten-lows (the losing hands with which your opponent would call), it is no longer worth a bet for value, because you get beat with his nine-lows and better. And since this opponent never bets on a bluff, you should fold in the face of a bet. The odds that you are beat are overwhelming.

Against the aggressive player, you would also check, but you would call a bet since there are many hands this opponent might be betting that you can beat. In other words, a call against this type of player would have positive expectation.

First Position Play in Terms of the Strength of Your Hand

We'll wrap up play in first position by summarizing it according to the strength of your hand.

If your hand is a cinch or a near cinch, you have two options. One is to bet, and one is to check-raise. You would decide which to do according to the check-raise formula presented earlier. However, if you are sure you have the best hand but suspect your opponent will raise if you bet, you should bet out in an attempt to win three bets when your opponent raises and you reraise.

If your hand figures to be a favorite when called but is not good enough to check-raise, you have two options — to bet or to check and then call. Basically you bet if your opponent will call with more hands than he'll bet with and you check and call if he'll bet with more hands than he'll call with.

If your hand is an underdog when called, you have three options. One is to bet, a second is to check and call, and the third is to check and fold. (A bluff check-raise is a remote possibility against very tough players who are capable of very tough folds.) You should check and call if your opponent will bet more hands than he will call with, including some hands you can beat. You should also check and call when your opponent will check many hands that will beat you but might come out bluffing with some hands you can beat. And you should come out betting if you have a calling hand but your opponent will call with more hands than he will bet.

Finally, if you have virtually no chance of winning if you check and your opponent bets and you are an underdog if you bet and he calls, then the proper play is to check and fold if he bets.

Summary

The concepts in this long chapter are important and slippery enough to warrant a final framing in an outline summary. The essence of each play is a judgment of its expectation.

I. *Last Position Play*
A. If you are second to act when all the cards are out and your opponent bets:
    1. Call if your hand is not worth a raise but has a better chance of winning than the pot odds you are getting. Your chances of winning are the sum of the chances that your opponent is bluffing, plus the chances that your hand can beat his legitimate hand.
    2. Raise if your opponent will still be the underdog after calling your raise. Raise also as a bluff if you think it will work often enough to have positive expectation. Also consider raising with what appears to be a calling hand if your opponent is capable of throwing away a better hand than yours for one more bet.
B. If you are second to act when all the cards are out and your opponent checks:
    1. Bluff if you think it will work often enough, remembering that a bluff does not tend to work as often in second position as it might in first position.
    2. Bet your hand for value if you are a favorite to have the best hand, even when your opponent calls your bet. Don't bet in close situations to avoid a check-raise.

II. *First Position Play*
A. If you are first to act when all the cards are out and have a very strong hand:
    1. Try to check-raise if your opponent will bet and call your raise more than half as often as he will call you when you bet.
    2. Come out betting if you don't think a check-raise will work often enough to be profitable or if you think you can win three bets when your opponent raises and you reraise.
B. If you are first to act and have a bad hand:
    1. Bluff if you can get away with it often enough for the play to have positive expectation.
    2. Otherwise check and fold if your opponent bets.
C. If you are first to act and have a hand that is a favorite to win if called but not strong enough for you to try a check-raise:
    1. Bet if your opponent will call with more hands than he will bet with if you check.
    2. Check and call if your opponent will bet with more hands than he will call with.
    3. Never check and fold.
D. If you are first to act and have a hand that is a small underdog to win when your bet is called:
    1. Bet if your opponent will call with more hands than he will bet, as long as some of the hands he would have bet, had you checked, would be worse than yours. Check and call if you think your opponent will check behind you with a significant number of hands better than yours but might still bluff with some hands you can beat.
    2. Check and call if your opponent will bet with more hands than he will call with, as long as your pot odds make it worth calling when he does bet.
    3. Check and fold if your opponent will almost never bet a hand worse than yours.

Chapter Twenty-two

Reading Hands

The ability to read hands may be the most important weapon a poker player can have. As the Fundamental Theorem of Poker suggests, the key mistake in poker is to play your hand differently from the way you would play it if you knew what your opponent had. The more often you play your hand correctly on the basis of what your opponent has the less you give up and the more you gain. If you somehow knew what your opponent had every time, you almost couldn't lose because you would always play correctly. It follows, then, that the better you are at reading your opponents' hands, the closer you come to perfect play, and the closer you come to perfect play, the less you lose and the more you win.

Reading hands is both an art and a science. It is an art because you must know your opponents. Before you can technically analyze what your opponents might have, you must have played with them for a considerable length of time, seen how they play their hands against you, and most importantly, watched them play hands in which you are not involved. Even when you are not in a hand, you should not relax your concentration. You want to discover how your opponents tend to play the various hands they might have. Will a particular opponent raise with strong hands in early position, or will he slowplay? Will he raise on a draw? How does he play his big hands from one round of betting to the next? How often does he bluff? The more you know about an opponent's general playing habits, the less difficulty you will have reading what he might be holding in a specific situation.

Ironically, it is not as hard to read good players as it is to read a bunch of incompetents. When a good player makes a play, there is a sensible reason for it, and your job is to find the reason and put that player on a hand. But there is no pattern to the play of a

221

weak player, and so you must do a great deal of tentative guesswork to put him on a hand. Nevertheless, by playing solidly against weak, unpredictable players, you have to win eventually. Sooner or later a sound, logical poker player must beat someone playing by the seat of his pants. The latter may get lucky for a while, catching the inside straights he draws to, winning with two small pair when you raised with aces on third street, but percentages are bound to catch up with him. Many good players get upset when a sucker draws out on them. While it's never pleasant to lose a pot you were favored to win, you should nevertheless welcome these beats. Congratulate such players on hanging in there to make their hands. Encourage them so they play even more sloppily. It shouldn't be long before you have their money.

The more you play against average-to-good players, the easier it becomes to read your opponents' hands because they tend to check, bet, and raise for logical reasons and with a certain consistency to their play. However, as your opponents get tougher and tougher, your ability to read hands starts to fall off because tough players disguise their hands and they are sometimes intentionally inconsistent. They make tricky, ambiguous plays like semi-bluffing, like raising with the second-best hand, like slowplaying right to the end and then check-raising you. They may even play a hand as it would normally be played, which can sometimes be the most deceptive play of all. In a word, they do all the sorts of things we have been discussing in this book. They are trying as hard to deceive you about what they have as you are trying to discover what they have. And of course, you are presumably playing your hands equally hard against them, even as you are trying to read their hands.

Reading Hands on the Basis of Your Opponents' Play and Exposed Cards

There are two universally applicable techniques for reading hands in all poker games and one more for open-handed games like seven-card stud, razz, and hold 'em. Most commonly you analyze the meaning of an opponent's check, bet, or raise, and in open-handed games you look at his exposed cards and try to judge from them what his entire hand might be. You then combine the plays he has made *throughout the hand* with his exposed cards and come to a determination about his most likely hand.

Here is a simple problem in reading hands that should make this point clear. The game is seven-card stud, and your opponents are decent players:

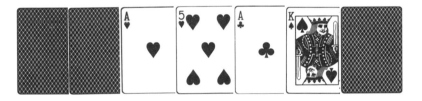

Player A

Player B

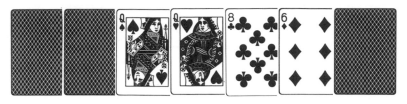

Player C

You

Player A with the pair of aces showing bets; Player B with the pair of kings showing calls; and Player C with the pair of queens showing calls. There are no raises. You are last to act. How should you play your three 7s?

If you combine what you see on board with what your opponents have done, there should be no doubt in your mind that you must fold; your three 7s have no chance whatsoever. The crucial factor is that the pair of queens overcalled. Player A may be betting with aces alone. But when Player B calls him, Player B must have at least kings up. Being a decent player, Player C knows this. Therefore, C could not call without having kings up beat. What are C's possible hands? Well, C cannot have aces and queens or kings and queens because there's a third ace and a third king out, making it impossible for C to have two of either. So, he must have three queens or better, and while your three 7s might beat the first two hands, they cannot beat C's three queens or better. Therefore, you fold.

Here is a good example of this kind of hand reading, which to my chagrin cost me half a pot. I was playing five-card stud high-low split with a replace on the end. With an ace and an 8 showing, I called the maximum raises on third street even though two other players each had a 6 and a 5 showing. There was another player in the pot with an obvious pair of kings. When it got down to the last card, I had A,8,6,3 showing. One 6,5 had folded, but despite the strength of my board, the other stayed with a ragged 6,5,10,Q showing. And of course, the pair of kings stayed. Now I was betting and raising, hoping the Q,10 low would get out. But that player read me too well. He didn't even take the opportunity to replace one of his cards.

What I was trying to do was win the whole pot, the high and the low, from the two kings, but the Q,10 low was clever enough to figure out my hand. He said to himself, "Sklansky is representing an 8 low, but could he have an 8 low? No, he couldn't. Why? Because he would never have called all those raises on third street with three cards to an 8 low when there were two other players in the pot who looked as if they had three cards to a 6 low. Therefore, he must have another ace in the hole." He was, of course, absolutely right. I won the high with my two aces, beating the two kings, but the Q,10 low was rewarded for his accurate reading with the low half of the pot (which I would have won against the two kings with my two aces counting also as a low pair). The player with the Q,10 low considered the way I played the hand not just at the end, but from the beginning, and he combined my play with the cards showing to arrive at the correct conclusion about what I was holding. He also analyzed the *order* in which I received my upcards. He knew I started with A,8 and then caught the 6 and the 3. If he had not known that — if, for example, he had not been sure whether I started with A,8 or A,6 — it would have been impossible for him to conclude with such certainty that I had a pair of aces.

It is in this way that you use logic to read hands. You interpret your opponents' plays on each round, and in open-handed games you note the cards they catch on each round, paying close attention to the order in which they catch them. You then put these two pieces of evidence together — the plays and the upcards — to draw a conclusion about an opponent's most likely hand.

In that high-low split hand, the Q,10 low was able to put me on a specific hand quite early. However, it is generally a mistake to put someone on a specific hand early and then stick to your initial conclusion no matter how things develop. A player who raises on third street in seven-card stud with a king showing may have two kings, but he may also have a small pair in the hole with the king kicker or a three-flush or a J,Q,K or a number of other hands as well. Drawing a narrow, irreversible conclusion early can lead to costly mistakes later, either because you fold with the best hand or because you stay in as a big underdog.

What you do in a game like seven-card stud or hold 'em or razz is to put an opponent on a variety of hands at the start of play, and as the hand continues, you eliminate some of those hands based on his later play and on the cards he catches. Through this process of elimination, you should have a good idea of what that opponent has (or is drawing to) when the last card is dealt.

Suppose, for instance, in seven-card stud a player starts with a queen of spades, then catches the deuce of spades, then the 7 of spades, then the 5 of hearts, and he's betting all the way. You have a pair of 10s which does not improve. Your opponent bets on the end, and clearly you can beat only a bluff. The question is — might your opponent be bluffing? With something like a four-flush and a small pair, he would probably have played the hand exactly the same way — semi-bluffing right to the end, assuming you didn't catch any dangerous-looking cards. Therefore, while your opponent may, in fact, have a pair of queens or queens up, there's also a chance he has a busted hand. Very possibly you should call his final bet, given the pot odds you're getting — but realizing at the same time that he may indeed have been semi-bluffing yet still caught his hand on the last card.

Suppose, on the other hand, your seven-stud opponent started with that same queen of spades and you with that same pair of 10s. Once again your opponent is betting all the way. But this time he catches the 7 of diamonds, then the 4 of clubs, then the jack of hearts. Now when he bets on the end, you should almost certainly fold your two unimproved 10s because when he caught the 7♦ and 4♣ but continued betting, you had to eliminate the flush draw as one of his possible hands. Therefore, he is almost certainly betting on the end for value with at least a pair of queens — more likely two pair. Ironically, it can sometimes occur that because your opponent's hand looks less dangerous on board it is more of a threat to have you beat when your opponent bets on the end, because nothing showing suggests he might have been semi-bluffing as the hand progressed.

At the end of a hand it becomes especially crucial to have a good idea of what your opponent has. The more accurately you can read hands on the end, the better you can decide whether you have, for example, a 20 percent chance of having your opponent beat or a 60 percent chance or whatever. You use your ability to read hands to come up with these percentages and then decide how to play your own hand.

In practice, most players don't arrive at exact figures like 20 percent or 60 percent, but at the very least they try to decide whether their opponent has a bad hand, a mediocre hand, a good hand, or a great hand. Let's say your opponent bets on the end. Usually when a person bets, it represents either a bluff, a good hand, or a great hand, but not a mediocre hand. If your opponent had a mediocre hand, he would probably check. If you have only a mediocre hand yourself, you have to decide what the chances are that your opponent is bluffing and whether those chances warrant a call in relation to the pot odds. If you have a very good hand, you must decide whether your opponent has a good hand or a great hand. If you think the chances are high he has only a good hand, you would raise. But if you think he may very well have a great hand, you would just call. If you are virtually certain he has a great hand, you might even fold your very good hand, depending upon the size of the pot. You ask yourself two questions: What does it look like my opponent is representing? Could he have the hand he's representing and have played it the way he did? Once you draw your conclusions about your opponent's hand on the basis of his play and his upcards, you decide on the basis of your own holding and the size of the pot whether to bet, check, call, raise, or whatever.

We have seen that in open-handed games one way to read hands is to start by considering a variety of possible hands an opponent might have and then eliminate some of those possibilities as the hand develops. A second or, more accurately, a complementary way to read hands is to work backward. It is that sort of thing my high-low split opponent did. If, for instance, the last card in hold 'em is a deuce and an opponent who'd been quiet from the start suddenly bets, you think back on his play in earlier rounds. If there was betting on the flop or on fourth street, that player would not have called with nothing but two 2s in the hole. So he is betting now either as a bluff or because he has something other than three 2s. If, on the other hand, everyone checked on the flop and on fourth street, it's very possible the player caught three 2s on the end. Every step of the way you must work forward and backward to zero in on your opponent's most likely hand.

Using Mathematics to Read Hands

When you can't actually put a person on a hand but have reduced his possible hands to a limited number, you try to use mathematics to determine the chances of his having certain hands rather than others. Then you decide what kind of hand you must have to continue playing. Using mathematics is particularly important in draw poker, where your main clue to what an opponent might have is what you know about his opening, calling, and raising requirements.

If, for example, you know an opponent will raise you with three 2s or better before the draw, you can resort to mathematics to determine what hand is favored to have him beat. It works out to something like three queens. Obviously, then, if you have three 3s, it's not worth calling that opponent's raise on the chance that he has specifically three 2s. But if you have something like three 5s or three 6s, the pot odds make it correct to call because now not only might you draw out on a better hand by making a full house or four-of-a-kind, but there are a few hands your opponent could have which you already have beat.

Sometimes you can use a mathematical procedure based on Bayes' Theorem to determine the chances an opponent has one or another hand. After deciding upon the kinds of hands your opponent would be betting in a particular situation, you determine the probability of his holding each of those hands. Then you compare those probabilities. If, for instance, in draw poker you know a particular player will open either with three-of-a-kind or two pair but will not open with one pair and will check as a slowplay with a pat hand, then it is 5-to-2 against that player's having trips when he does open. Why is this so? On average, according to draw poker distribution, a player will be dealt two pair 5 percent of the time and trips 2 percent of the time. When you compare these two percentages, you arrive at a ratio of 5-to-2. Therefore, the player is a 5-to-2 favorite to have two pair.

Let's say in hold 'em an opponent puts in a big raise before the flop, and you read him for the type of player who will raise only with two aces, two kings, or ace, king. The probability that a player gets two aces on the first two cards is 0.45 percent. The probability of his getting two kings is also 0.45 percent. So he will get two aces or two kings 0.9 percent of the time on average. The probability of his getting an ace, king is 1.2 percent. By comparing these two probabilities — 1.2 percent and .9 percent — you deduce that the chances are 4-to-3 in favor of your opponent's having ace, king rather than two aces or two kings. Of course, knowing your opponent is a 4-to-3 favorite to have ace, king is not enough by itself to justify calling his raise with, say, two queens. You are a small favorite if he does have ace, king, but you're a big underdog if he has two aces or two kings. Nevertheless, the more you know about the chances of an opponent's having one hand rather than another when he bets or raises, the easier it is for you to decide whether to fold, call, or raise.

Earlier in this chapter we talked about a player in seven-card stud raising on third street with a king showing, and we pointed out that he might have two kings, but he might also have a small pair or a three-flush or something like J,Q,K. To simplify, we'll assume you know this particular player will raise only with a pair of kings or a three-flush. You have a pair of queens. The probability is about 11 percent before the raise that your opponent has another king in the hole to make a pair of kings, and it's about 5 percent that he has three of the same suit. This is simply the *mathematical* probability based on card distribution and has nothing to do with any action the player takes. Therefore, when your opponent raises, which now limits his possible hands on the basis of what you know about him to either two kings or a three-flush, he is an 11-to-5 favorite to have the two kings, and you would probably fold your two queens. However, another king showing somewhere on the table radically reduces the mathematical probability of your opponent's having two kings before he raises because there are only two kings instead of three among the unseen cards. The probability of your opponent's having two kings is cut to about 7½ percent. A raise now makes it about 40 percent that your opponent has a three-flush rather than two kings. Depending upon your position, your queens may be strong enough to justify a call. In this case you read your opponent's hand not just on the basis of what you know about him, the action he takes, and the exposed card you see, but also on the basis of a mathematical comparison of his possible hands.

It does not, of course, take a mathematical genius to realize that another king on the table decreases the chances of an opponent's having two kings before he raises, so using math to read hands does not always require the precise knowledge of card-distribution probabilities presented here. Furthermore, you need to complement mathematical conclusions with what you know about a player. For example, in a relatively small-ante game, some players might not raise with two kings when there is no other king showing in hopes of making a big hand, but they will raise with two kings when there is a king showing to try to win the pot right there. They decide to go for the pot right away precisely because of the presence of that other king, which reduces their chances of improving. When you are up against such players, the presence of another king might actually increase the probability of their having two kings *after* they raise — not on the basis of mathematics but on the basis of the action they have taken and what you know about the way they play.

Reading Hands in Multi-Way Pots

Another factor in reading hands and deciding how to play your own is the number of players in the pot. Any time someone bets and someone else calls, you are in a more precarious position than when it is just up to you to call. In general, a caller ahead of you makes it necessary for you to tighten up significantly because you no longer have the extra equity that the bettor may be bluffing. Whether he is bluffing or not, the second player must have something to call. Therefore, when your hand is barely worth a call in a heads-up situation because of the extra chance of catching a bluff, it is not worth an overcall when someone else has called ahead of you.

Here is an example of such a situation that came up in a small ante razz game I was playing. On the first three cards I had an:

A decent hand but not a great one. The high card brought it in, and a player called with a 5 showing. I was prepared to call or possibly raise. However, a player ahead of me, who was playing tight, raised with a 4 showing. Had the first player with the 5 showing not called the initial bet, I would have called the raiser with my 8,5,2 because, though the raiser was playing tight, there would have been a chance he was semi-bluffing. But since the raiser raised another low card that had already called, it was almost a certainty he had a better hand than I did; and there was also the probability the first caller had a good hand. Therefore, given the small ante, my hand was no longer worth a call.

The same sort of thinking must be employed when deciding whether to call a raise cold. With very few exceptions, you need a better hand to call a raise cold than you would need to raise yourself. The simple logic of this principle can be set forth through an example from draw poker. Let's say in the game you are playing you decide to raise before the draw with aces up or better. You look at your hand and find you have three 2s. You're prepared to raise, but all of a sudden the player to your right, who will also raise with aces up or better, puts in a raise. Now instead of raising, you can't even call. You must fold because the chances are too good that the raiser has you beat.

This principle applies to any game. When you have a minimum or near-minimum raising hand and the player to your right, who has the same standards as yours, raises ahead of you, then his hand is probably better than yours, and your correct play is to fold.

Summary

Reading hands well is a powerful poker weapon because it allows you to play correctly more often, according to the Fundamental Theorem of Poker. The better you read your opponents' hands, the less likely you are to play your hand differently from the way you would play it if you could actually see what your opponents had. Weak players are difficult to read because there is little pattern to their play. Good players are easier because there is logic to their play. However, very tough players are more difficult to read because of their ability to disguise their hands.

One way to read hands is to put opponents on a variety of possible hands and eliminate some of them on the basis of their play and the cards they catch from one round to the next, keeping track of the order in which they catch their cards. A second, complementary way is to work backward, looking at an opponent's later plays in terms of how he played his hand in earlier rounds.

You can also read hands by using mathematics, by comparing possible hands on the basis of Bayes' Theorem. If you know an opponent will bet only certain hands, you form a ratio based on the probability of that opponent being dealt each of those hands. To simplify, you can divide his possible hands between those you can beat and those you can't beat. The ratio tells you which of the hands he is favored to have.

Finally, when reading hands you must consider the number of people in the pot. When there is a caller ahead of you, the caller and the original bettor cannot both be bluffing, so you must play on the assumption that you are up against at least one legitimate hand. When there is a raiser ahead of you with the same standards as yours, you should have more than your minimum raising hand to call that raiser because you have to figure your minimal raising hand is beat.

Throughout this chapter it has been implicitly suggested that a significant aspect of reading hands is knowing your opponents. Which leads us to the next chapter, "The Psychology of Poker."

Chapter Twenty-three

The Psychology of Poker

Psychological Plays

The late John Crawford was one of the great game players and gamblers of all time. His best games were bridge and backgammon, but he was also an excellent gin rummy player. He and the legendary games expert Oswald Jacoby used to play gin rummy against each other constantly. They were close in ability, but there was no question Crawford had the psychological edge. He would needle Jacoby, taunt him, even laugh at his play, until Jacoby sometimes became so enraged he could hardly see the cards in front of him.

Along the same lines, Los Angeles backgammon pro Gaby Horowitz is well-known for his glib, sometimes disparaging talk during a game, which is calculated to put his opponents on tilt. Seven-card stud poker pro Danny Robinson is equally famous for his nonstop patter during a hand, which is used to distract and confuse his opponents.

These are all psychological ploys, and there are an endless number of such ploys. Some people approve of them. Some don't. While they have a definite place in poker, they are not what we mean by the psychology of poker. They are psychological devices that apply to all games or, for that matter, to all forms of competition. Chess champion Bobby Fischer used them in his famous match against Soviet master Boris Spassky. Managers like Earl Weaver and Billy Martin use them on the baseball diamond. And the late Soviet Premier Nikita Khrushchev was notorious for using them as tactics of cold war diplomacy.

The Thought Processes of Poker

What we mean by the psychology of poker is getting into your opponents' heads, analyzing how they think, figuring out what they think you think, and even determining what they think you think they think. In this sense the psychology of poker is an extension of reading opponents' hands, and it is also an extension of using deception in the way you play your own hand.

Recently, while I was working on this book, a friend ran up to me and said, "I made a great play in seven-stud last night at the Castaways." We had recently been talking about using deception by betting a second-best hand to make an opponent think you are stronger than you really are in hopes he will fold if you improve.

"Low card brought it in, and I called with a pair of kings," my friend began. "One of the kings was showing. Behind me a guy who was steaming and almost all-in called with an ace showing. He could have anything. Another guy, A.D., the best player in the game, raised with an ace showing. We all called.

"On fourth street I catch a 5. I have a king, 5 showing — still only a pair of kings. The guy who's steaming has ace, 10, and he bets. Maybe he has a small pair. The good player calls. Now I know for sure the good player has aces because he would never call another ace unless he had aces himself, especially with me sitting behind him with, maybe, two kings. He's played with me a lot, and he knows how I play."

"So you folded your pair of kings."

"No, I raised!"

"That's pretty dangerous in that spot," I said.

"Well, I knew A.D. had aces," My friend continued, "and I knew *he* knew I knew he had aces. So when I raise, he has to figure that since I know he has aces, I must have made kings up. The guy who's steaming calls, and A.D. reluctantly calls. Then I get lucky. I make an open pair of 5s on fifth street, and I bet out. The guy who's steaming goes all-in, but A.D. shakes his head and folds his two aces because now he's worried I've made a full house — 5s full of kings. I end up winning the hand with kings and 5s against a pair of 10s. A.D. grumbled afterward that he's the one who should have been raising."

My friend did get lucky when he paired the 5s. However, in playing the hand he demonstrated the kind of thought processes that are the principal subject of this chapter. He went three steps beyond what he saw on the board. First, he thought about what his opponents might have. He tentatively put the steamer on a small pair, and with more assurance he put A.D. on a pair of aces. Then he went one step further. He thought about what A.D. thought he had — namely, a pair of kings. Then he went a step beyond that. He thought about what A.D. thought he thought A.D. had — and he knew A.D. knew that he thought A.D. had two aces. It was only after reaching this third level that he decided to raise with a pair of kings to make A.D. think he had kings up. Of course, it was also important that A.D. was a good enough player to think on a second and third level himself. Otherwise the play would make no sense. Just as you can't put a weak player on a hand, you can't put him on a thought either. A weak player might reraise with two aces, without analyzing the possibility that the other man might have kings up.

Very sophisticated poker play can go considerably beyond the third level. An instance of such play came up at the Sahara in Las Vegas in a tough seven-card stud game. One player had:

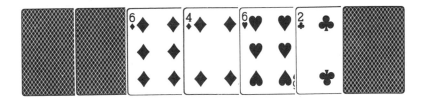

Another had:

The pair of 6s bet on the end; the A,K raised with aces and kings; and the pair of 6s called with 6s up. On the surface it may seem as if the 6s up made a sucker play in betting, that the aces and kings took a big chance in raising a possible flush or trips, and that the 6s up made another sucker play in calling the raise. In a typical game, the two small pair would no doubt check on the end, and the aces and kings might very well check behind him to avoid a check-raise. However, the thinking of the two players in this game was much more complicated.

First, the 6♦4♦ was betting all the way; that player knew, therefore, that his opponent put him on a four-flush. So with two small pair he bet for value on the end because he knew his opponent thought he had a four-flush, and he figured the opponent would call with one pair to snap off a bluff. The A,K took it a step further. He thought the pair of 6s might in fact be betting two pair for value because he knew the man with the two 6s thought he put him on a four-flush and that therefore the man with two 6s would bet two pair to get a call from one pair. So the A,K raised for value, thinking his opponent might think he was raising with only one pair. The man with the 6s up was hoping exactly that, and given the size of the pot, he felt his hand had enough of a chance to justify calling the raise. If the pair of 6s' first two up-cards had not been the same suit, the aces and kings would never have considered raising the bet on the end. At best, he would only have had a *crying call* because with two small pair the other player would probably have checked since he couldn't represent a flush draw. But with those diamonds showing each opponent was trying to outwit the other, and the aces and kings ended up getting the best of the situation. The 6s up didn't reraise, of course, representing a flush, because he knew that at that point the pot was so large his opponent would certainly call with something like aces up.

At the expert level of poker, the dialectic of trying to outwit your opponent can sometimes extend to so many levels that you must finally abandon psychology altogether and rely on game theory. It is precisely when judgment fails that game theory becomes so useful. However, in ordinary play against good players, you should think at least up to the third level. First, think about what your opponent has. Second, think about what your opponent thinks you have. And third, think about what your opponent thinks you think he has. Only when you are playing against weak players, who might not bother to think about what you have and who almost certainly don't think about what you think they have, does it not necessarily pay to go through such thought processes. Against all others it is crucial to successful play, especially when deception is a big part of the game.

Calling on the Basis of What Your Opponent Thinks

There is a very important principle based on thinking about what your opponent thinks you have, and it is this: When an opponent bets in a situation where he is sure you are going to call, he is not bluffing. This point is obvious, yet many players overlook it. What it means is if you create the impression — by the way you have played your hand, by the look of your board, by the action you have put in the pot, or even by artificial means — that you are going to call a bet, an opponent who bets is betting for value. He figures to have you beat because he knows you are going to call. Therefore, you should fold if he bets unless your hand warrants a call on the value of the hand. You should certainly fold a mediocre hand that can beat only a bluff; clearly no one but an idiot would bluff when he is sure he's going to get called.

A prime example of such a situation arises when you bet on the end and a player raises you. It is very rare to find an opponent who is capable of raising on the end as a bluff. It is even rarer to find an opponent who would raise on a bluff when you have been betting all the way and have, therefore, given every indication of paying off a raise. So against all but very tough players capable of such a bluff raise, you should fold a routine hand because your opponent wouldn't raise without a good hand. Similarly, if you raise on the end and your opponent reraises, you should usually fold unless your hand can beat some of the legitimate hands with which he might be reraising.[11] In sum, when deciding whether to call a bet or a raise, it is important to think about what your opponent thinks you're going to do. An opponent who is sure you're going to call will not be bluffing when he bets or raises.

A corollary to this principle is if your opponent bets when there appears to be a good chance you will fold, that opponent may very well be bluffing. What this means in practice is that if your opponent bets in a situation where he thinks he might be able to get away with a bluff, you have to give more consideration to calling him even with a mediocre hand.

Astute readers will have noticed that this principle and corollary are the bases of stopping and inducing bluffs, which were discussed in Chapter Twenty. When you show strength, especially more strength than you really have, to stop a bluff, you must be prepared to fold when your opponent bets into you because that opponent is expecting you to call; therefore he has a hand. Conversely, when you have shown more weakness than you really have, you must automatically call a player who bets on the end because you have induced a bluff: That player may be betting because he thinks you will fold.

---

[11] These suggestions violate the precepts of Game Theory but they are valid for all but the wildest or toughest games.

Betting on the Basis of What Your Opponent Thinks

In deciding whether to bet, it is equally important to think about what your opponent thinks you have. If you know your opponent suspects you have a strong hand, you would tend to bluff more with a weak hand because the chances are good your opponent will fold. However, you should not bet a fair hand for value in this situation. Your opponent's fear of your strong hand will probably make him fold all the hands he might have except those which have you beat.

Conversely, if you know your opponent suspects you are weak, you should not try to bluff because you'll get caught, but you should bet your fair hands for value because he'll pay you off.

Psychology and Future Impressions

Varying your play and making an "incorrect" play intentionally are also part of the psychology of poker because you are trying to affect the thinking of your opponents for future hands. To take a simple example, you might make three-of-a-kind on fourth street in seven-card stud with two of the cards showing and check your open pair on a slowplay. Assuming your opponents saw your hand in a showdown, if you make a similar three-of-a-kind later in the session, you might bet it then. Since you checked three-of-a-kind before, your opponents are now likely to think you do not have three-of-a-kind, but something like two small pair or one pair and a three-flush. In other words, you are taking advantage of the impression you created earlier to get paid off later when you bet.

By the same token, let's say you make an open pair on fourth street, but this time that's all you have. You check. Now your opponents will be suspicious that you may have three-of-a-kind.

They may give you a free card, and if one of them bets, you can be fairly certain that player has a good hand.

In general, you should evaluate any play you make on its merits alone — that is, on its expectation in a given situation. However, as we suggested in the chapter on bluffing, you might occasionally want to do something that is theoretically incorrect, especially in a no-limit game. You might either bluff a hand when you are almost sure you won't get away with it or fold a legitimate hand when you think you are getting bluffed and then show the hand. What you are trying to do is create an impression for the future. You are making a bad play so that it sticks in everybody's mind. Once you have opponents thinking one way, you take advantage of that thinking later. These types of plays will work against players who are good enough to try to take advantage of their new-found knowledge but who are not good enough to realize that you know they are going to try to take advantage of it and that they should therefore ignore it. Once again it comes down to knowing your opponents. You have to know how they think and whether they are capable of thinking on the level you are giving them credit for. If they think on a still higher level, you have to step up to that level too.

Summary

The psychology of poker is an important aspect of the game. You should think not only about what your opponents have, but about what they think you have and about what they think you think they have. You must go through such thought processes against good players in particular, but the better they are, the more difficult it is to figure them out. When you get to the expert level, the process sometimes becomes so complex and tenuous that you have to fall back on game theory.

On the other hand, these thought processes can be costly against weak players — as we saw in Chapter Eight — because your opponents are not thinking on such an advanced level.

Against weak players the best strategy is to play your cards in a basic, straightforward way.

Thinking about what your opponent is thinking will improve your calling and betting strategy. If an opponent is sure you will call his bet, he is not bluffing; if he thinks you will fold, he may be bluffing. By the same token, if an opponent thinks you are strong, you may be able to bluff, but you should not bet a fair hand for value. If an opponent thinks you are weak, you can't bluff, but you can bet your fair hands for value.

Ordinarily you evaluate a poker play solely on its own merits, but you can occasionally make a bad play for psychological effect — to create an impression for the future.

The psychology of poker is an extension of reading hands and using deception in the play of your own hands, and thus it is an extension of the Fundamental Theorem of Poker.

Chapter Twenty-four

Analysis at the Table

Like any other gambling game, poker is a game of risks versus rewards. Any decision you make at the poker table can be thought of as a comparison of the risk involved in a particular play and the possible reward for the play. There are three questions involved in arriving at a decision: How great is the risk? How great is the reward? Is the reward great enough to justify the risk?

When deciding whether to bluff, your risk is a bet. Your reward is the pot (as well as advertising value if you show the bluff). When deciding whether to bet a mediocre hand before all the cards are out, you risk a bet. If successful, your reward (when your opponent doesn't simply fold) is that you didn't give a lesser hand a free card to outdraw you. When you check a big hand, you risk losing a bet on that round as well as losing the pot to a hand that would have folded if you bet. Your reward is a check-raise or future bets on later rounds. When deciding whether to call, your risk is a bet, and your reward is the pot. Any poker decision can be put into these terms. What do you have to gain (including future benefits on subsequent hands) by making a particular play? What do you have to lose? The ability to evaluate properly the risk-reward ratio for any poker decision is the ultimate test on the road to becoming a champion poker player.

The trouble is that unlike chess and many other games, poker is a game of speed. Every once in a while you are allowed to think about a hand, but in general you have to make decisions in a few seconds. You can't sit there for two minutes calculating odds, trying to read your opponents' hands, trying to figure out what they are thinking, and then deciding upon your best play. For one thing the other players at the table wouldn't tolerate your dawdling. For another, you would be giving away information about your hand, since any time you paused unduly long to reflect, your opponents would know you had some kind of problem. (Consequently, when you find, despite your best efforts, you have to pause often when you're playing, you should also pause when you have no reason, to throw your opponents off.)

Poker tends to be a game for quick-thinking people. Some geniuses are plodding thinkers, unable to come to quick decisions, and they can never become great poker players. On the other hand, some of the best poker players in the world are not super minds, but they are super-quick minds and can remember any mistake they and their opponents make. Some combination of quick thinking and instant recall has to be developed if you want to become a poker champion.

Analysis in Theory

One of the most difficult things for the average poker player to do is to make accurate decisions at the game in the heat of a hand. Many good and bad players alike simply decide what they think their opponent has and then go on to determine their best play on the assumption that their opponent has the hand they're assuming he has. However, as we saw in the chapter on reading hands, this is a bad and potentially costly way of going about the business of decision-making. There is a better way, which is employed by most good players. They ask, "What are the various hands my opponent could have, and what are the chances he has each of them?" They determine the best play for each of the possible hands, and they usually choose the best play against their opponent's most likely hand or hands.

Sometimes it works out that no matter what your opponent has, you wind up with the same best play. This is especially true in the relatively easy decisions — for example, deciding to fold when you have nothing in seven-card stud, the pot is small, and your opponent with an open pair of aces bets on the end.

If, on the other hand, the pot were large — hence the reward would be large — you might want to determine the chances of a bluff raise working if your opponent has nothing but two aces.

And, of course, those chances depend upon the chances that your opponent has in fact only aces.

Frequently, then, a different play becomes correct depending upon what your opponent has. For example, a bluff raise might have a reasonable chance of working if your opponent has nothing but two aces. It has less chance of working if that opponent has aces up. It has little to no chance of working if he's made a straight and no chance whatsoever against aces full. Therefore, determining whether the risk of two bets (calling and raising) is worth the possible reward of the pot depends:

1. Upon the chances that your opponent has only two aces rather than any of his other possible hands.
2. On whether that opponent is the type of player who would fold them if you raise.

Let's say you decide there's only about a 25 percent chance that your opponent has two aces and a 75 percent chance he has aces up or better. Furthermore, if that player does have only aces, you think there's only about a 50 percent chance he will fold if you raise. Then the reward of the pot is probably not worth the risk of two bets, and you should fold. In general, when you have alternate plays dependent upon your opponent's hand, you choose the best play against his most likely hand or hands.

Let's say you figure an opponent to have Hand A 40 percent of the time, Hand B 35 percent of the time, and Hand C 25 percent of the time. Usually you would pick the best play against Hand A, which is your opponent's most likely hand. However, if Hand A requires one play, while both Hand B and Hand C require quite another play, you would ordinarily make the second play since it would be right 60 percent of the time — 35 percent of the time when your opponent has Hand B and 25 percent of the time when he has Hand C.

When analyzing a poker situation, you go through four steps in deciding on your best play.

1. Determine the possible hands your opponent may have.
2. Assess the chances of his having each of his possible hands.

3. Determine your best play against each of his possible hands.
4. In most cases, pick the play that will most often be correct.

Analysis in Practice

To see how this sort of analysis works in practice, we'll look at a couple of examples.

Draw Poker
$5-$10 Limit

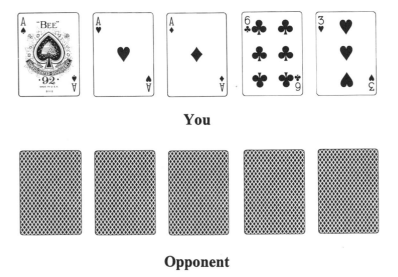

You

Opponent

You open for $5 in early position. Everyone folds except the player under the gun who originally checked to you and who now raises another $5. We'll assume you know this player will never make such a play without three-of-a-kind or better. We'll also assume that with the antes and your implied odds it would be incorrect to fold even if you knew your opponent had a pat hand. So the question is whether you should simply call the $5 raise or reraise another $5.

Your opponent's raise tells you he has either trips, which must necessarily be smaller than your three aces, or a pat hand. If he has trips, you have the best hand and are the favorite to win the pot; if he has a pat hand, you have the second-best hand and are an underdog to win the pot. According to draw poker distribution, your opponent will have three-of-a-kind about 65 percent of the time and a pat hand about 35 percent of the time. When he has a pat hand, you should obviously not reraise. However, it's nearly 2-to-1 he has trips. Should you therefore reraise?

The answer is no because when you only call and your opponent draws cards, you can draw one card, as though you had two pair, and check-raise after the draw. Assuming he calls your raise, which he will almost always do, and neglecting the slight chance of your opponent improving to a full house when you don't, you win $30 (plus the antes) by playing this way — $10 before the draw and $20 afterward when you check, your opponent bets $10, and you raise to $20. In contrast, by reraising $5 before the draw and coming out betting $10 afterward, you win a total of $25 — $15 before the draw and $10 afterward. Thus, the 65 percent of the time your opponent has three-of-a-kind, you win $5 more by calling instead of reraising. At the same time, the 35 percent of the time he has a pat hand (and you don't improve to a full house), you lose only $10 instead of $15, a savings of $5. Therefore, in this situation a call is the correct play since it is right all the time — whether your opponent has three-of-a-kind or a pat hand.

Here is a trickier situation from hold 'em:

Hold 'em
$10-$20 Limit (Small Pot)

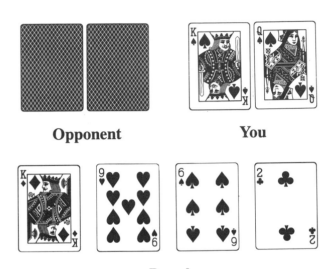

Opponent   **You**

Board

Your opponent, who is a good player, checked and called your bet on the flop. When the deuce falls, your opponent checks again. Should you check or bet your pair of kings?

In hold 'em, any time an opponent bets, calls, or raises, good players ask, "What could my opponent have done that with?" Then they think of the various hands the opponent might have to do what he did. So when your opponent called your bet on the flop and then checked on fourth street, you try to determine what hands he might have that prompted him to play the way he did.

Your opponent could be slowplaying a better hand than yours — say, K,9 or 6,6. You estimate there's a 25 percent chance he has such a hand. He might have a fairly good hand such as K,J or K,10. You figure those hands at 25 percent, too. Your opponent might have a mediocre hand like K,4 or A,9 or 10,10. The chances of those hands you put at 35 percent. And you figure there's a 15 percent chance your opponent has 8,7 and is drawing to a straight.

You know that if you bet on fourth street after his check, your opponent will probably call with his fair hands, with a straight draw and at least call with his big hands. However this player will probably fold his mediocre hands because the pot is not big enough to justify calling with them. Therefore, after your opponent checks on fourth street, it turns out the correct play may be to check it right back.[12] Your intentions are to bet on the end if your opponent checks and call if he bets.

The rationale for this play is that, like many players, this opponent will fold his mediocre hands if you bet on fourth street to avoid having to call twice to see what you have. Your checking on fourth street makes it easier for him to call on the end, not only because you have made it cheaper but also because you have shown weakness. Obviously checking is also the better play that 25 percent of the time you have the worse hand. Finally, checking on fourth street induces a bluff on the end.

The drawbacks to checking on fourth street are:
1.   It gives your opponent a free card to outdraw you.
2.   There's a 25 percent chance your opponent has a hand like K,J or K,10, with which he would probably call twice.

It is important that the pot be small — say, under $60 in a $10-$20 game — to make checking right because you gain only one bet by checking and betting on the end into your opponent's mediocre hands, but you lose the whole pot if the free card gives your opponent the best hand.

---

[12] Changes in the structure of hold 'em since this was first written has made this play debatable. However, the thinking process behind it remains valid.

Notice that the percentages support checking as the correct play on fourth street.

Opponent's Possible Hands	Approximate Chances	Best Play
Better than Yours	25 percent	Check
Mediocre hand	35 percent	Check
Fair hand (K,J or K,10)	25 percent	Bet
Straight Draw	15 percent	Bet

Because you expect your opponent to fold his mediocre hands if you bet on fourth street, and you want to win at least one more bet from those hands, the correct play 60 percent of the time is to check. It is correct to bet only 40 percent of the time. You usually pick the play that is likely to be right most of the time: Therefore, you check.

Analyzing the Cost of a Mistake

Unfortunately, the play that is likely to be right most of the time is not always the correct play. When you have a choice of plays, you also have to decide how bad it will be if you make a mistake. Here is an obvious example. If your opponent bets on the end and you think the chances are better than 50-50 that that opponent has the best hand, the correct play most of the time is to fold and save a bet. However, it costs you not just one bet but the whole pot when folding turns out to be a mistake — that is, when you fold the best hand. Therefore, you would call, even though the chances are that you are making a mistake. The reason you call is that this mistake costs you only one bet, while the opposite mistake — folding when you have the best hand — costs you the whole pot. (This is simply another way of stating that you should call when the pot odds you are getting in relation to your chances of having the best hand make calling a play with positive expectation.)

There are other situations, as well, where making the wrong play can cost you a considerable amount of money, so you should not necessarily choose that play though it is favored to be right over 50 percent of the time. Such situations come up particularly in no-limit poker. Suppose, for example, you have two queens in no-limit hold 'em, and you put in a small raise before the flop. Everyone folds except one player, who fires back with a gigantic reraise. You know that this player will make such a play not only with two aces and two kings but also with ace, king. Assuming you have nothing other than Bayes' Theorem available to put your opponent on one of these three hands, the odds work out to be 4-to-3 in favor of your opponent's having ace, king rather than a pair of aces or a pair of kings. Thus, 4/7 of the time your pair of queens is the favorite, and 3/7 of the time it is the underdog. However, when your opponent does have ace, king, your queens are only a 13-to-10 favorite since there are five cards to come, any one of which could give your opponent either a pair of kings or a pair of aces. So while you will average winning 13 times, the other 10 out of 23 times you will lose the hand when you call the raise and your opponent has ace, king. On the other hand, those three times out of seven when your opponent has two aces or two kings, your two queens are a big 4½-to-1 underdog, meaning in those instances you will lose 18 hands out of every 22 you play on average.

Therefore, you cannot say, "My queens are 4-to-3 favorites to be the best hand. So I must call." It works out that the 3/7 of the time your opponent has two aces or two kings, you hurt yourself so much that you don't gain it back the 4/7 of the time when he has ace, king.

The general principle operating here is the following: When one alternative will have slightly bad consequences if it's wrong and another second alternative will have terrible consequences if it's wrong, you may be right to choose the first alternative even when the second is slightly favored to be the correct play.

Here is an example of the same principle in a limit game, where the consequences of making the wrong play are not nearly so severe as in the no-limit example:

Seven-Card Razz
$15-$30 Limit

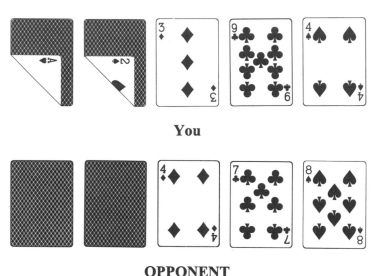

You

OPPONENT

Your opponent bets $30, and you know this opponent will bet anything in this spot except two pair. Should you call or raise?

Probability tells us your opponent is a slight favorite — about 55 percent — to have his 8,7 low made when he bets, assuming he started with three small cards. When he does have an 8,7 low, you should not raise since you are a slight underdog and will probably get reraised. However, when one of your opponent's upcards has paired one of his hole cards the remaining 45 percent of the time, a raise is very profitable since you are a big favorite. Thus, a call is correct 55 percent of the time, and a raise is the better play 45 percent of the time. Nevertheless, the best play is to raise because raising will be slightly wrong 55 percent of the time, but calling will be very wrong 45 percent of the time. In other words, even when your opponent does have an 8,7 made and reraises, you still have a good chance of outdrawing him. However, when he has paired, he has only a slim chance of beating you since your 9 low is already the best hand and you have an excellent chance of improving to beat your opponent — even if he makes his 8,7. In the long run then, you do better by raising than by calling though raising will be right only 45 percent of the time.

SUMMARY

Accurately and quickly analyzing risk-reward decisions at the poker table in the heat of a hand comes only with experience. Some top players do it intuitively. In this chapter we have presented the theoretical basis for these decisions. Most of the time, when the choice of plays is problematic, your best play is the one likely to be correct more than 50 percent of the time. However, when the favored play has very bad consequences when it is wrong, and the less-favored play has only slightly bad consequences when it is wrong, it may be correct to choose the less favored play.

Chapter Twenty-five

Evaluating the Game

Before sitting down, good poker players stop and evaluate the game, especially when they have many games to choose from as they do in Las Vegas, California, or New Jersey. However, a serious player should evaluate even a weekly private game before deciding whether to become a regular.

There are two reasons for evaluating a game. One is to determine whether the game is worth playing. The second is to determine how to play in that particular game. When professional players consider whether a game is worth playing, they estimate their expected hourly rate and decide whether that rate is satisfactory.

Social players in a home game are not generally so concerned with hourly rate. However, even they do not want to become regulars in a game where they have much the worst of it; nor do they want to get involved in a game whose stakes are either too high for their financial position or too low to be interesting. Additionally, social players should consider the game — or games, if it's dealer's choice — that are played and be sure they're comfortable with them. They should also consider the speed of the game. If they're really interested in playing cards, they probably do not want to become involved in a game in which there's a new deal only about every four or five minutes.

To determine whether a game is worth playing and how to play in a particular game, the two most important considerations are the structure of the game and the *players* in the game.

Evaluating the
Structure and Adjusting to It

By the *structure* of the game, we mean principally the ante, the betting limits, and the rules of betting. The structure may deter an average or even an above-average player from sitting down, but it should rarely deter a good player. The good player should be able to adjust his play to suit any structure he happens to confront.

There is however one instance where the structure might cause even a very good player to stay out of a game: When it has made fair players into good players by accident. Most players don't sufficiently alter their style of play according to the structure; they tend to play a fairly consistent game. However, sometimes the structure is exactly suited to the style of a group of players. Specifically the ante and/or the blind might by coincidence be an amount that makes these players' style of play approximately correct. For instance, there are some very aggressive seven-card stud players in Las Vegas who play a little bit too loose in an ordinary game, but in a game with a very high ante, their style of play is almost perfect.

The Ante and Other Forced Bets

The key question to ask about the ante and other forced bets like the blinds in hold 'em is: How big are they in relation to the betting limits? As we saw in Chapter Four, when the ante is large, you must loosen up, try to steal more antes, and almost never slowplay. When the ante is small, you tighten up, steal fewer antes, and slowplay more. If you find you do better and are more comfortable in a tighter, small-ante game, that's what you should look for, and vice versa. For example, if you are especially good at disguising your hand, at slow laying, and at trapping opponents, then a small-ante game suits your style. If on the other hand you are an aggressive player with a keen sense of when to bluff and when not to, a large-ante game is likely to produce the best results. However, whatever your style of play, you should avoid a game where the ante is simply enormous in relation to the betting limits. In that case, the pot is so large to begin with that it's worth calling with almost anything, and the game may almost be reduced to dealing out the cards and seeing who has the best hand.

An important aspect of the ante structure is the size of the initial bet and the size of the initial raise after the initial bet. Changes in these two bets can mean significant changes in strategy. To illustrate, we will use the standard $15-$30 razz game in Las Vegas and a $15-$30 razz game I've played in Reno.

Usually, a $15-$30 Las Vegas razz game has a $1 ante, and the high card has a forced bet of $5. Anyone can then raise $10 to make it $15. With this structure, it is almost always correct when you have a good hand to raise with the next-to-last low card if everyone else has folded. If you just call the $5 forced bet with a decent hand, the last low card is correct in calling behind you, even with nothing at all, simply because that player is getting about 3½-to-1 odds on his $5 and figures to win if he catches a baby and you don't. However, by raising in this spot, you cut down the last low card's odds to about 2-to-1. Now if that player wants to take the chance of outdrawing you on the next round, he is taking the worst of it unless he has a good hand himself.

In the Reno $15-$30 game, on the other hand, the high card brings it in for $10, and then anyone can raise and make it $25. That structure dictates a completely different strategy in the situation just described. Under these circumstances it becomes almost always correct to simply call the initial $10 bet with the next-to-last low card when you have a hand. You are hoping for an overcall behind you since the player is no longer getting sufficient pot odds to gamble on outdrawing you.

The difference in strategy is based on the Fundamental Theorem of Poker. By calling, you have not only induced your opponent to make a mistake with a weak hand, but you've given the impression that your hand is weaker than it is. If your opponent calls, you welcome it. If he raises, that's fine too.

The interworking of different structures and strategies can also be seen by comparing the old $10-$20 hold 'em game in Reno and the $10-$20 hold 'em game in Las Vegas. In Vegas the first bet is $5, and a raiser can make it $10. In Reno the first bet is $4, and the raiser can make it $14. The first effect of these differences is to make you play somewhat tighter in Vegas since your initial investment is a dollar more. However, in Reno you must have a somewhat better hand to raise since you are investing a total of $14 — $4 more than a raiser in Vegas invests — and the initial pot that you are raising is smaller. That is, the ratio of the raiser's money to the first bettor's money is $14-to-$4 as opposed to $10-to-$5 in Las Vegas. Thus, in Las Vegas it is frequently correct to throw in a $5 raise to deceive your opponents and get them to check to you on the flop; but in Reno it is usually too expensive to raise simply for deception. Additionally, when you call the initial $5 bet in Vegas, you are almost always committed to come in for a second $5. However, in Reno you may very well have a hand that is worth a $4 call but should be thrown away before calling $10 more.

The Betting Limits

The first thing to consider about the betting limits is whether you can afford them. Even if you think you have much the best of it, you should not play in a game whose limits are so high in relation to your bankroll that you cannot play your hands correctly because you don't want to risk going broke. At the same time, when you think you have the best of it, you should play at the highest limits you can afford whenever possible.

The excellent nonprofessional player Jay Heimowitz, from Monticello, New York, tells the story of how he started playing in a 25-50-cent poker game in the early 1960s. "I noticed I was winning about $20 a week, and that $20 a week was the difference between my wife Carol and I going out to dinner," Heimowitz says. "Then I got the brainstorm that if I played in a $1 limit game, maybe I'd win $40 a week, and we could go out to dinner twice." Today Heimowitz, a successful Budweiser beer distributor, plays no-limit hold 'em for tens of thousands of dollars against the very best hold 'em players in the world, but the point of his story is that, everything else being equal, when you have the best of it, the higher you play, the more you will average winning.

Assuming you are playing at a limit that suits you, the important question is the ratio of bet sizes from early rounds to late rounds. If the betting limits increase drastically from the early rounds to the later rounds, you must play quite a bit differently than if the limits remain fairly steady. In mathematical terms, the greater the escalation of the limits, the higher your implied odds on early rounds. Thus, you tend to play looser early in games where you may win bigger bets later. When we say looser, we mean you take chances with hands that have some chance of improving to big hands. You do not play mediocre hands that can only improve to fairly good hands. In other words, if you cannot be reasonably sure that a hand will be the best hand, even if it improves, that hand is not playable. However, a hand like a high inside straight draw, which you would not play if the bets remained fairly steady, may be worth playing if you figure to win a big bet later on when you hit.

Of course, the games with the greatest escalation in limits from early to late rounds are pot-limit and no-limit. No-limit poker does not technically have an escalating limit since anyone may bet any amount right from the start, but usually the bets become increasingly larger as the hand progresses. Thus, as we saw in Chapter Seven, in pot-limit and no-limit games implied odds — not the odds a player is getting from the pot — often become the primary consideration in betting or calling a bet.

When a game has fairly steady betting limits — most commonly limits like $2-$4, $5-$10, $10-$20, which increase only two fold from the first round to the last — you must start off with a good hand and throw away hands that require you to get lucky. You have to pay too high a price to stay in, in proportion to what you might win the few times you hit. It is especially important to get rid of such hands in games where there is a great deal of raising on the first round. Frequently you find people putting in two and three raises before the flop in limit hold 'em games. In games like these, it is important to play high pairs and high cards and to stay away from hands like

For those starting hands to be played profitably you need a game with low early betting and high later betting. That is, you need a game where it doesn't cost you much to draw to a big hand that can make you a lot of money in the later betting rounds.

The Betting Rules

Some of the questions you should ask before sitting down to play are: Is check-raising allowed? Is a flat bet imposed, or is there variable betting? In seven-card stud, does the low card bring it in or the high card? How many raises are allowed? Does the player who opens the pot have to bet first next round?

Whatever the rules, you should be thoroughly familiar with them before you sit down to play. Don't make the mistake a friend of mine made the first time he ever played draw poker in Gardena. He is the only man I know who made a royal flush but lost the hand. In Gardena you need jacks or better to open, and a joker is used as a bug. That is, the joker may be used with straights, flushes, and aces; it cannot be used to make a pair except with aces.

My friend N.S. bought into a $2-$4 draw poker game for $40, and the first hand he picked up was an ace-high straight:

He was in third position behind the dealer. The man under the gun checked, the second man checked, and N.S. gleefully bet $2. Everyone behind him folded, but then bang! The man in first position raised, and the man in second position reraised. Stupefied, N.S. called the double raise, and the first raiser called the reraise.

When it came time to draw cards, the first man stood pat. The second man stood pat. N.S. was smart enough to realize his straight was beat, if not by the man in first position, certainly by the man in second position. So he cleverly discarded the ace of clubs to draw to a straight flush in hearts — or any kind of flush, since with the joker he'd have an A,Q high.

Drawing to 10♥J♥Q♥Jk, N.S. actually had four cards that would make the straight flush — the 8♥, 9♥, K♥, and A♥. When he looked at the card he'd drawn, there it was — the king of hearts! He'd made a royal flush, the pure nuts of pure nuts.

The man in second position bet. N.S. raised. The man in first position called. The man in second position reraised. N.S. reraised. The man in first position eventually folded his jack-high flush, but the reraising continued until the entire $40 with which N.S. bought into the game was in the pot. The second player turned over a full house — kings full of 9s. With a broad smile N.S. revealed his royal flush.

He was about to gather in the pot when his opponent asked, "Where are your openers?"

"Openers?" N.S. said. "I had a straight."

"But you drew one card," said his opponent. "You don't have openers."

Remember that in Gardena card rooms you need jacks or better to open. The joker can be used only with aces, straights, and flushes. Since N.S. had thrown away his ace of clubs and had indeed drawn one card to make the royal, he had no proof whatsoever that he had opened with a legal opening hand. Of course, there's a posted rule in Gardena card rooms to cover such situations: "When splitting openers, player must declare same and protect split card by turning it face up under a chip." N.S. had not informed himself of this rule, his royal flush was declared dead, and the full house won the pot.

Beyond knowing the rules, it's important to use them to your advantage — as the man in Gardena with the full house certainly did. However, here we're not talking about exploiting technicalities but rather adjusting your play to suit the rules of the game. Suppose, for example, the game does not allow check-raising. Well, that rule takes away a very effective tool, which presumably you can use better than other players in the game. But it changes your playing strategy in that it gives more power to the player in last position. Therefore, when you are in last position, you must bet quite a lot more since you are no longer putting yourself in jeopardy of a check-raise. You would semi-bluff more on earlier rounds because the worst that could happen would be that you'd get called — not raised. Even in first position you must bet more often than you ordinarily would since you can't check-raise. (However, against tough players it may be still better to check and call, rather than bet out with a very good hand in first position, because you may induce them to bet with a hand they would have folded if you had bet.)

Adjusting Properly to the Structure

The important thing is to adjust your play to the betting rules, the betting limits, and the ante structure with which you are confronted. This ability to adjust is one of your greatest edges against the good but nontheoretical player. It takes quite a while for the nontheoretical player to find instinctively the correct method of play in an unfamiliar structure. In the meantime, that player makes costly mistakes.

For example, the $15-$30 hold 'em game that used to be played at the Golden Nugget in downtown Las Vegas attracted some of the toughest hold 'em players in the country. However, as good and as solid as they were, most of them didn't realize that the structure of this game, compared to that of the more common $10-$20 hold 'em games they knew, necessitated a change in strategy.

In the $10-$20 games there is ordinarily a 50-cent ante and a $5 blind. It costs $5 to come in and another $5 to raise. However, in the $15-$30 Golden Nugget game, there was no ante, but there were two blinds — $5 and $10. It cost $10 to come in, and to raise it cost another $15 for a total of $25. Thus, in this game it cost considerably more to come in, relative to the betting limits, than it did in the $10-$20 game — especially when there was a raise. When you call the $5 blind in the $10-$20 game, you are investing half of the $10 bet on the flop; but when you called the $10 blind in the Golden Nugget $15-$30 game, you were investing two-thirds of the $15 flop bet. When you raise (or call a raise) in the $10-$20, you are investing as much as the bet on the flop — namely, $10; but when you raised or called a raise in $15-$30, you were investing almost twice as much as the bet on the flop — $25. Additionally, when you call the $5 blind in early position in $10-$20, you risk being raised only the amount of the initial bet; but when you called the $10 blind in $15-$30 in early position, you risked being raised another $15 — one-and-a-half times the initial bet.

The effect of these structural changes in the $15-$30 game, which made it more expensive to come in, was that you had to play very tightly and play only hands that didn't depend on high implied odds. Hands like ace, king and big pairs went up in value, while hands like 6,7 suited and baby pairs, which are playable in $10-$20, went down in value. These differences were so significant that anyone who understood them and adjusted to them properly had an edge in the $15-$30 hold 'em over players who may have been great in $10-$20 but who insisted on playing the same way in the $15-$30 game.

Evaluating the
Players and Adjusting to Them

When you are deciding whether to play and how to play, the other players in a given game are much more significant than the structure. Rarely will the structure deter good players from sitting down, but if they look around the table and see nothing but top players, relative to their own abilities, they should probably find another game. There is an old and true adage in poker: If you look around and don't see a sucker in the game, you're it.

At the same time, everybody in the game does not have to be worse than you. For a game to be potentially profitable, all you need are one or two bad players or five or six mediocre players. However, if everyone in the game is as good as you or nearly as good, you may not be taking the worst of it, but you cannot expect your hourly rate to be very high.

Players Who Play Too Loose

Once you have decided that the caliber of your opponents allows you to sit down and play profitably, your next step is to evaluate their mistakes and see how you can best take advantage of those mistakes. The most common mistake players make is playing too many hands. In Las Vegas I frequently find this tendency to be the only weakness in some opponents. Everything else about their play is top-notch. Consequently, there is little I can actively do to take advantage of these players' mistakes other than not play as loosely as they do. Yet just playing better starting hands than they do on average is a decent edge. Sometimes I play a very unimaginative game against them, simply to make them think I'm not much of a player. I thereby encourage them to play even more hands. When the night is over, I usually have the money, and they are shaking their heads, wondering how I beat them. Well, I didn't outplay them, just as they suspect, nor did I get lucky. I simply played better openers than they did, and so when I was in a pot against them, more often than not I ended up with a better hand than theirs.

Often players who play too many hands will make many other mistakes as well. A typical loose player will call too much, not just on the first round but on all rounds. These players are the kind you encounter most often in home games. They play poker only once a week, and they want action. Against such opponents, conservatism and patience pay big dividends. You play your solid cards, and you don't bluff nearly as much as game theory indicates to be correct. There is clearly no value in bluffing when you know you'll be called — except perhaps once or twice early in a session for advertising purposes, to make doubly sure you'll get called later with your legitimate hands.

Players Who Play Too Tight

Occasionally you'll run into the opposite type of player — the player who plays too tight. These players may play too tight on the first round or on every round, but the tighter they play, the more they are giving away. You take advantage of the player who's too tight on the first round by stealing antes with more frequency than game theory would indicate to be correct. In fact, you should test such a player by raising the forced bet just about every time you and he are the only players left in the pot. You shouldn't raise every single time the situation comes up, because eventually that tight player will realize you're robbing him and he'll loosen up, which you don't want him to do. However, you should try making a play on that player at least two times out of three when he is the only person left behind you on the first round.

Many players who play too tight on the opening round tend to play too loose later on. Since they're playing only good starting cards, they hate to throw them away. Consequently, if you get called by such a player when you try to steal the antes on the opening round, it is very important to give up your bluff because this type will not fold on later rounds, having called your raise. However, if you have a legitimate hand which you figure to be the best hand, bet it out since this player will probably give you crying calls all the way.

Much rarer are the tight players who throw away too many hands on all rounds. Against them, you should semi-bluff just about any time you're able to represent a good hand, and you should bluff more than game theory would indicate to be correct.

Other Mistakes to Look For

As we saw in the first section of this chapter, some otherwise excellent players are incapable of adjusting to different structures. Therefore, you may sometimes decide to sit down in a game with them specifically because you know they are playing on unfamiliar turf. You take advantage of their weakness by playing more correctly, according to the structure, than they do.

One of my favorite types of player is the one who never bluffs. You have a tremendous advantage over these players because you just about always know where you're at. Against most players you have to call with a marginal hand since you usually have two ways of winning — either by improving to the best hand or by having them beat when they're bluffing. However, you can assume that players who never bluff have hands when they bet, and you only call when your hand has a fair chance of beating theirs or when you're getting good enough pot odds to chase. You never need to consider calling on the chance that they may be bluffing. Even players who bluff much less frequently than they should offer you a big advantage, especially when you make plays to stop the few bluffs they might be tempted to try against you.

Over a period of time, you can save a tremendous number of bets by not having to call such players. At the same time, you are likely to make money from them since you only play against them with a legitimate hand that has a reasonable chance of beating theirs. Ironically, though, against such players you face the psychologically upsetting fact that you only profit from their mistakes when you fold and lose the pot to them. Your profit comes from having lost less to them than you would have lost to players whose legitimate hands you might have paid off. This is an example of the poker principle that any bet saved means more money earned at the end of the session and at the end of the year.

Sometimes the only weakness I can discern in opponents is that they will never check-raise bluff. Even this relatively small flaw gives me an edge. Knowing that these opponents always have good hands allows me to fold hands I might otherwise have called with when I do get check-raised. Anytime I can do this I save money, and these savings add up in the long run. Other players will never make any kind of bluff raise; against them I can save even more money since I always know they have good hands when they raise.

Occasionally you encounter players who never check-raise. You take advantage of this major mistake by betting more hands after they check than you would against other players who have checked. Since these players don't check-raise, you know they are checking because they have only fair hands at best. You are actually in a better position than you would be when a hand is checked to you in a non-check-raising game, because in these games a player will occasionally check a good hand to induce you to bet a weaker hand. The players who never check-raise will hardly be so cute: When they check, it's because their hands are not worth betting.

Players who bluff much more than they should give you a tremendous opportunity for a profitable session. You should do everything you can to induce them to bluff even more and then call them. There is one player whom I run into now and then in Las Vegas who bluffs much too much. I never bet into that player because he will usually fold. Instead I check, and he will almost automatically bet; then, depending upon my hand, I either call or raise. It's true that by playing against him this way, I give him many chances for a free card, but that risk is more than compensated for by the times he just keeps on bluffing at the pot.

(Though players who bluff too much can produce a profitable session for you, they are also much more dangerous than players who never bluff, especially if you are on any kind of limited bankroll. To take advantage of these players' mistakes, you must induce bluffs and nearly always call them, even when you have a mediocre hand. Obviously players who bluff too much get their share of good hands like the rest of us. When they get more than their share, you will tend to pay them off when you wouldn't pay off others. Therefore, up to a point, were I on a limited bankroll, I would prefer my opponents to be tight, nonbluffing players rather than wild, bluffing players.)

There are endless kinds of mistakes you can detect in your opponents' play, and when you detect them, there is always a way to take advantage of them. Following is a list of the most common mistakes poker players make, accompanied by the best strategies to use to take advantage of the mistakes.

Type of Mistake	Best Strategy
1. Bluffs too much.	1. Induce a bluff, then call.
2. Bluffs too little.	2. Stop a bluff, then fold if you cannot beat a hand (unless there are more cards to come and you are getting good enough odds to chase).
3. Never folds any fair hand on the end.	3. Never bluff, but be sure to come out betting with a decent hand.
4. Rarely folds a fair hand on any round.	4. Don't slowplay. Bet your decent hands for value.

Type of Mistake	Best Strategy
5. Folds too often on the end.	5. Bluff more than you normally would, but don't bet your fair hands for value.
6. Plays very tight on the first round, but then won't throw a hand away	6. If this player has not yet called and no one else is left, try to steal the antes no matter what you have. If the player calls your raise, give up on a bluff. However, you can play a fair hand for one card. If the next card improves you, the player still won't fold.
7. Never check-raises.	7. Bet many more hands behind this player than you would behind someone who does check-raise.
8. Never bluff raises.	8. Fold fair-to-good hands when this player raises. Bet weaker hands than normal into him since his response will give you more information than you usually get.

Type of Mistake	Best Strategy
9. Never slowplays.	9. If you are first and have little, check to see what this player does. If he also checks, you can be pretty sure a bluff will work the next round.
10. Plays too loose.	10. Play solid poker, and cut down on your bluffs.
11. Plays too loose on early rounds and too aggressively later on.	11. Play solid cards, but play them meekly. Make this player think he can run over you.
12. Semi-bluffs too much.	12. Semi-bluff raise.
13. Plays weakly and in a way that gives away his hand.	13. Play as many hands as possible against this type of player, just as you would if you were using marked cards.

Rules of Play

Five-Card Draw

After the ante each player is dealt five cards face down. Starting with the player to the dealer's left, each player checks, bets, or raises. To open, a player must usually hold a pair of jacks or better. In many games a joker is used, usually as a bug but sometimes as a wild card.

Once the first round of betting is complete, each active player, starting to the dealer's left, has the option of discarding from one to five cards and receiving replacements from the dealer. Sometimes the rules of a game restrict to three the number of cards any player may replace.

After the draw, there is a final round of betting, usually starting with the player who opened the pot. In the showdown the best high hand wins.

Seven-Card Stud

Three cards are dealt to each player, two face down and one face up. Depending on the betting rules, either the low card or the high card on board starts the action. When there are two low (or high) cards of the same rank, either the card of the lowest ranking suit (clubs, then diamonds, then hearts) or the card closest to the dealer's left starts the action, once again depending on the betting rules in effect.

After the first round of betting, a fourth card is dealt face up, and now the high hand on board starts a second round of betting. (If there are two identical high hands, the one closest to the dealer's left begins.)

A fifth and then a sixth card are dealt face up with a round of betting after each. A seventh card is dealt face down, followed by a final round of betting. In each case the high hand on board starts the action. In the showdown the best high hand wins.

Hold 'em

Hold 'em is most easily described as a variation of seven-card stud. Two cards are dealt face down to each player, and then a total of five community cards are dealt face up in the center of the table. Each player uses the five community cards in combination with his hole cards to form the best five-card hand.

After the first two cards are dealt to each player, there is a round of betting, beginning with a forced, blind bet by one, two, and sometimes three players to the immediate left of the dealer or the button if there is a house dealer. In limit hold 'em there is usually only one forced blind.

After that first round of betting, the dealer turns over three cards, called the flop, in the center of the table. These are the first three community cards. Thus, if the flop is A♥8♥5♣ a player holding A♣5♦ in the hole has two pair; a player holding 7♥6♥ in the hole has a four-flush and an open-ended straight; and a player holding 8♠8♦ in the hole has three 8s.

Following the flop, there is a round of betting, followed by a fourth community card, then another round of betting, then a fifth and final community card and a final round of betting. Each round of betting begins with the first active player to the left of the dealer or button. In the showdown the best high hand wins.

Five-Card Stud

Two cards are dealt to each player, one face down and the other face up. There is a round of betting, starting either with the lowest card or thc highest card un board, depending on the betting rules. A third card is dealt face up, and there is a round of betting, starting with the best high hand on board. A fourth and fifth card are dealt face up with a round of betting after each. After the final round of betting, the best high hand in the showdown wins the pot.

Draw Lowball

In standard lowball (also called California lowball) the best low hand is A,2,3,4,5, followed by A,2,3,4,6; then A,2,3,5,6; etc. Frequently the joker is used as a wild card. In deuce-to-seven lowball the best low hand is 2,3,4,5,7.

Each player receives five cards face down. There is a round of betting, starting with the player to the dealer's left. Ordinarily the rules require that the player to the dealer's left bet blind.

After that betting round, players may draw up to five cards. Following the draw, there is a final round of betting. Usually the rules of play require a 7 low or better to bet in order to win any money put into the pot after the draw.

The lowest ranking hand in the showdown wins the pot. In standard lowball, straights and flushes are ignored. However, in deuce-to-seven lowball they count and therefore are not considered a low hand. In standard lowball the ace is a low card; in deuce-to-seven it is a high card. Another lowball variation makes A,2,3,4,6 the best low hand and counts straights and flushes as high hands.

When I discuss lowball in this book, I am always referring to standard or California lowball.

Razz

Razz is seven-card stud lowball with A,2,3,4,5 the best hand. Straights and flushes are ignored.

Two cards are dealt face down and one face up to each player. Usually the high card on board (excluding the ace, which counts as low) starts the action. A fourth card is dealt face up, and there is a round of betting, beginning with the best two-card low on board. A fifth and sixth card are dealt face up with a round of betting after each, starting with the best low hand on board. A seventh and final card is dealt face down, followed by a final round of betting. In the showdown the best low hand wins.

High-Low Split

This name covers several popular forms of poker. The game may be five-card draw, five-card stud, or seven-card stud, and in the showdown the best low hand and the best high hand split the pot. Sometimes, however, the rules may require that players have to declare — either simultaneously or consecutively — whether they are going for high, for low, or for both.

In five-card high-low split games the best low hand is always A,2,3,4,5, as in draw lowball. In seven stud games the best low hand is sometimes A,2,3,4,6, with straights and flushes counted as high. Aces always count both as low cards and high cards. (Hence, two aces may be a low pair as well as a high pair.) In stud high-low split games, the high hand on board usually starts each betting round.

A variation of high-low split requires a player to have an 8 low or better to qualify for low. If no one has an 8 low or better, the best high hand wins the whole pot.

Glossary of Poker Terms

Action: The betting in a particular hand or game. A game with a lot of action is a game with a lot of betting. The player who starts the action is the player who makes the first bet.

Active player: A player still in the pot.

All-in: Having all one's money in the pot.

Ante: A bet required from all players before the start of a hand.

Baby: A small card, specifically an ace, 2, 3, 4, or 5. The term is used especially in razz and high-low split.

Back door: In seven-card stud and hold 'em, three cards to a flush or a straight after five cards have been dealt. In general, the term is used for a hand made on the end, which a player was not originally trying to make.

Bad beat: Having a hand that is a big favorite defeated as the result of a lucky draw, especially when the person drawing was playing incorrectly by being in the pot in the first place.

Bad game: A game in which your opponents are too good for you to expect to win; a game in which you're an underdog.

Bankroll: The amount of money you have available to wager.

Belly buster: A draw to an inside-straight. Also called a gut shot.

Best of it: A situation in which a wager can be expected to be profitable in the long run.

Bet: To put money in the pot before anyone else on any given round.

Bettor: The person who first puts money in the pot on any given round.

Bet for value: To bet in order to be called by a lesser hand. You are betting to make money, not to make your opponents fold.

Bicycle: Ace, 2, 3, 4, 5 — the best possible hand in lowball. Also called a *wheel* and a *baby straight*. The term is used in all games.

Blank: A card that is not of any value to a player's hand.

Blind: In hold 'em, draw lowball, and some other games, a forced bet that one or more players must make to start the action on the first round of betting. The blind rotates around the table with each new deal. The person whose turn it is to bet is said to be in the blind.

Bluff: A bet or raise with a hand you do not think is the best hand.

Board: The cards that are face up in a player's hand. In hold 'em, the community cards.

Bring it in: To start the betting on the first round.

Bug: A joker that can be used to make straights and flushes and can also be used to make a pair with aces, but not with any other cards.

Busted hand: A hand that does not develop into anything of value.

Button: When there is a house dealer, as in the card rooms of Las Vegas, the *button* is a round disc that rotates around the table to represent the dealer for the purposes of indicating which player is to be first to act. A button is necessary in hold 'em, draw lowball, and five card draw.

Buy in: The minimum amount of money required to sit down in a particular game.

Call: To put in the pot an amount of money equal to an opponent's bet or raise.

Call a raise cold: To call a double bet — that is, a bet and a raise.

Caller: A person who calls a bet or raise.

Chase: To continue in a hand trying to outdraw an opponent's hand you are quite sure is better than yours.

Card room: The area in a casino where poker (and sometimes panguingue) are played.

Check: To decline to bet when it is your turn.

Check-raise: To check and then raise after an opponent bets.

Chip: A round token in various denominations representing money. Among many professional gamblers it is also called a check.

Cinch: The best possible hand, given the cards on board, when all the cards are out.

Closed hand: A hand in which all the cards are concealed from one's opponents.

Come hand: A hand that has not yet been made, with more cards still to be dealt. Thus, a four-card flush would be a come hand.

Crying call: A call with a hand you think has a small chance of winning.

Cut the pot: To take a percentage from each pot as the profits for the person or the casino running the game.

Dead hand: A hand a player may not continue to play because of an irregularity.

Dead money: Money put in the pot by players who have already folded their hands.

Dealer's choice: Poker in which the player whose turn it is to deal may choose the game for that particular hand.

Draw: 1. To take one or more cards. 2. A form of poker in which each player receives five cards and then has the option of discarding one or more of them and receiving new cards in their place.

Drawing dead: Drawing to try to make a hand that cannot possibly win because an opponent already holds a bigger hand. A player drawing to make a flush when an opponent already has a full house is drawing dead.

Draw lowball: A form of poker in which the best low hand wins. See Appendix A.

Draw out: To improve your hand so that it beats an opponent who had a better hand than yours prior to your draw.

Door card: In stud games, the first exposed card in a player's hand.

Double belly buster: *See* Open-ended straight.

Early position: A position on a round of betting in which you must act before most of the other players.

Edge: An advantage over an opponent.

Effective odds: The ratio of the total amount of money you expect to win if you make your hand to the total amount of bets you will have to call to continue from the present round of betting to the end of the hand.

Equity: The value of a particular hand or combination of cards.

Even money: A wager in which you hope to win the same amount as you bet. The term is also used to describe situations in which the chances that one result will occur are the same as the chances the opposite result will occur. Hence, whether an honest coin comes up heads or tails is an even-money proposition.

Expectation: The average profit (or loss) of any bet over the long run.

Favorite: In poker, before all the cards are out, a hand that has the best chance of winning.

Fifth street: In stud poker, the fifth card to be dealt to each player. In hold 'em the fifth and final community card on board.

Fill: To draw a card that makes a hand. For example, to fill a flush is to draw a fifth card of that suit.

Fill up: To make a full house.

Five-card draw: A form of poker in which players start with five cards and then may draw to replace them. *See* Appendix A.

Five-card stud: A form of poker in which each player gets one concealed card and four exposed cards. *See* Appendix A.

Flat call: To call a bet without raising.

Flat limit: A betting limit in a poker game that does not escalate from one round to the next.

Flop: In hold 'em the first three exposed community cards, which are dealt simultaneously. The word is also used as a verb. For example, to flop a set is to make three-of-a-kind on the flop.

Flush: Five cards of the same suit.

Fold: To drop out of a pot rather than call a bet or raise.

Forced bet: A required bet to start the action on the first round of a poker hand. In seven-card stud, for example, usually the low card on board must make a forced bet.

Four-flush: Four cards to a flush.

Four-of-a-kind: Four cards of the same rank. Four jacks is four-of-a-kind.

Fourth street: In stud games, the fourth card dealt to each player. In hold 'em, the fourth community card on board.

Free card: A card that a player gets without having to call a bet.

Freeze out: A game in which the players involved continue play until only one player has all the money.

Full house: Three cards of one rank and two of another. Three aces and two 10s is a full house.

Gardena: A city in the Los Angeles greater metropolitan area with public card rooms in which draw poker and panguingue are played.

Giving a hand away: Playing your hand in such a way that your opponents should know what you have.

Good game: A game in which there are enough players worse than you for you to be a substantial favorite.

Gut shot: A draw to an inside straight. Also called a belly buster.

Heads-up: Playing against a single opponent.

High-low split: A form of poker in which the best high hand and the best low hand in the showdown normally split the pot. *See* Appendix A.

Hold 'em: Also called *Texas hold 'em*. An increasingly popular form of poker in which players use five community cards in combination with their two hole cards to form the best five-card hand. See Appendix A.

Hole: In seven-stud games, the first two concealed cards. In five-card stud games, the first and only concealed card.

Hourly rate: The amount of money a player expects to win per hour on average.

Implied odds: The ratio of the total amount of money you expect to win if you make your hand to the bet you must now call to continue in the hand.

Inside straight: A straight which can be made only with a card of one rank, usually somewhere in the middle of the straight. When you hold 6,7,9,10, only an 8 will give you a straight. Thus, you are drawing to an inside straight, or you have an inside-straight draw.

Jacks or better to open: Draw poker in which a player needs at least a pair of jacks to start the betting.

Joker: A fifty-third card in the deck, which may be used either as a wild card or as a bug.

Kicker: A side card, usually a high one. Someone holding 9,9,A has a pair of 9s with an ace *kicker*.

Late position: A position on a round of betting in which you act after most of the other players have acted.

Lay the odds: To wager more money on a proposition than you hope to win.

Legitimate hand: A hand with value; a hand that is not a bluffing hand.

Limit: The amount a player may bet or raise on any round of betting.

Limit poker: A poker game where the minimum and maximum amounts a player may bet or raise on any given round of betting are fixed.

Live card: In stud games a card that has not yet been seen and is therefore presumed likely to be still in play.

Live one: A loose, weak player with a lot of money to lose. A rich sucker. There is a story, perhaps apocryphal, about a poker game in Gardena in which one player had a heart attack and died. The player to his left shouted to the floorman, "Hey, Louie, bring us a live one."

Lock: A cinch hand. A hand that cannot lose.

Long odds: The odds for an event that has a relatively small chance of occurring.

Long shot: An event that has little chance of occurring. Hence, in poker a hand that has little chance of being made.

Loose: Playing more hands than the norm.

Lowball: A variety of poker games in which the best low hand wins in the showdown. *See* Draw Lowball and Razz in Appendix A.

Mathematical expectation: The mathematical calculation of what a bet can be expected to win or lose on average.

Middle position: A position on a round of betting somewhere in the middle. In an eight-handed game, the fourth, fifth, and sixth players to act would be said to be in middle position.

Move all-in: To bet all the money one has on the table.

Multi-way pot: A pot in which more than two players are involved.

Negative expectation: The amount a wager may be expected to lose on average. A play with negative expectation is a play that will lose money over the long run.

No-limit poker: Poker in which players may wager any amount up to what they have in front of them on any given round.

Nuts: The best possible hand at any given point in a pot.

Odds: The chances, expressed mathematically, that an event will occur. Also, in the term *pot odds,* the ratio of the size of the pot to the amount of the bet you must call to continue.

Off-suit: Not of the same suit.

On the come: Playing a hand that has not yet been made. For instance, if you bet with four cards to a flush, you are betting on the come.

On tilt: Playing much worse than usual because, for one reason or another, you have become emotionally upset.

Open: To make the first bet in a poker hand. The term is used especially in draw poker.

Open-ended straight: Four cards to a straight, which can be made with cards of two different ranks. Thus, 6,7,8,9 is an open-ended straight, which can be made with either a 5 or a 10. Theoretically, 5,7,8,9,J is also open-ended in that either a 6 or a 10 will make the hand. The latter hand is also called a double belly buster.

Open-handed: A poker game like seven-card stud or razz in which some cards in each player's hand are exposed.

Open pair: An exposed pair.

Out: Cards which will improve your hand. Also, ways of improving your hand. The term is used particularly in reference to a hand that needs to improve to become the best hand.

Outdraw: *See* Draw Out.

Overcall: A call of a bet after another player has already called.

Overcard: In stud games, a card higher than any card your opponent has showing.

Pair: Two cards of the same rank. Two 8s is a *pair*.

Pass: To check. Also, to fold.

Pat hand: In draw poker games, a complete hand before the draw. A pat flush would be a five-card flush before the draw.

Pay off: To call a bet or raise when you don't think you have the best hand.

Pay station: A player who calls bets and raises much more than is correct. He's also referred to as a *calling station*. This type is great when you have a legitimate hand, but he's just about impossible to bluff out of a pot.

Pocket: Another term for hole. Thus, two aces in the pocket means two aces in the hole.

Position: The spot in the sequence of betting in which a player is located. A player in first position would be the first person to act; a player in last position would be the last person to act.

Positive expectation: The amount a wager may be expected to win on average. A play with positive expectation is a play that will win money over the long run.

Pot: The total amount of money wagered at any point in a hand. A hand itself is also referred to as a pot. Thus, three people in the pot means there are three active players still playing the hand.

Pot-limit poker: Poker in which players may bet or raise any amount up to the current size of the pot.

Pot odds: The ratio of the amount of money in the pot to the bet you must call to continue in the hand.

Pure nuts: The best possible hand. In lowball, A,2,3,4,5 is the pure nuts. If in hold 'em the board is A♥7♦8♦K♣4♠ a player holding a 5,6 has the pure nuts.

Put someone on a hand: To determine as best you can the hand (or hands) an opponent is most likely to have.

Rag: *See* Blank.

Raise: To bet an additional amount after someone else has bet.

Raiser: A player who raises.

Rake: An amount retained by a casino from each pot, usually no more than $2 or $3.

Razz: Seven-card stud lowball. The original name of the game was razzle dazzle. *See* Appendix A.

Represent: To make your opponents believe you have a bigger hand than you are showing on board. Thus, if in seven-card stud you raise with an ace showing, you are representing a pair of aces. You may or may not in fact have a pair of aces.

Reraise: To raise after an opponent has raised.

Reverse implied odds: The ratio of the amount of money now in the pot to the amount of money you will have to call to continue from the present round to the end of the hand.

River: The seventh and last card, dealt face down, in seven-card stud and razz.

Rolled up: In seven-card stud, three-of-a-kind on the first three cards.

Round of betting: A sequence of betting after one or more cards have been dealt. A round of betting continues until each active player has either folded or called.

Rough: A lowball hand that is not perfect. Thus, an 8,4,3,2,A is a perfect eight. An 8,7,4,2,A is a rough eight.

Royal flush: An ace-high straight flush. A♠K♠Q♠J♠10♠ is a royal flush.

Sandbag: To play weakly with a strong hand. To check-raise or slowplay with the probable best hand.

Score: A big win.

Seat charge: In public card rooms, primarily those of California, an hourly fee for playing poker.

Semi-bluff: To bet with a hand which you do not think is the best hand but which has a reasonable chance of improving to the best hand.

Set: Three-of-a-kind. The term is used particularly in hold 'em.

Short odds: The odds for an event that has a good chance of occurring.

Short-stacked: Playing in a game with a relatively small number of chips remaining.

Showdown: The turning up of all active players' cards at the end of the final round of betting to see who has the best hand.

Side pot: A second pot for the other active players when one player is all-in.

Seventh street: In seven-stud games, the seventh card dealt to each player.

Sixth street: In seven-stud games, the sixth card dealt to each player.

Slowplay: To check or just call an opponent's bet with a big hand in order to win more money on later rounds of betting.

Starting requirement: The minimum initial hand a player considers he needs to continue in a pot.

Start the action: To make the first bet in a particular hand.

Steal: To cause your opponents to fold when you probably do not have the best hand. The term is used especially in reference to stealing the antes — that is, raising on the first round of betting so that everyone remaining in the pot folds.

Steal the antes: *See* above.

Steam: To play badly because you are emotionally upset — especially to play considerably more pots than you normally would when your hands do not justify it.

Straight: Five cards of mixed suits in sequence. 6♥7♦8♥9♣10♦ is a straight.

Straight flush: Five cards of the same suit in sequence. 6♥7♥8♥9♥10♥ is a straight flush.

Structure: The limits set upon the ante, forced bets, and subsequent bets and raises in any given game.

Stuck: Losing money, especially a substantial amount of money, in a given session or over a period of time. We might say, "Sammy is stuck $1,500 in the game." That is, Sammy has lost $1,500.

Stud: Poker games in which some of each player's cards are exposed.

Sucker: A player who can be expected to lose money, especially one who is not as good as he thinks.

Suited: Two or more cards of the same suit.

Take the odds: To wager less money on a proposition than you hope to win.

Texas hold 'em: Another name for hold 'em.

Three-of-a-kind: Three cards of the same rank. 7♠7♦7♥ is *three-of-a-kind.*

Third street: In stud games, the third card dealt to each player.

Three-flush: Three cards of the same suit.

Tight: Playing fewer hands than the norm.

Trips: Three-of-a-kind.

Turn: The flop in hold 'em. Also the fourth card in seven-card stud, and sometimes the fourth community card in hold 'em.

Two-flush: Two cards of the same suit.

Underdog: In poker, before all the cards are out, a hand that does not have the best chance of winning.

Under the gun: The first person to act on the first round of betting is under the gun. On later betting rounds, the player to the immediate left of the bettor is said to be under the gun.

Up: Expressions like aces up, kings up, and 6s up mean two pair with two aces, two kings, or two 6s as the highest of the two pair. Unless an opponent has a top pair of the same rank, the rank of the second pair is of no importance.

Up-card: A card that is dealt face up.

Value: What a hand is worth in terms of its chances of being the best hand.

Wager: A bet.

Wheel: *See* Bicycle.

Wild card: A joker or any other card mutually agreed upon by the players in the game which can be used to represent any card needed.

Wired pair: A pair in the hole.

World Series of Poker: An annual series of some fifteen poker tournaments with buy-ins ranging up to $10,000, which is held each spring at the Horseshoe Casino in Las Vegas. The competition is generally recognized as the premier competition among the best poker players in the world.

Worst of it: A situation in which a wager will be unprofitable in the long run.

Index

NOTES

NOTES

NOTES